WRITING AGAINST WAR

CULTURAL EXPRESSIONS OF WORLD WAR II

INTERWAR PRELUDES, RESPONSES, MEMORY

PHYLLIS LASSNER, SERIES EDITOR

WRITING AGAINST WAR

LITERATURE, ACTIVISM, AND THE BRITISH PEACE MOVEMENT

CHARLES ANDREWS

NORTHWESTERN UNIVERSITY PRESS | EVANSTON, ILLINOIS

Northwestern University Press
www.nupress.northwestern.edu

Printed in the United States of America

10 9 8 7 6 5 4 3 2 1

Library of Congress Cataloging-in-Publication Data

Names: Andrews, Charles, 1979– author.
Title: Writing against war : literature, activism, and the British peace movement /
Charles Andrews.
Other titles: Cultural expressions of World War II.
Description: Evanston, Ill. : Northwestern University Press, 2017. | Series: Cultural
expressions of World War II: interwar preludes, responses, memory | Includes
bibliographical references and index.
Identifiers: LCCN 2017000573 | ISBN 9780810134997 (cloth : alk. paper) |
ISBN 9780810134980 (pbk. : alk. paper) | ISBN 9780810135000 (e-book)
Subjects: LCSH: English fiction — 20th century — History and criticism. | Peace
movements in literature. | Experimental fiction, English — History and criticism. |
Peace movements — Great Britain — 20th century.
Classification: LCC PR888.P42 A53 2017 | DDC 823.912093581 — dc23
LC record available at https://lccn.loc.gov/2017000573

For Liv, Arlo, and Robin

CONTENTS

ACKNOWLEDGMENTS

Long gestating projects accrue many debts, and the following is, inevitably, a partial list of thanks to the many people who have enabled this research. I have benefited immensely from the support of my local intellectual community, which gave verbal and written feedback. My colleagues Laura Bloxham, Vic Bobb, Thom Caraway, LuElla D'Amico, Fred Johnson, Stacey Moo, Leonard Oakland, Pamela Corpron Parker, John Pell, Nicole Sheets, Dale Soden, Annie Stillar, and Douglas Sugano have been a dependable network. Especially noteworthy is Anthony E. Clark, who read and commented on substantial portions of the manuscript from its earliest stages, providing much advice and *yǐn chá*. I am also grateful for the critical readings given by friends and former students, including Jake Jacobs, Shannon Kelly, Claire LePage, Ana Quiring, and Jakob Rinderknecht. Pamela L. Caughie's expertise in Woolf studies and careful reading of my fifth chapter were invaluable; her support for former students is a model to which I aspire. Among the professional colleagues whose mutual interests have catalyzed my thinking, I would mention in particular J. Ashley Foster, Nancy Knowles, Jean Mills, Tammy Proctor, Richard Rankin Russell, Cynthia Wallace, and Rebecca Wisor. As a friend and professional advocate of many years, Patrick R. Query remains unsurpassed, and I have learned much from his thoughts on peace and war in a context in which these phenomena are far beyond merely academic. Finally, without the initial mentorship and guidance of peace activist and educator Tim Peebles, this project would never have begun.

Archival research and library support significantly affected this study. Specifically, I wish to thank the archivists at the Peace Pledge Union, the British Library, the William Ready Research Division of McMaster University, and the Swarthmore College Peace Collection. First-rate librarians at Whitworth University enabled what would otherwise have been virtually impossible tasks, and I gratefully acknowledge the particular assistance of Barbara Carden, Amanda C. R. Clark, and Christina Dolan-Derks.

Research support was provided by Whitworth University in the form of a year's sabbatical from teaching as well as several travel and research grants. My project also received the 2015 Provost's Award for Scholarship. Special thanks is due to the Graves Award committee for a generous grant enabling work in the humanities from scholars teaching at liberal arts colleges.

The use of Vera Brittain material is by permission of Mark Bostridge and T. J. Brittain-Catlin, Literary Executors for the Estate of Vera Brittain 1970. Extracts from various letters by Storm Jameson in the Vera Brittain Collection, McMaster University Library are reprinted by permission of Peters Fraser & Dunlop (www.petersfraserdunlop.com) on behalf of the Estate of Storm Jameson. An early version of chapter 1 appeared in *The Space Between: Literature and Culture 1914–1945*, vol. 8 (2012), edited by Kristin Bluemel. My thanks to current journal editor Janine Utell for her assistance. A portion of chapter 5 was published in *Virginia Woolf Writing the World* (2015), edited by Pamela L. Caughie and Diana L. Swanson. I am grateful to Wayne K. Chapman and Clemson University Press for permission to use this material.

Having a life in which the workday is never really over but the scheduled hours are flexible and variable means that my time with family is greater than most. And yet, there are always sacrifices. For making those concessions to my schedule, either willingly or of necessity, I am forever grateful to Liv—and also for her unwavering belief in this work. My parents, Tom and Ann Andrews, have also celebrated this journey through many of its vagaries, enriching the experience considerably. To Arlo and Robin, I wish the knowledge, spirit, and practices of peacemaking.

ABBREVIATIONS

Aldous Huxley

EG   *Eyeless in Gaza* (1936; New York: HarperPerennial, 2009)

EM   *Ends and Means: An Inquiry into the Nature of Ideals*
            (1937; New Brunswick, N.J.: Transaction, 2012)

HH   *The Hidden Huxley*, ed. David Bradshaw (London: Faber,
            1994)

LAH   *Letters of Aldous Huxley*, ed. Grover Smith (New York:
            Harper and Row, 1969)

Storm Jameson

CP   *Company Parade* (1934; London: Virago, 1982)

CTD   *Challenge to Death* (New York: Dutton, 1935)

JN   *Journey from the North: The Autobiography of Storm Jame-
            son* (New York: Harper and Row, 1970)

LIW   *Love in Winter* (1935; London: Capuchin Classics, 2009)

NTB   *None Turn Back* (1936; London: Virago, 1984)

Rose Macaulay

ANMW   *And No Man's Wit* (Boston: Little, Brown, 1940)

LTS   *Letters to a Sister*, ed. Constance Babington-Smith (New
            York: Atheneum, 1964)

OL   *An Open Letter to a Non-Pacifist* (London: Collins and
            PPU, 1937)

Siegfried Sassoon

CP 1908–56 *Collected Poems 1908–1956* (London: Faber, 1961)

LTC   *Letters to a Critic* (London: John Roberts, 1976)

CMGS   *The Complete Memoirs of George Sherston* (1937; London:
            Faber, 1972)

SLSB   *Selected Letters of Siegfried Sassoon and Edmund Blunden.* Volume 2: *Letters 1932–1947,* ed. Carol Z. Rothkopf (London: Pickering and Chatto, 2012)

Virginia Woolf

D   *The Diary of Virginia Woolf,* ed. Anne Olivier Bell (San Diego: Harvest/Harcourt, 1977–1984)

E   *The Essays of Virginia Woolf,* ed. Andrew McNeillie and Stuart N. Clarke (Orlando: Harcourt Brace Jovanovich, 1987–2011)

L   *The Letters of Virginia Woolf,* vol. 6, 1936–1941, ed. Nigel Nicolson and Joanne Trautmann (Orlando: Harcourt Brace Jovanovich, 1980)

MOB   *Moments of Being: Unpublished Autobiographical Writings,* ed. Jeanne Schulkind (New York: Harcourt Brace Jovanovich, 1976)

TG   *Three Guineas,* ed. Jane Marcus (1938; Orlando: Harvest/Harcourt, 2006)

TY   *The Years,* ed. Eleanor McNees (1937; Orlando: Harvest/Harcourt, 2008)

"Throwing Sand"

The decline of enthusiasm for pacifist movements, the growing strength of aggressive nationalism, the setting up of dictators in one after another of the states of Europe—all these testify to the failure of our ceremonies, our war-books, our peace propaganda as yet to bring about that great reformation which they set out to achieve in the hearts of men. How to preserve the memory of our suffering in such a way that our successors may understand it and refrain from the temptations offered by glamour and glory—that is the problem which we, the war generation, have still to solve before the darkness covers us.

—VERA BRITTAIN, *MANCHESTER GUARDIAN*, NOVEMBER 11, 1930

A young woman was talking to me about my Peace Movement
    the other day.
"And do you really want to abolish war?" she asked.
"I do," was my emphatic reply.
"But don't you think it would be rather a pity?" she objected.
    "You know, peace is rather dull, isn't it? And war is so
    romantic!"

—DICK SHEPPARD, *WE SAY "NO": THE PLAIN MAN'S GUIDE TO PACIFISM* (1935)

Storm Jameson's *No Time like the Present* (1933) begins like a conventional memoir, describing her youth in Whitby with her characteristic style, brisk and fierce and sharply detailed. Then, nearly without warning, the book shifts from story to screed. As her narrative moves closer and closer toward the Great War years, Jameson's outrage at the waste, callousness, and misbegotten sentimentality of the time, as well as her unshackled grief over all the loved ones lost for no good reason, almost entirely derail the book. Her brother, a decorated and successful fighter pilot, was killed in action in January 1917, and as Jameson describes the reactions of the Whitby townsfolk to his death, her prose adopts a free indirect mode for their often heard platitudes: "He was a very nervous boy and he did these things to prove himself. He was reserved but had great ambitions" (*No Time*, 42). Abruptly, as though her rage is uncontainable, the paragraph breaks and she interrogates her reader: "In 1932, what lying, gaping mouth will say that it was worth while to kill my brother in his nineteenth year? You may say that the world's account is balanced by the item that we have with us still a number of elderly patriots, politicians, army contractors, women who obscenely presented white feathers. You will forgive me if, as courteously as is possible in the circumstances, I say that a field latrine is more use to humanity than these leavings" (42–43). This furious explosion, with its lists and its spiteful use of decorous vulgarity, is emblematic of *No Time like the Present*, a book whose structure literally gets bent out of shape in fits of anger. The war has done so much to Jameson, her family, and the provincial community she recollects that every memory is lacerated by violence. Like many of her generation, the war changed everything, and—at least during the early 1930s—opposition to future wars became her primary motivating force, the catalyst for a host of political and creative activities.

Jameson would later reconsider her views about war and betray doubts about her approach to antiwar writing. For so many of the "war generation," Hitler would spoil pacifist absolutes, and Nazism would become the one force that justified another war. Jameson did autobiographical penance for her earlier views in the circumspect and self-censorious *Journey from the North* (1969–1970), which reproaches her previous memoir and much of her literary writing for lacking restraint and blatantly indulging in political advocacy. Many writers followed a similar path, abandoning the "Never Again!" mantra of the 1920s and embracing a range of positions that allowed for violent force in response to Nazism. From the well-known supporters of militant antifascism such as Elizabeth Bowen, George Orwell, and Rebecca West to less well-remembered figures such as Phyllis Bottome, Katharine Burdekin, Sarah Campion, and Sally Carson, the problem of Hitler's regime and its growing menace throughout Europe raised cries for military intervention.[1] The growing body of scholarship on literary responses to World War II has understandably focused on this dominant strain, the change from broad antiwar sentiment to complex, qualified support for this one particular war. My analysis concentrates on a less frequently discussed dimension of 1930s literary culture: the voices of pacifist writers, whose positions were as complicated and various as those of their peers who fully supported the war.

Though the structure of No Time like the Present may seem haphazard and unhinged, it was part of Jameson's original plan, described in a letter to Vera Brittain as a "trick" to get people in 1933 to read antiwar writing when she was unsure of the genre's commercial viability.[2] Employing narrative as subterfuge for a political broadside is an intriguing though somewhat crude solution to a creative problem Jameson faced in much of her writing as she and many other interwar British writers undertook experimental works that fused literary artistry with antiwar propaganda. Peace activist writers like Jameson were wary of either simplistic didacticism or artistic isolationism, and the threat of these twin perils stimulated many of their experiments with literary form. The formal mutation of No Time like the Present is a vivid example of the pressures political convictions and passions exerted upon creative expression, and the five writers I focus on in this study—Aldous Huxley, Storm Jameson, Siegfried Sassoon, Rose Macaulay, and Virginia Woolf—each in their various ways exhibit activist ideals through formally experimental fiction.

Form and politics were united preoccupations for 1930s writers, but the resulting literature did not always satisfy its creators. In Journey from the North, Jameson recalls her skepticism about a gathering of antiwar activists she was asked to convene in 1933 and from which she recruited contributions to an edited collection, Challenge to Death (1935). Though she was ardently committed to peace activism, she realized that wars were not likely prevented by conferences and book projects, and she described these activities as "children throwing sand against the wind" (JN, 326). She presumably intended self-deprecation with this phrase, but another trace of meaning is pertinent too. Children throwing sand may be unable to redefine international relations, protect victims of fascism, or stop bomber planes over European metropoles, but the grains might be useful irritants, a nonlethal force for change. In a wide variety of ways, the authors and works examined in this study are throwing sand, striving toward a peaceable world despite apparent futility. My account of literary peace activism in the 1930s offers a new light in which to see experimental fiction by interwar British writers through integrating the resources of peace studies and literary analysis.

On Pacifism, Nonviolence, and Peace Activism

Before turning to the 1930s peace movement, some discussion is necessary about the murky definition of "pacifism." Several overlapping concepts exist within the current field of peace studies, and nomenclature has been variously applied throughout the history of the peace movement. Even the label "British Peace Movement" is more convenient than precise, a catchall for the many pacifist, internationalist, and antiwar organizations and individual activists who sought to prevent, curtail, or end war.[3] Martin Ceadel, the most thorough chronicler of the interwar peace movement in Britain, has shown that pacifism in the strictest, most absolute sense became conflated with a more pragmatic view that accepts in the short term some necessary wars on the way toward an eventual, completely diplomatic internationalism (*Semi-Detached*, 243). Borrowing from A. J. P. Taylor, Ceadel employs the terms "pacifist" and "pacific-ist" to distinguish between absolute renunciation of violence and the pragmatic acceptance of limited violence. Even though the term "pacific-ist" does appear in some works from the interwar period, its definition was less precise than Taylor's and Ceadel's usage, and for this reason as well as the sheer unwieldiness of the term in both speech and print, I will follow the usual scholarly practice by avoiding it.[4] Among the figures in this study whose thinking changed through the 1930s and into the war years (Jameson and Macaulay most overtly), the term "pacifist" shifted from self-description to a label for others who remained active in peace organizations. And yet, these figures did not adopt new language of the "just war" or "political realist" traditions. Partly, this is because those concepts became more rigorously theorized and employed after the Second World

War, but it is also because these writers continued to identify themselves with pacifism on qualified terms.[5] What Jameson and Macaulay's positions reveal, along with the other writers in this book, is that "pacifism" is not a static or homogenous category but instead names a range of antiwar convictions derived from various humanitarian, religious, affective, or philosophical bases.[6]

Often sharing the conceptual field alongside pacifism is the concept of "nonviolence," a term that has its own history of haphazard usage and consequent misunderstanding. Among its earliest manifestations is *ahimsa*, the Sanskrit term meaning "not injure" found in Hindu and Buddhist religious circles and famously promoted by Gandhi, the figure whose theories and practices bulk large in virtually all twentieth-century peace activism.[7] Later peace activists and scholars have separated "pacifism" from "nonviolence" with a division akin to Ceadel's distinction between "*inspiration* or basis" and "*orientation* or attitude towards society and the problem of war prevention" (*Pacifism in Britain*, 11). Dustin Ells Howes provides an admirably clear definition along these lines: "pacifism is the *ideological* and principled rejection of war and violence, whereas nonviolence refers to *methods* of political action that eschew violence."[8] Gene Sharp, the leading theorist of nonviolence, refines the term further, suggesting that too often "nonviolence" itself becomes an ideological conviction rather than naming strategies and practices, and he prefers "nonviolent action" or "nonviolent struggle" when speaking of methods used to achieve political goals without resorting to "passivity or violence."[9] Consistent in Sharp's voluminous writings is an emphasis on nonviolent action used by people and groups who do not subscribe to any absolute renunciation of violent means but who have found nonviolence a superior weapon in the political arsenal, even against regimes that freely exercise violent force.

My analysis of British writers in the 1930s sorts through the prevailing inspirations of their pacifism, considers how they retained or rejected nonviolence, and situates their positions within contemporary debates about peace and war prevention. Concomitant with this analysis is the recognition that many 1930s activists were not as sophisticated in their theories of pacifism and nonviolence as peace researchers have become since World War II. To some extent this reflects a symptom of that war and its aftermath: the failure of the peace movement to prevent war or produce wide-scale nonviolent actions became a focal point for later theorists and activists determined to learn from past mistakes.[10] Learning from failure certainly has its merits, but my interest in the ways British writers of the thirties theorized peacemaking goes beyond simply pointing out the errors of judgment, faulty reasoning, inadequate foresight, or theoretical and strategic flaws in their proposals. Rather, I encourage us to see these writers' engagement in nascent forms of peace and nonviolence theory as interesting on its own terms, valuable as projections into future methodologies, and demonstrative of aesthetic practices that have rarely been considered as participating in peace work. For many of these novelists, fiction was a crucial vehicle for raising awareness of social injustices and belligerent ideologies and for calling readers into active engagement with these increasing threats of violence.

Activism remains the overarching concern of this study, especially as conducted through literary writing. This focus refutes the tenacious and erroneous conflation of pacifism with passivity that persists despite scholarly interventions in peace studies, theological ethics, political science, and modern history. This conflation was no less pronounced in the 1930s. Cecil Day Lewis, for instance, responded to Aldous Huxley's antiwar pamphlet *What Are You Going to Do about It?* with his own *We're Not Going to Do Nothing!* (both 1936), as if "nothing" were Huxley's proposal. Likewise, Gerald K. Hibbert's edited collection *The New Pacifism* (1936), with essays by Huxley, A. A. Milne, and Dick Sheppard, expressed its primary mission as a reinvigoration of "active" pacifism. While I do not deny the existence of a completely passive strain of pacifism, it is overshadowed by the record of active, engaged pacifism more appropriately called peacemaking or peacebuilding.[11]

Among 1930s peacemakers, one organization holds pride of place throughout this study: Britain's one-time largest and still extant secular pacifist group, the Peace Pledge Union (PPU).[12] Its origins and effects will be described in fuller detail later, but in brief, all five writers were connected to the PPU. Huxley, Jameson, Sassoon, and Macaulay were sponsors or founder members, and Woolf, though characteristically removed from official membership, discussed, wrote about, and interacted with the group. The PPU offers a microcosm of the thirties peace movement, with its heterogeneous makeup and conflicting approaches toward understanding pacifism and enacting nonviolence. For much of the interwar period, the British populace maintained a wide-spread, even normative, resistance to war and desire for better international organization—positions that came at the expense of any detailed, shared vision. In Richard Overy's words, "to be anti-war in the 1920s and 1930s was to acquire membership in a broad church, though scarcely a united front" (*Morbid Age*, 221). General agreement that war should be eliminated (or at least strenuously avoided) and that some better form of international relationship might be the key to this goal opened the possibility for radical, separatist Christians to join with Marxist revolutionaries, but it offered little guidance about how divided visions could be reconciled. What was problematic for the peace movement's political cohesion provides a major source of interest for the present study. The five writers examined in these pages are united in writing against war but distinct in their motivations and their strategies for crafting what I refer to as "pacifist aesthetics."

Pacifist Aesthetics in 1930s Literature

One of the crucial interventions made by Phyllis Lassner's *British Women Writers of World War II* is a disruption of the prowar/antiwar binary prevalent in scholarly discussions. For the years surrounding World War II, Lassner argues, this reductive view of women's positions has obscured a wider range of attitudes and activities through leaning too heavily on a paradigm derived from World War I and from Virginia Woolf's "metahistorical and pancultural construction of fascism as well as essentialist theories that women are only passive victims, war protestors, or complicit with the power of a masculinist war machine" (4). What Lassner offers in her critique of other scholars' "universalist anti-war conclusions" is the recovery of many voices conflicted about war and also those who wrote to support the Allied military effort.

Writing against War pursues Lassner's conclusions with a different scope, challenging antiwar universalism not by attending to nonpacifists but by showing how pacifism itself is more capacious and varied than is often supposed. All of the writers I discuss were active in the peace movement and all were in differing ways engaged in war prevention, violence reduction, and conflict resolution debates. Calling these "debates" is not a figure of speech; there were sharp disagreements within and among peace organizations throughout the thirties about underlying convictions as well as specific policies and responses to an array of political crises that marked the decade. Though Huxley, Jameson, Sassoon, Macaulay, and Woolf were energetic peace activist writers and shared many values as well as strategic objectives, they were also in contentious dialogue with each other and with many intellectuals in the movement. Their efforts toward literary peace work, while sharing some formal and stylistic traits, were distinctive contributions toward politically committed literature.

Political commitment has long been seen as a defining feature of British writing in the 1930s, a time, as Samuel Hynes influentially describes it, when writers produced "worlds of the imagination which would consist in new, significant forms, and through which literature could play a moral role in a time of crisis" (*Auden Generation*, 13). The combination of literary art and political agenda profoundly troubled many writers. While writing her now canonical modernist novels of the 1920s, Virginia Woolf famously accused Edwardian social realists of making "incomplete" books, novels whose completion could only be achieved by a reader compelled "to do something—to join a society, or, more desperately, to write a cheque" (*E*, 3:427). In her critique, she does not deny that there is pleasure to be found in this sort of writing, but she is reluctant to call it fiction, a form that ought not to "preach doctrines, sing songs, or celebrate the glories of the British Empire" (*E*, 3:425). But by the thirties, Woolf would find the lure of politicized art and even propaganda impossible to avoid.[13] Even among avowedly activist writers, there remained throughout the decade a nagging sense of what Benjamin Kohlmann calls an "apolitical unconscious," or "the fraught attraction to the idea of a supposedly self-contained writing among authors variously associated with the political left" (*Committed Styles*, 4–5). From either of these positions, then, the relationship between artistic representation and political didacticism was far from harmonious.

Since Hynes's study, many scholars have expanded the range of his archive, challenged his view of Auden's predominance for the period, and pointed to the centrality of women writers and middlebrow works.[14] My research is indebted to this expansive view of thirties writing and broadened understanding of political and aesthetic commitment, but within that rich field of recovery and recuperation, relatively little has been written by literary scholars about the peace movement. Scholarship on the thirties often treats pacifist and antiwar writing as a side issue, at best a single feature of a crowded landscape. In some cases, there is noticeable dismissiveness, emblematized by Valentine Cunningham's claim that violent and sadistic fixations during this decade made the PPU "really such a non-starter among '30s intellectuals" (*British Writers*, 69). This presumed lack of influence obscures the rich and complicated range of positions and aesthetic practices at work among pacifists of the 1930s.

Another important effect of reading peace activist fiction as a unit rather than a subsidiary element of another project—the political left, writing about war, feminist literature, etc.—is that it yields a crop of writers who might not ordinarily seem to be linked. The concept of intermodernism promoted by Kristin Bluemel has among its hallmarks a reconsideration of writers with "eccentric political alliances" or whose work was in "genres of writing that fall far outside formal markers of modernism" (*Intermodernism*, 5). This categorization is apt for several of the authors I examine, and indeed, Bluemel's appendix, "Who Are the Intermodernists?," includes minibiographies of Huxley, Jameson, and Macaulay. Placing Sassoon and Woolf alongside these others gives the opportunity to reconsider their importance for understanding 1930s political writing. The heterogeneity within the peace movement enables a complicated picture to emerge within the broader understanding of the thirties as a time of politically engaged literature in crisis.

The peace movement's contribution to political literature of the 1930s has been eclipsed by several factors, including simplistic conceptions of pacifism and narrow critical orthodoxies about 1930s politics. Also, throughout the discipline, there is much greater interest in the philosophical, political, and cultural dynamics of war. Though certainly not celebratory of war per se, this large body of work testifies to the perennial fascination with the cultural functions of horror, trauma, and violence.[15] As Dick Sheppard's interlocutor points out in the epigraph to this chapter, war seems far more romantic—and compellingly literary—than peace (*We Say NO!*, 43). R. S. White, author of the widest survey of pacifism and British literature, observes that scholars disproportionately focus on militarism and violence rather than peace. He notes that "libraries are filled with vast sections on military history and theory" and that in researching pacifism, he routinely "encountered the phrase in book indexes, 'Peace: see War'" (*Pacifism*, 4). Sarah Cole explains this phenomenon, claiming that for the Great War generation, "the great goal was to see that such wars could never happen again; for ours, it may simply be to comprehend them."[16] Cole's point is trenchant, making visible the purpose of humanistic studies during our present age of perpetual war. Attending, however, to the imaginative ways literary writers enacted their peace witness arrives at the problem of war from another direction, not just (or not always) examining the workings of violence but exploring the possibilities of nonviolence and peacemaking.

Responding to violence through art was a continual problem for peace activist writers. To explain the special dynamics of warfare, Cole theorizes two types of violence: "either the fuel for generativity or the emblem of grotesque loss" (*Violet Hour*, 39). Following Max Weber, she describes these modes as "enchanted" (producing a magical or quasi-religious redemption) or "disenchanted" (leaving only traumatic, abject despair). War is a special case, spectacular as "a fertile field for imagining art as a legacy of enchanted and disenchanted violence" (40). She argues that pacifist artists often use disenchanted violence as their primary tool for convincing readers or spectators, and she shows how trench poets, memoirists, and novelists of the Great War continually return to "carefully chosen images of bodily rupture and pain" as the centerpiece of their "disenchanting agenda" (64). As an argument about the dynamics of represented violence, Cole's theory is quite persuasive and informs my thinking, but in the pages that follow, I will show how disenchanting violence is only one of many devices peace activist writers use to convey an antiwar message while retaining literary complexity. The writers I examine recognized that brutal representations of violence, though possibly achieving their desired rhetorical effect, might just as easily stimulate bloodlust. Fredric Jameson has noted that many Great War works intended as warnings "occasionally had the opposite effect, fascinating young people bored and frustrated by peacetime."[17] Moreover, believing that war is hell is not confined to a pacifist faith. All combatants know that warfare is horrible, and demonstrating through fiction the extent of those horrors may not sway readers convinced of a particular war's necessity. As a pacifist device, "disenchanting violence" can rest too heavily on horrific images, using descriptions of bodies in pain as the sole method for revealing the viciousness of war and making graphic content the basis of a peace witness.

Overemphasizing content remains one of the hazards in the emerging cross-disciplinary work of peace studies and literary criticism.[18] Antony Adolf, in his theorization of "peace literature," claims that "content and process are paramount, and thus take precedence over formal and structural traits" ("What Does Peace Literature Do?, 12). Though Adolf's goal is to argue for the importance of historical context and against "pure" formalism when defining a genre of "peace literature," placing the stress solely on context and content can obscure the ways literary form advances a peace witness. Similar to Adolf's insistence on content is R. S. White's attempt, in *Pacifism and English Literature: Minstrels of Peace*, to show "that literature can be read and analysed from a pacifist perspective when its subject celebrates peace as a natural precondition for human existence and condemns war as an unnatural death wish" (1). White's theory rests squarely on his commitment to natural law, in which nature inclines toward life and away from death, and his survey of many centuries of English literature works largely by accretion, demonstrating through multiple examples the presence of pacifist ideas in British cultural texts.[19] The greatest value of his study is its response to the kind of argument C. S. Lewis makes in his essay "Why I Am Not a Pacifist" (1940), claiming that pacifism commands the rejection of most great literature. According to Lewis, "If I am a Pacifist, I have Arthur and Aelfred, Elizabeth and Cromwell, Walpole and Burke, against me. I have the literature of my country against me, and cannot even open my *Beowulf*, my Shakespeare, my Johnson, or my Wordsworth without being reproved."[20] The reproach Lewis believes awaits the literate pacifist seems predicated on the notion that Shakespeare and company affirm the wars they describe, and White's rejoinder is a wealth of antiwar sentiment quoted from Shakespearean characters, romantic poetry, and many other English cultural artifacts Lewis deems inherently antipacifist.[21] Both White and Lewis suggest that the critical task in reading about war involves gleaning messages of "celebration" or "condemnation"—determined by authorial or contextual clues and discernable attitudes about represented violence.

I share the conviction that context is essential for interpreting the political agendas of literature, and my analyses in this study strive for thick description of contemporary peace movement debates circulating around and through activists' fiction. But I also show through formal analysis how often these novels resist simplistic didacticism, trouble authorial statements found in extraliterary writings, and manifest the messy realities of a peace witness. White's attempt to read "as a pacifist" risks construing pacifism as simple "affirmation of life" that effaces many nuanced and conflicted views about war and peace that are expressed through the innovative literary forms of 1930s novels.

Despite White's intervention, the interdisciplinary field of peace studies remains more immersed in social scientific methodologies than in theories and practices of the humanities.[22] One major exception is the eminent peace activist and researcher John Paul Lederach, who has been an important voice calling for more "literary" approaches to peace work. In *The Moral Imagination: The Art and Soul of Building Peace*, Lederach suggests that cyclical patterns of violence persist, in part, because of a failure to imagine, and that rigidly schematized approaches to peacebuilding can sometimes lack the creativity needed to transcend violence: "we must explore the creative process itself, not as a tangential inquiry, but as the wellspring that feeds the building of peace . . . we must venture into the mostly uncharted territory of the artist's way as applied to social change" (5). This contention has understandably found favor in humanistic disciplines, but while Lederach's book is an interesting starting point for interdisciplinary inquiry, his attention to "the artist's way" focuses more on how ideas are generated than on examining the ways that literary forms engage with the problems of warfare and peacemaking.[23]

Writing against War supplements peace research like Lederach's, which relies too heavily on romantic notions of the "artist," and literary analysis like White's, which traffics too casually with an ahistorical "pacifist impulse" found in content-based readings of literature. A compelling model is Grace Brockington's *Above the Battlefield: Modernism and the Peace Movement in Britain, 1900–1918*, which goes beyond cataloguing belligerent images or the effects of disenchanting violence to show how artistic forms within a particular historical context were engaged in peace witness. Brockington recovers a forgotten core of pacifism within modernist art by attending to "non-combatant artists and writers who asked far-reaching questions about the nature of civilization and how it should be defended, but whose principled objection to war is frequently interpreted as the shirking of civic responsibility or indifference to suffering"

(*Above the Battlefield*, 2). She demonstrates how seemingly apolitical avant-garde works of visual, plastic, and theatrical arts were through their experimental forms contributing to antiwar activism in the years surrounding World War I. Brockington's concern for historically grounded formal analysis is exemplary, and I follow her lead while analyzing a different period and medium.

One of the most promising frameworks for examining pacifist literary forms is Nancy Knowles's theory of "narrative pacifism."[24] Knowles derives from Woolf's *Three Guineas* a theoretical model with four interrelated components: social inequality in the foreground, militarism in the background, a fragmentary and "unconventional narrative structure," and a gesture toward art as a redemptive force in this conflictual mix ("Active Pacifism," 242). Knowles extracts from *Three Guineas* a formalist approach to politics, gleaning the best of Woolf's contribution to pacifist thinking while largely shedding the gender essentialism that has been pointedly criticized by later readers.[25] My fictional analyses do not attempt to filter all critical interpretations through Knowles's narrative pacifism, but when appropriate I will return to specific aspects of her theory, testing how particular novels employ or deviate from the structures she identifies.

Vital to my analysis is showing how literary works engage with matters of peacemaking and conflict resolution apart from explicit representations of violence. Knowles's attention to conflict within the fictional form correlates with the views of critics such as Mia Spiro, who argues that modernist writers in the thirties used "experimental novelization" for "anti-Nazi strategies" (*Anti-Nazi Modernism*, 11). Resistance to Hitler, Spiro contends, was performed audaciously (if imperfectly) through novelistic forms that deviated from conventional, realist approaches to plotting and characterization, without relying on overt discussions of Nazism or its victims. Among the five writers I consider, self-conscious experimentation with established novelistic conventions offers a solution to the problem of combining artistic integrity and political advocacy. These writers convey antiwar and pacifist messages with fictional devices that include nonlinear chronologies, divided points of view, authorial interjection, and displaced or sublimated violence. Each of the following chapters traces the ways a given literary work thwarts conventional expectations, challenging readers to confront the social structures that facilitate war. Formal experiments not only complicate and give artistic richness to the political agendas of each work but also enact pacifist agendas.

Reading the British Peace Movement

The British peace movement of the 1930s offers a virtually peerless example within the history of peace activism, when impassioned, creative energies from absolute pacifists found broad-based sympathy among the general populace. The so-called Peace Ballot that the internationalist League of Nations Union (LNU) conducted during 1934 and 1935 became what David Cortright describes as "one of the largest and most successful mobilizations of peace sentiment in history" (*Peace*, 77). The LNU polled 38 percent of adult British people about their views regarding the League of Nations, decrease of armaments, abolition of military and naval aircraft, and other measures seeking international and cooperative forms of collective security and violence reduction. The results showed that the majority of those surveyed supported realistic peace-minded measures.[26] More equivocal was the nearly 59 percent favorable response to using military intervention if absolutely necessary, a mirror of debates within the peace movement proper about pacifist absolutism versus armament-based strategies such as collective security. Many peace activist organizations were founded or dramatically increased in membership during this time, including the Peace Pledge Union, which reached its peak in 1940 with roughly 136,000 members, despite the death or defection of many of its leading figures (Ceadel, *Semi-Detached*, 400). What exactly this "peace sentiment" amounted to in practice was quite varied, of course, and the general antipathy to war did not crystallize into unified strategies or policies.

Despite widespread antiwar feelings and leadership from intellectuals and artists in the pacifist vanguard, the 1930s peace movement is perhaps best remembered for its resounding failure to achieve what many felt was its essential goal: preventing another war. The collapse of that common platform has had a lasting influence on discussions about the viability of nonviolence against supremely violent regimes, and historians and political theorists continue to debate the possibilities for avoiding World War II, especially regarding the infamous appeasement campaign led by Neville Chamberlain.[27] The peace movement's relationship with appeasement was as complex and various as any other policy, as Cecelia Lynch notes, ranging "from lukewarm support of avoiding war to outright opposition to annexation" (*Beyond Appeasement*, 97). None of the authors in this study saw appeasement as a perfect solution, and their novels do not advocate any single government-led plan of war prevention. In fact, optimism of any kind is fleeting in these novels, which take the high probability of failure as an animating theme. Impending war was a perennial fear, at least as far back as the rebarbative Treaty of Versailles, which J. M. Keynes and many others argued would only ensure more international conflict. Writing in 1930, before Hitler's assumption of the chancellorship and the many violent crises of the midthirties, Vera Brittain identified several factors as leading Europe toward another war: militant nationalism, dictatorial leaders, and declining pacifist activism.[28] Brittain forewarns that the responsibility for war prevention belongs to the "war generation" of the 1910s, whose "war books" and "peace propaganda" must combat militarism by preserving the memory of their suffering. She observes that "a mass of literature has already grown up around the war," but "despite the fact that the immense civilian armies were more articulate than actual fighters have ever been before," this literature is "inadequate to save from self-destruction a new generation" (*Testament of a Generation*, 210). Implied is her belief that political literature by the war generation can be prophetic for their children, serving as cautionary tales to avoid the devastations their parents brought upon themselves. Failure is looming, Brittain contends, because the warnings are unheeded, and the inexorable rush of history inclines toward repetition.

Unforeseen in Brittain's commentary, however, is that the recurrence of war would not only be a matter of bloated patriotism and alliances gone awry but would involve militant aggression seemingly immune to diplomacy and willfully destructive in ways far surpassing the previous war. This new kind of threat intersects with what Sarah Cole identifies as the three related problems for the peace movement: passivity, complicity, and efficacy (*Violet Hour*, 228). As I noted earlier, the charge that pacifism is merely passive tenaciously holds fast, and many peace activist writings in the 1930s positioned themselves against this perception. Complicity may be even harder to shake because it registers a conflict of values between those who believe war is necessary and useful and those who persist with advocating nonviolence. After the war, Rebecca West reflected in *The Meaning of Treason* that the PPU was "that ambiguous organisation which in the name of peace was performing many actions certain to benefit Hitler" (qtd. in Morrison, *I Renounce War*, 51).[29] And, with his typical bluntness, George Orwell wrote: "Pacifism is objectively pro-Fascist" (*My Country Right or Left*, 220).[30] Orwell's claim assumes that pacifism is either passive, and thus ineffectual, or obstructionist, impeding military actions needed for victory. In either case, the enemy gains from pacifist collusion. This view assumes that violence is more effective than nonviolence, especially when confronting forces eager to use violence for their own goals. The writers in this study expended a great deal of intellectual energy responding to the challenges of passivity, complicity, and effectiveness from both opponents of the peace movement and their own internal reservations. That there emerged no definitive rebuttal to these charges signifies another dimension of the British peace movement's failure.

It is possible, however, to reframe the notion of "failure," as some activists did, by refusing to see the start of World War II as the only index of the peace movement's worth. I have mentioned the approach of later theorists who use the 1930s as a case study, a negative example valuable for future activists, and there are also studies of the small, often impromptu, successful nonviolent actions against the Nazis in places such as Norway and Denmark.[31] Additionally, there is a "long view" notion of peace activism, which recognizes that violent conflict will not suddenly vanish but requires instead a slow process of violence reduction based on a larger, less immediate goal of a just peace.[32] In the long view, each particular war is a tragic and lamentable setback but not a definitive proof of the ineptitude of nonviolence. There is unquestionably a utopian dimension to this way of thinking insofar as it calls for a better way of being than currently exists, and large-scale revolution also hovers in its prophecies. As John Middleton Murry wrote in 1937 during his pacifist period and while promoting a socialism derived in equal parts from Marx and Christ, "pacifism cannot be less than a revolutionary faith: it involves a revolution in the inward man and compels a revolution in the society to which it belongs" (*The Pledge of Peace*, 116).[33] For the five British writers in this study, there is noticeable competition between the desire for short-term efficacy and a long view commitment to pacifism, and my arguments trace how these writers grappled with internal conflicts over these two positions. Returning to antiwar writing of the 1930s is partly an investigation of how to live with political failure and how literature reveals the fissures and contradictions inherent in political advocacy. What separates literary art from propaganda in peace activist novels is the willingness to dwell deeply in uncertainty, internal conflict, and even likely defeat, all the while extending glimpses of a better world along with offering a penetrating critique of the one we have.

Five Peace Activist Writers

Propelling the narrative of *Writing against War* is the variety of reactions within the peace movement to several political crises of the long 1930s. Hitler's assumption of power, rearmament of the Rhineland, appeasement at Munich, and invasion of Poland, plus Italy's conquest of Abyssinia and the civil war in Spain were events that forced peace activists to reckon with the lived realities of their convictions. The five central authors in this study respond to these political crises and record the often painful confrontations between deeply held pacifist convictions and seemingly insurmountable military force. In their various responses to this time of crisis, these literary writers enable a microcosmic view of the British peace movement.

My principle of inclusion is to attend to writers known primarily for literary writing rather than memoir, philosophy, criticism, journalism, etc., and who were clearly involved in peace activism. Much interwar literature can be seen as "against war" at some level—Ford Madox Ford even prefaced the second volume of *Parade's End* by saying that like other combatants, he hoped his novel could create "such a state of mind as should end wars as possibilities" (4). Like Ford, literary writers such as Richard Aldington, Helen Zenna Smith (Evadne Price), and Christopher Isherwood all created broadly antiwar works but did not match this writing with dedicated peace activism; others, such as Bertrand Russell, Maude Royden, and John Middleton Murry were peace activist writers but did not specialize in literary genres. My five primary authors are representative rather than exhaustive, though few writers from this period were as successful at combining peace work and fiction writing. Each knew of the others and several were friends or social acquaintances, but there is little suggestion in their diaries and letters that they were aware of the full extent of their shared intellectual, creative, and political project. My critical recovery work shows how novelists who felt isolated in their politically committed creative pursuits were in fact united by a common cause and struggling with similar aesthetic problems.

The following five chapters concentrate on a single author and work or "project" to provide a multifocal lens for considering the range of pacifist literature during the height of the British peace movement. Huxley is my starting point because no other major literary figure was as central to the movement. Not only did his full-blown, absolute pacifist conversion coincide with the formation of the Peace Pledge Union, but his charter membership quickly grew into active campaigning against war on PPU platforms. Through his pamphlets and books on peace, Huxley engineered much of the PPU's philosophical infrastructure. *Eyeless in Gaza* (1936), with its fractured chronological structure, is formally experimental and explicitly pacifist, and it explores the agonistic tensions of living for peace while surrounded by violence.

The second chapter analyzes a trilogy of novels by Storm Jameson, a figure whose political profile rivals Huxley's and whose total literary output surpasses all the others considered in this study. Among Jameson's nearly seventy books are more than forty novels, which engage a vast range of styles and interests and which document her changing political sensibilities across a sixty-year career. Jameson's deep commitment to antiwar, antifascist, and socialist political organizations was integral to her fiction in the 1930s, and her voluminous writing leaves a record of an intense struggle to reconcile pacifism and antifascism. Her *Mirror in Darkness* trilogy (1934–36) is a panoramic look at the 1920s, a projected roman-fleuve of half a dozen novels that she abandoned when she felt that she had lost the form. Yet what remains is a testament to her lively experiment in socialist fiction that could critique the fascist and militarist ideologies of interwar Britain.

From Jameson's highly engaged political writing, which charts in linear, chronological fashion her turn from staunch pacifist into cautious war supporter, we turn in chapter 3 to Siegfried Sassoon and his *Memoirs of George Sherston* (1928–36), which creates a much more hybrid relationship between the peace activist and the warrior. In this chapter, I treat hybridity in multiple aspects of Sassoon's career—especially his veteran-pacifism, which combines emotional and ethical commitment to brothers-in-arms while vehemently resisting the war machine, and also his experimental approach to genre, which produced his unconventional "autobiographical novel" or "fictional memoir" well in advance of today's creative nonfiction. *The Memoirs of George Sherston*, in many respects more avant-garde than his better known trench poetry, enacts a narrative pacifism rich with political ambivalence and formal complexity.

Following my exploration of Huxley's philosophical mysticism, Jameson's antifascist socialism and Sassoon's ambivalent veteran-pacifism, chapter 4 analyzes the war writings of Rose Macaulay, whose ardent pacifist activism changed during the Spanish Civil War to a qualified support of militant antifascism and ultimately into a mournful postwar effort to tend the ruins of London. Much of the attention to Macaulay's works has focused on her middlebrow comic writing or, when seriously considering her politics, her early pacifist novel *Non-Combatants and Others* (1916) and her postwar bombsites novel *The World My Wilderness* (1950). I examine instead her Spanish Civil War novel, *And No Man's Wit* (1940), which takes head-on the severe challenge to absolute pacifism occasioned by the war in Spain and its premonition of the global fight against Fascism and Nazism. In Macaulay's fiction we find the best example of a combination of public activism, popular writing, satire against war, and finally lament—a process that retains its peace advocacy in new forms despite the loss of absolute pacifism.

As far as activism goes, Virginia Woolf is the most marginal figure in this study, but my reasons for including her are several. With the exception of Tolstoy, it is hard to think of a writer as highly regarded today who was as unabashed about her pacifist convictions. Though she never joined any particular peace organization, she spoke publically on behalf of peace right up to the last years of her life, and she published major works espousing her pacifist convictions, most notably the sibling texts *The Years* (1937) and *Three Guineas* (1938). Though many critics share Leonard Woolf's view that *The Years* is among her weakest novels, chapter 5 offers an analysis of the subtly provocative ways that Woolf attempted a mode of literary nonviolence evident in her rhetorical and narrative forms.

Linking these diverse approaches is the demand placed on readers to engage with unconventional forms and to mount interior resistance to what Judith Butler calls war's "daily effort at conscription" (*Frames of War*, xiv). Though reading books on peace may be one more action equivalent to throwing sand against the wind, this intellectual effort may begin the process of immersing in Lederach's idea of the moral imagination, which, as he describes it, "requires the capacity to imagine ourselves in a web of relationships that includes our enemies; the ability to sustain a paradoxical curiosity that embraces complexity without reliance on dualistic polarity; the fundamental belief in and pursuit of the creative act; and the acceptance of the inherent risk of stepping into the mystery of the unknown that lies beyond the far too familiar landscape of violence" (*Moral Imagination*, 5). With the five writers analyzed in *Writing against War*, we can encounter that relational web, complex curiosity, creative pursuit, and acceptance of mystery. In doing so, we may uncover the ways that political activism involves choices made at specific times with only the limited information we have at hand. A universal pacifist conviction offers merely the starting point for a set of lived actions that manifest this pacifism. The novel becomes a key cultural record of how various lives are worked out—literary constructions of pacifist beliefs put into practice.

CHAPTER 1

Pledging Peace in Aldous Huxley's *Eyeless in Gaza*

Prominent among the various cultural attitudes in Britain during the interwar years was a widely held and often deeply felt revulsion to war. The living memory of the Great War, despite certain efforts to move beyond its legacy, was profoundly memorialized in the 1920s and transformed into cultural myth through a host of media on stage, page, and screen.[1] This cultural exploration of recent history and concomitant wave of antiwar sentiment stood in close kinship with a growing fear that another, worse war was imminent. Storm Jameson captured the mood in the title of her *New Clarion* essay from October 1933: "Fifteen Years Ago—We Said 'NEVER AGAIN!'" Jameson, like many others, recorded a sickening sense that the dark days of 1914 were returning. Putting the fearful mood in terms of a medical condition, Aldous Huxley described the condition of Europe in 1936: "Four and a half years of homicidal and suicidal mania were followed by seventeen of more or less acute neurosis during the last reign. At the start of a new reign our civilisation is showing symptoms of physical and mental disease even more alarming than those which were discernable before 1914. The new reign opens upon a momentous question: will the disease be allowed to run its course, or shall we decide that it is time to begin a new epoch of history and try to cure the present symptoms and prevent their recurrence?" (*HH*, 215). Only with a thoroughgoing change in the sociopolitical order might there be some relief from the disease of war.

The hoped for peace in Europe grew especially tenuous in 1933 with Hitler's assumption of power that January and growing signs of his aggression—Jameson's *New Clarion* article names German rearmament, persecution of socialists and Jews, and rejection of the League of Nations. But Hitler's ascent may be seen as a turning point rather than the sole source of the European crisis. The flaws in the Versailles treaties made themselves ever more apparent, and the economic crash of the late 1920s spread its deleterious effects on international relations, greatly diminishing the capacity to secure lasting peace. As Patrick O. Cohrs argues, the "Achilles' heel of the unfinished peace order after the Great War" was to be found in British and American stabilization policies, which "came to fail because those who shaped these policies did not, or could not, do enough in a period of 'relative stability' to buttress the newly republican Germany and to back those in Berlin who were struggling to pursue peaceful change and a *rapprochement* with the west" (*Unfinished Peace*, 574). At precisely this time of escalating militarism amid social and economic hardship, the peace movement galvanized popular animosity to war, and along with the rallies, demonstrations, pamphleteering, and protests were literary efforts heralding that cry of "never again!" As we will see in the next chapter, Jameson's responses to the crises in Europe would grow and change, modifying according to her acute sense of justice during the Nazis' systematic devastations of the continent. Huxley's views also developed through the 1930s, but his unwavering commitment to pacifism and his celebrity within the peace movement make him an especially good starting point for analyzing the strategies of peace activist literature.

Amid the vagaries of popular and critical fashion, no writer as thoroughly and publically engaged with the British peace movement remains as well known today as Aldous Huxley. Others were equally active in the political movement and some were arguably more popular in their day, but Huxley, largely through the enduring taste for his influential dystopia *Brave New World* (1932), has kept a foothold in the public consciousness—albeit shorn of many of his true political beliefs.[2] As David Bradshaw has shown in *The Hidden Huxley*, the 1930s were a period of intellectual sea change for Huxley, moving from an elitist champion of eugenics enamored with H. L. Mencken and flirting with intellectual authoritarianism, as did Yeats, Pound, and Lawrence, to becoming what Bradshaw calls "a fugelman of the anti-fascist intelligentsia and a spokesman for the dispossessed" (*HH*, viii).[3]

Along with his growing concern for the poor and recognition of the blight of fascism was an intensifying of his pacifist convictions, which had roots in his involvement with the literary celebrities of Bloomsbury, many of whom he had met at Ottoline Morrell's invitation to Garsington Manor.[4] His early reactions to the outbreak of the First World War had been consistent with stereotypically patriotic peers, writing to his father on September 14, 1914 that news of war was "splendid" (*LAH*, 62). He was pronounced "totally unfit," however, because of eye problems, and his disqualification from active combat in January 1916 occasioned his turn toward the pacifist views of many in Morrell's circle (Murray, *Huxley*, 60). During the war, he performed alternative service at Garsington, clearing brush and doing other yardwork, sharing this post with Bertrand Russell and John Middleton Murry, and he became acquainted with Russell's pacifist writings, such as *Principles of Social Reconstruction* (1916), also published under the more obviously war-themed title *Why Men Fight*.[5] By March 1916 he was writing to his brother Julian that if it were possible, "I think I'd be a conscientious objector" (*LAH*, 97).

This halfway commitment to a position he would never need to test sustained him through the immediate postwar years, and though it is risky to assign too much weight to any one moment in a person's life, we can conveniently note that 1936 was a pivotal year for Huxley. Much of his creative energy before this year was spent writing the five largely satirical novels on which his reputation still rests: *Crome Yellow* (1921), *Antic Hay* (1923), *Those Barren Leaves* (1925), *Point Counter Point* (1928), and the work typically seen as his magnum opus—*Brave New World*. Over his lifetime, Huxley produced many of his nearly fifty books under contractual obligations to write two or even three books per year, a pace that seemed to cause him little concern. Yet *Eyeless in Gaza*, his underread masterpiece, took four years to complete. Begun in 1932 and published in 1936, *Eyeless* is in most ways typical of Huxley's fiction—erudite, philosophical, and semiautobiographical. His title alludes to Milton's *Samson Agonistes*, and his characters each take competing positions on the issues most important to Huxley and his cohort of artists and intellectuals: human relations, mystical spirituality, and radical politics. *Eyeless in Gaza* also shows off some of Huxley's most formally adventurous writing, particularly with regard to narrative chronology. Each of the novel's fifty-four chapters is set on a specific day between November 6,

1902, and February 23, 1935. Lacking any readily discernible pattern, the chapters jump back and forth within this thirty-three year range. The earliest dates show our main character Anthony Beavis as a young boy at his mother's funeral; by the 1910s we see him at Oxford; by the 1920s Anthony is a struggling writer; and by the 1930s he is in a love affair with Helen, briefly involved in a Mexican revolution, and ultimately converts to pacifism.

Many critics focus on the novel's form, treating its convolutions as a stand-alone point of interest divorced from content.[6] The avant-garde time structure of the novel was part of Huxley's long and difficult struggle with the text, and the consistent critical attention to this feature is understandable. In February 1934 Huxley wrote to Mary Hutchinson, saying: "I dodder along with my book, rather exasperated because I can't quite get the formal relations between parts that I'm looking for . . . I am looking for a device to present two epochs of a life simultaneously so as to show their relations with one another—and also their lack of relationship. For when one considers life one is equally struck by both facts—that one has remained the same and become totally different" (*LAH*, 292). Staging a contradictory, possibly even self-defeating, narrative of discovery was Huxley's goal, but his aims were more than just producing a formally flashy bildungsroman. The composition of this book may be seen as a form of spiritual discipline, a key component of his own gradual conversion to pacifism as an article of faith. With *Eyeless in Gaza*, Huxley seems to have marked a new aesthetic, philosophical, and political direction. I will explore this shift to show how 1936 was not only a turning point for Huxley but also for the peace movement in the build-up to World War II. Subsequent chapters will add to this portrait of the changing fortunes of the peace movement, but in this chapter we will consider how Huxley's pacifist activism provides a context for his narrative experiments in order to better understand his complicated expression of a newfound politics.

Critics attentive to this new politics often diverge from formalist readings by regarding *Eyeless in Gaza* as essentially synonymous with the pacifist tracts Huxley wrote during the same period. George Woodcock confesses the disillusionment he felt when as a young man he read *Eyeless* and found its narrative of "conversion to mystical religion" to be Huxley's suggestion "with obvious didactic intent—that such a spiritual evolution was not merely compatible with the pacifist and decentralist politics that he had recently been preaching in print and on public platforms, but was perhaps the only condition under which they could become effective" (*Dawn and the Darkest Hour*, 3). In this interpretation, Huxley's supposed didacticism — made especially repellent by his espousing a suspicious and/or foolish creed — overwhelms the novel's formal innovations and undermines Huxley's credentials as a prophet for some new, quasi-libertarian society.

Disillusionment over Huxley's mystical turn resonates with the broader disillusionment within the peace movement. The challenge of the Spanish Civil War, which presented a clear case of violence against innocents and military defense requiring broader European support, shook the confidence of many peace activists, and the Munich crisis, with the indelible black mark of appeasement, further divided the disparate groups working to prevent war. Huxley's own position at this crisis point in the late thirties is open to deep criticism. By 1938 he had abandoned Britain for the United States, where he lived the rest of his life as a screenwriter, public intellectual, narcotics voyager, and countercultural sage. The introverted mysticism of Huxley's later years can seem like a dodge, shirking political exigencies in Europe for the seclusion of the American West, and in his lifetime it was met with mockery, disappointment, and bafflement.[7] Differing from many peace movement luminaries, Huxley never abandoned the pacifist convictions he espoused before the Second World War, but his life narrative also lacks any heroic, nonviolent confrontation with the belligerent and genocidal forces surging through Europe.

Before entering the late phase of his life and career as a self-styled guru, at the pivot point of 1936, Huxley sought an integrated life of literary expression, personal discipline, and public peace activism. Huxley's experimental literary pursuits, rather than being a separate function of his intellectual interests, were essential to his peace activism in the 1930s and to his ongoing search for a coherent and totalizing system for living life well. Many of Huxley's contemporaries and later critics, mistakenly view *Eyeless in Gaza* as merely didactic. The critical treatment of *Eyeless in Gaza* seems contradictory, reading it as an avant-garde formalist exercise *or* as merely a pacifist tract. I focus instead on how the radical form of the novel, particularly its fractured chronology, is Huxley's method for producing his pacifist aesthetics. His activist literature is richer and more densely agonistic than it first appears to be, obscured by a superficially preachy style. The avant-garde form permits a much more tentative, complicated politics to emerge, one that presents self-questioning at the core of even a very active politics of peacemaking.

Beyond "Case-Hardened"

Huxley's leading biographer portrays him as a last remnant of the Victorian sage tradition, embodied by his grandfather Thomas Henry Huxley and great-uncle Matthew Arnold, and his efforts to realize his philosophies became a large part of his public intellectualism and celebrity (Murray, *Huxley*, 7). Some of his practices have aged rather badly, such as his commitment to a quack who taught that physical exercises could cure his blindness.[8] Critical evaluations of his life tend to include his pacifism in the same category as his other dubious, shameful, or laughable convictions, and many readers have detected in Huxley's inability to articulate a persuasive utopian vision the vestiges of his privileged, snobbish, satisfied life. For instance, Christopher Hitchens, in his less than glowing foreword to *Brave New World*, calls the book "didactic and pedagogic and faintly superior" and written in "the tone of voice of an Etonian schoolmaster. It is also somewhat contradictory and even self-defeating" (xi). Thus, even Huxley's most widely read novel is packaged as a kind of smug failure. While the charges of arrogance and didacticism in Huxley's works are not entirely refutable, it is at least worth noting that he was aware of these problems. He frequently observed that he was not a first-rate novelist, and in 1925 wrote to Hutchinson: "I have lived so long and so exclusively in a private literary-intellectual world, that I am case-hardened" (qtd. in Murray, *Huxley*, 171).

This "case-hardening" and intellectual isolation dogged Huxley throughout his life, but his peace work in the mid-1930s can be seen as his most substantial effort to push beyond his elitist milieu, the position from which he had articulated his most callous eugenicist views and contempt for the masses and popular culture. In 1934, still wrestling with his unfinished novel, he became deeply involved with the most important affiliation of his political life: the Peace Pledge Union. The genesis of this organization was a sermon by the prominent New York City clergyman Harry Emerson Fosdick, who preached on Armistice Sunday 1933 about renouncing war "for its consequences, the lies it lives on and propagates, for the undying hatred it arouses, for the dictatorships it puts in the place of democracy" (qtd. in Morrison, *I Renounce*, 8). This charge was taken up wholeheartedly by the well-known Anglican Canon H. R. L. Sheppard who published an open letter in the *Manchester Guardian* on October 16, 1934, inviting men to join the largely female peace movement by signing this resolution: "We renounce war and never again, directly or indirectly, will we support or sanction another" (qtd. in ibid., 100). Within the next two days, thousands of postcards had arrived at Sheppard's door, including one from Aldous Huxley (Murray, *Huxley*, 284).

Sheppard's initial plan was not to create yet another antiwar or pacifist group of the type that had proliferated through the 1920s. Pacifist organizations such as the No More War Movement, the Fellowship of Reconciliation, and the War Resisters' International alongside internationalist war prevention groups such as the League of Nations Union and the Union of Democratic Control were a few of the many collectives formed in response to the Great War, each having slightly different inspirational bases and orientational agendas. After his first call for the peace pledge, nine months would elapse before Sheppard followed the urging of friends as well as his own drive toward advancing his Christian pacifist views in a broadly secular arena. Partly because of the prodding of Laurence Housman, who would remain a lifelong peace activist, the Dick Sheppard Peace Movement, as it was initially called, held its first rally at the Royal Albert Hall on July 14, 1935, with seven thousand men in attendance (Ceadel, *Pacifism in Britain*, 222; Hetherington, *Swimming*, 6). This show of support indicated to Sheppard and his cohort a potential groundswell, and the official PPU began with the immediate invitation of women into the sponsors committee and membership ranks.[9] As Ceadel describes the situation, the PPU came into existence as the leading voice of "the New Pacifism," combining an absolutist commitment with a stalwart mission of nonviolent practice, and grew into the largest peace group, with peak membership of around 136,000 members (Ceadel, *Semi-Detached*, 400). One reason for this growth was the deliberate minimalism of its official requirements and the openness of its official pledge, which allowed antiwar people of all stripes to unite. Early members included former soldiers, such as Frank Crozier and Edmund Blunden; socialists such as Laurence Housman and G. D. H. Cole; Christian pacifists, such as Charles Raven and Donald Soper; and many other artists, intellectuals, and religious leaders, including John Middleton Murry, A. A. Milne, Bertrand Russell, Max Plowman, Arthur Ponsonby, and later Vera Brittain, Storm Jameson, and Rose Macaulay (Hetherington, *Swimming*, 6–7). The broad appeal of the PPU may also have been its weakness because there was neither consensus about the basis for the membership's pacifism nor (more important) were there uniform ideas about how the group should proceed. Within the broad umbrella category of "antiwar movements" were internationalists who believed that collective security from a multinational police force was the best hope for peaceful coexistence working alongside Tolstoyan absolute pacifists who resisted any form of coercion. In its early years, however, from the time of Sheppard's initial call for men to renounce war through his sudden death in October 1937, the PPU saw a remarkable surge in membership and popularity—a growth spurt that peaked in 1940, when the demands of open warfare shifted public opinion.

Huxley was central to the PPU's first phase, beginning with his post-card pledge, developing through his pamphlet-writing and public lectures, and culminating in his *Ends and Means* (1937). This book, sub-titled "An Inquiry into the Nature of Ideals," is the fullest expression of his pacifist social vision, an engagement with the reigning sociological theories of the time, and a treatise once revered as the "Bible of the PPU."[10] It would also be his swansong as an active member of the peace movement. Though he remained on the official roster for the rest of his life, his move to America—concurrent with the publication of *Ends and Means*—significantly altered any chance of personally testing his ideas while living in a war zone.

Originally planned as a collaborative effort with Gerald Heard, *Ends and Means* reflects its basis in theories about the "New Pacifism," which was promoted through Gerald Hibbert's edited collection of that name and embraced by the PPU. Heard mandated that a viable pacifism must reject quietism and become "thorough, dynamic, constructive and creative" through its essential mission of "securing peace through social reconstruction" (Eros, "Sort of Mutt and Jeff," 88). Though pacifism is a central part of *Ends and Means*, its scope is deliberately broader, attempting what Bernfried Nugel identifies as a full-fledged moral philosophy akin to Heard's *The Third Morality* (1937).[11] Crucial to the new moral order that Huxley envisions is a complete revolutionizing of the world system through nonviolent means. His argument stakes out a wide range of forces that condition all subjects within a society, including government, nationalism, education, religion, and war.

To begin, he assumes a universal consensus about the goals of civilization: "liberty, peace, justice and brotherly love" (*EM*, 1). Though these values sound a bit clichéd, his provocative and idiosyncratic edge comes from his assertion that once we recognize our universal, mutual collective interest, we might move closer to these ends by means of nonviolent social reforms. War is the result of many factors in Huxley's analysis: the alleviation of boredom, "pseudo-religious faith" in a "deified nation," desires for glory, and economic acquisitiveness (114–16). Most concerning to Huxley, however, is the drive toward war urged by "politically powerful minorities"—that is, weapons manufacturers (118). To remedy this social conditioning, he proposes a series of reforms, drastic enough to count as revolutionary and idealistic enough to be called utopian.[12] Arms manufacturing should be first nationalized to deincentivize the profit motive and then rapidly abolished (119). Huxley insists that the "machinery of peaceful settlement and international cooperation," such as border dispute arbitrations, "securing the elementary rights of individuals belonging to minorities," and third world assistance through a mandate system are all excellent, proven, nonviolent strategies (130–38). They simply lack widespread application.

Proposals such as these have been criticized by today's social scientists, much as they were attacked in Huxley's own day, for seeming disconnected from reality. Howard Schneiderman, introducing the recent Transaction edition of the book, affirms Talcott Parsons's 1938 review in the *American Journal of Sociology*, which asserts that *Ends and Means* "cannot fail to arouse greatest interest" (qtd. in Schneiderman, "Introduction," xxii). This damnation through faint praise matches the overall tone of Schneiderman's introduction, which commends Huxley for attempting a serious engagement with contemporary sociology but faults him for utopianism and concludes that his lack of a nonviolent rejoinder for Nazi antisemitism is "morally and politically distasteful, in a world in which the struggle between good and evil continues on a daily basis" (xxii).[13] There is no question that Huxley is largely silent about Nazi persecutions and that tyrannical ascendency in Germany, Italy, and Spain are offered as exemplary case studies in violent nationalism rather than as direct threats to which a pacifist philosophy must respond. This relative silence, given our current vantage point, does seem short sighted (if not just irresponsible). As Tony Kushner has pointed out, an inability to see antisemitic violence as an international problem was widespread among British liberals through the 1930s (*Holocaust*, 31–60).

Despite the shortcomings of *Ends and Means* as an empirical study of engaged civic action, it successfully identifies the underlying structures and ideologies that promote dictatorships, appeals broadly for remedies to injustice, and provocatively calls for massive social change. It is idealistic, perhaps, but undoubtedly revolutionary. Among the many changes Huxley wants to see is a reorientation of nations toward achieving the "elementary rights of individuals belonging to minorities, racially or linguistically distinct from the majority of the inhabitants of their country" (*EM*, 138). This concern for marginalized groups resonates with Kushner's explanation of refugee policies in Britain in the 1930s, which were shaped by "fear of antisemitism and of the dilution of national identity" (*Holocaust*, 34), and Huxley's call for wider acceptance of and basic rights for nonassimilated national minorities counters the general British national sentiment. That Huxley does not extend the logic of his claims into direct advocacy for particular minorities is lamentable given that 1937 was the height of his popularity and political clout. But the lack of a specific response to current events signals his aspirations for *Ends and Means*—that it would be a lasting philosophical and sociological treatise rather than an occasional essay on contemporary matters of political concern.

All in all, Huxley has been deemed a purveyor of "anti-politics," a judgment that seems apt insofar as we view "politics" as a matter of governmental structures, legal institutions, and enforcement mechanisms as they currently exist (Schneiderman, "Introduction," xv). Rather than taking the growing crises in Europe head-on, *Ends and Means* gleans from geopolitical history a series of local cases in which diplomatic machinery was effective and sees in them the seeds for a larger transformation. Huxley offers nonviolent revolution as a strategy that will eliminate the root causes of war and fascism rather than a point-by-point analysis of the current political situation. This revolutionary utopianism may seem implausible and unrealistic. And yet, as a matter of identifying the extent of reform necessary to prevent war and totalitarian dominance, his book remains an important record and a cry—or last gasp perhaps—at a moment when a drastic measure like total revolution might snatch victory from defeat.

Arguing for nonviolent social reform is utopian, but it is consistent with what Jay Winter describes as the many "openings" in the twentieth century where "minor utopias" emerged and briefly gave hope for possibilities of peace (*Dreams*, 2). Events such as the 1937 Paris exposition used art and technology as a means toward unifying people through exhibiting the best of human creativity. Picasso's *Guernica* was first displayed at this world's fair to proclaim what he called his "abhorrence of the military caste which has sunk Spain into an ocean of pain and death" (qtd. in ibid., 83). And the centerpiece of the exposition was its Pavilion of Peace, representing the horrors of war and offering a venue for international veterans of World War I to announce their commitment to peace. Winter's description of the expo also examines its contradictions and "eloquent silences", noting the space granted to Nazi and British imperialist propaganda. These failures tell us much about the limitations of peaceful internationalism but also suggest the lengths to which well-meaning people throughout Europe desired to make amends for the tragedy of the Great War and prevent its duplication. The PPU and Huxley's closely related theorization of a nonviolent mission inhabit a place in twentieth-century history much like that occupied by the Paris expo: minor—but not insignificant. These minor utopian energies were eclipsed by what Winter calls the "major utopias" perpetrated by Hitler and Stalin, and public memory has lost sight of much of the optimism felt in the mid-1930s by antiwar advocates who saw their numbers increasing and felt that alternatives to war were within reach (ibid., 1).

A significant factor in this antiwar surge was fear of a future war, commonly envisioned as a replication of the Great War, only magnified and intensified, and fears about historical repetition shaped much of the rhetoric and theories of peace activists, as we will see in subsequent chapters. This feeling dominates Storm Jameson's "Fifteen Years Ago," in which she describes the news from Germany at the end of 1933 and has a flashback of being in the sunshine, reading a newspaper with friends in 1914: "In less than two years my friends were killed. That was my first thought. Next I thought of my son, who was eighteen, war age, a short time ago. Between these two moments, between the moment when I remembered my dead friends and the one in which I thought only of my son, I felt such anger, bitterness, and despair as I hope never to feel again" (325). For the rest of the article, she challenges her readers to consider what might be done when (not *if*) Germany starts another war. Huxley's *Ends and Means* also seems bound by the logic of repeating the Great War. In one of his only comments on Hitler's aggression, Huxley classifies the problem as essentially economic and a matter of territorial and boundary disagreement, using as evidence Hitler's own assertion that more room is needed for Germany's surplus population: "If Germany goes to war with Russia it will be, in part at least, to satisfy this real or imaginary craving for more and better land" (*EM*, 116).

With the benefit of analytical hindsight, historians today debate the precise relationship between the first and second world wars, but a prominent argument contends that a clear distinction must be maintained regarding the origins of these conflicts. In one of the major comprehensive histories of World War II, Gerhard L. Weinberg resists seeing 1914–1945 as "the age of a new European civil war, a Thirty-one Years War if you will," arguing that World War I was still a "traditional" conflict in terms of the war aims of the belligerents (*World at Arms*, 1). Though the destruction from this war and the effect it had on every level of national and international organization throughout Europe was unprecedented, these "massive changes" were not intentional; in World War II, however, "all this was very different indeed. The *intent* was different from the start. A total reordering of the globe was at stake from the very beginning, and the leadership on both sides recognized this" (2). Not just a war over territory, it was from the beginning "about who would live and control the resources of the globe and which peoples would vanish entirely because they were believed inferior or undesirable by the victors" (ibid.). Some historians have objected to Weinberg's approach to the material. Norman Davies, for instance, criticizes *A World at Arms* for being little more than "an honest summary of the Western view" and "conceived in the conventional mode of anti-Fascism," which "avoids most of the weighty political and moral teasers involved" (*Europe at War*, 5). Davies objects to histories that overlook the imperial and genocidal agendas of the Soviet regime, which rivaled Nazi atrocities, but he still accepts the basic premise that the aggressive forces in World War II had global ambitions that were greater than those of the preceding war.

Current historical appraisals like Weinberg's and Davies's stand in contrast to the perceptions of many Britons in the 1930s, but even among peace activists at the time there were concerns that this message of fearing the next war could undermine cogent political action. Canon Charles Raven, writing in 1938 from his position as Regius Professor of Divinity at Cambridge, decried the influx of novels and memoirs about horrific trench life in World War I and the extrapolation of these horrors into "imaginative forecasts of cities deluged with vesicants and thermite, of populations maddened by famine and disease, of civilization blasted into ruin . . . Disgust and fear, the accumulated effects of nervous exhaustion and disappointment, were responsible for many of the converts to pacifism; and such pacifism was in consequence negative and sentimental. It might, and did, delay the cry for re-armament: it might, but did not, give statesmen an opportunity for constructive peace-making: but its source was largely pathological and its influence consequently impermanent" (*War and the Christian*, 21). The mode of "disenchanted violence," as Sarah Cole calls it, had become stock-in-trade for many antiwar advocates as they recounted horrors and imagined their recurrence on a grander scale, but the effect of this fear mongering was thin and ultimately unsuited for durable nonviolent politics (*Violet Hour*, 36).

To avoid merely reactionary pacifism of the negative and sentimental kind that Raven criticized, Huxley advocated broad programmatic schemes for achieving a nonviolent way of life as an alternative to the current societal norms. His involvement with Sheppard's Peace Movement and the PPU represented for him the clearest way to mobilize his restless search for a totalizing philosophy sufficient for radical social renewal. Huxley was deeply influenced by the writings of the Dutch anarchist Barthélemy de Ligt, especially *Pour vaincre sans violence*, for which he supplied an introduction to the widely read English translation, and also by the American Gandhi disciple Richard Gregg, whose *The Power of Non-Violence* shaped many debates in the nascent PPU.[14] After witnessing Gandhi's work in India in 1925, Gregg sought to translate his practices into Western contexts, and though the whiff of spiritualism and superstition about some of his ideas proved divisive, *The Power of Non-Violence* had a long tenure as a sourcebook for peace activists.[15] Essential to Gregg's system was "moral jiu-jitsu," which avoids counterviolence and instead "offers resistance, but only in moral terms" (*Power of Non-Violence*, 26). By asserting one's moral authority in response to aggression, Gregg believed that the terms of a conflict could be shifted in favor of the victim. This grappling with an opponent through reversals of power had individual applications in resisting attackers or small-scale civil disobedience, but Gregg also contended that large-scale national conflicts could be handled this way if nonviolent combatants had sufficient training and discipline.

By the time he was completing *Ends and Means*, Huxley had begun moving beyond his "Greggist" phase, but he still cited both Gregg and de Ligt as practical guides for his claim that "the thing that makes for peace above all others is the systematic practice in all human relationships of non-violence" (*EM*, 158). Gregg's formulae for civil disobedience conducted with assertiveness and equanimity were less important for Huxley at this stage, partly because of his situation as an American émigré rather than a resident of militant Europe. Instead, Huxley traveled further into the visionary dimension of nonviolence, where "individual work for reform" may become the basis for socialistic enclaves—what he calls "associations"—preparing and training for nonviolent action. He remarks in passing on his distance from the PPU, criticizing them and the War Resisters' International because "their organization is too loose and their membership too large and too widely scattered" (173). The purpose of these groups, he suggests, is propaganda, bringing to public attention "a morally better and more effective alternative to revolution, to war, to violence and brutality of every kind" (174). This statement, though delivered as an aside rather than a centerpiece of the book, may be the strongest signal of Huxley's changing attitude, his implication that he no longer saw himself in the role of "propagandist" for peace and rather desired something more intellectual, philosophical, visionary, and quite possibly more eremitic. In the last months before the eruption of global war, Huxley's attention turned toward structural violence, the injustices and inequalities that lead to belligerence, and his work strived for "nonattachment" from these ills.

Huxley Agonistes

If *Ends and Means* is a culminating statement of Huxley's activist period, declaring his positions on war, nonviolence, and social reform, then his labors on *Eyeless in Gaza* can be seen as his process of forming these views. As his friend Gerald Heard reported, the novel was "begun before and finished after [Huxley] had crossed his watershed" (qtd. in Eros, "Mutt and Jeff," 86). While the commonest narrative among members of the peace movement is a reaction against the First World War either because of personal combat experience or its effect on loved ones, Huxley's pacifist awakening was more idiosyncratic. His formation among the conscientious objectors at Garsington had some lingering effect, but even in the early 1930s he was dismissive of nonviolence, regarding Gandhi's satyagraha as the dislikable purview of "religious enthusiasts" and in 1934 refusing to contribute to Storm Jameson's antiwar anthology *Challenge to Death* in what Elizabeth Maslen calls "a long letter of doom-laden prevarication about the threat of war" (*Life*, 132). By October 1935, however, the Italian invasion of Abyssinia had aroused in him a new sense of purpose, and after meeting Sheppard in November, he declared that his lofty highhandedness was a thing of the past: "That *I* should have talked so much to *you* — the theoretician to the man who knows the business of dealing with people by the process of self-dedication — is frankly comic . . . Thinking, reading, talking, and writing have been my opium and alcohol, and I am trying to get off them on to listening and doing" (qtd. in Bradshaw, "Flight," 13).[16] Once again, we find Huxley confessing his tendency toward posturing superiority, and his encounter with Sheppard convicts him of this flaw and pushes him toward praxis.

Huxley tested the waters gradually, refusing at first to speak publicly about his peace work because he hoped to avoid what he called "a campaign of religious and ethical preaching against war" (qtd. in Dunaway, *Hollywood*, 17). But he was soon drawn into its orbit and was schooled in the cost of nonviolence by hearing Oswald Mosley speak at a British Union of Fascists (BUF) rally on June 7, 1935. Mosley's Blackshirts beat civil protestors at the event in front of Huxley, brutally announcing that nonviolent activism carried serious consequences and that Huxley's pacifism was not merely a matter of abstract ideas. In his first public speech on behalf of the PPU, Huxley acknowledged the need for all people to face the empirical realities of violence: "Warlike passions burn most fiercely in minds which think about the problems of peace and war in terms of generalizations and abstractions . . . when those human beings are thought of merely as members of a class which has previously been defined as evil, then killing becomes a simple matter" (qtd. in ibid., 21).

This statement suggests not only a personal, ethical position but also commends the novelist's art to the realm of peace activism by working always in specifics. The attention paid in *Eyeless in Gaza* to Anthony and his soul's journey may be an effort to generate sympathy for an enemy class: the peace worker whose views are deemed disastrous and even treasonous.

Anthony's spiritual and political journey shows the influence of Huxley's own mentors and a willingness to embrace positions disdained by the mainstream religious and national institutions. Sheppard remained a key figure for Huxley, as he was for many PPU members, largely because of his widely recognized personal charisma and persuasiveness.[17] For founder members such as Sybil Morrison, Sheppard's untimely death in October 1937 was a blow difficult to overcome: "sitting quietly at his desk with his head upon his arms as though asleep his much strained heart had given out; Dick Sheppard, that man of many parts was dead, and there was no-one to replace him" (*I Renounce*, 26). Morrison's account of the PPU makes the best of this situation, claiming that the rank and file members were the true backbone of the organization, but there can be little denying that Sheppard's presiding presence was a vital energy source for its activism. In fiction, Huxley used Sheppard as the model in *Eyeless in Gaza* for Reverend John Purchas, whom Anthony describes as someone "who takes Christianity seriously and has started an organization of pacifists. Purchas by name. Middle-aged. Slightly the muscular-jocular Christian manner. (How hard to admit that a man can use clichés and yet be intelligent!) . . . The aim is to use and extend Purchas's organization. The unit is a small group, like the Early Christian *agape*" (*EG*, 12).[18] Like Purchas, the real-life Sheppard was adamant that the PPU should take Christian community and evangelistic techniques as its model but that its inspiration should not be theological. Though he insisted that the PPU was secular, Sheppard made no secret of his own motivation, which is evident in *100,000 Say No!*, a pamphlet that republishes a joint interview with Huxley from *Nash's Pall Mall Magazine*. Sheppard responds to a question, "On what principles is the Movement based?" by saying: "Speaking for myself, I believe this issue is a spiritual one. I am a pacifist because I am a Christian, and I think that a large number of our members have fundamentally the same convictions as myself. At the same time, we welcome every sincere pacifist, whatever his views. There is no kind of religious test. Personally, I repeat, I profoundly believe that the Movement has got to be founded on a spiritual basis" (4). This "spiritual basis" for a secular organization appealed greatly to Huxley, who was drawn to its method of emptying Christianity of theological content and redeploying religious forms for political and secular-mystical ends.

A revisionary, political faith seemed to many of Huxley's peers merely idiosyncratic and quirky, and his self-fashioning as a secular mystic was regarded with suspicion and derision. In 1936, Graham Greene wrote in the Catholic periodical the *Tablet* that he applauded Cyril Connolly's parody of Huxley as a man "gone a little 'gamey' and on the verge of discovering pacifism and a personal religion" (*Articles of Faith*, 95). For Greene, who took his religion with a heavy dose of obsession and penance, the idea of Huxley's ethereal and amorphous spirituality could only seem deranged. As Huxley began to publish his unfolding beliefs more widely, his arguments sparked debates throughout Britain about the impending war. As a leading voice in the PPU, Huxley wrote its first official tract, *What Are You Going to Do About It? The Case for Constructive Peace* (1936). This essay drew the ire of many people, including Cecil Day Lewis, whose rebuttal, *We're Not Going to Do Nothing!*, accused Huxley of constructing "a great, big, beautiful idealist bubble—lovely to look at, no doubt; charming to live in, perhaps: but with little reference to the real facts and inadequate protection against a four-engined bomber" (3).

Huxley saw Italy's conquest of Abyssinia as clearly evil, but his call to action was simply that: "the great monopolistic powers should immediately summon a conference at which the unsatisfied powers, great and small, should be invited to state their grievance and claims" (*What Are You?*, 27). Obviously, this grand conference idea never took hold in the public imagination. But if nothing else, Huxley's pamphleteering shows his abhorrence of the isolationist position as a form of "negative pacifism" assumed casually perhaps by people refusing to fight only because it would cause their own discomfort. A bad peace, such as that achieved in Versailles, cannot be the goal of the constructive pacifist. In his *Encyclopaedia of Pacifism* (1937), Huxley wrote that "non-violence does not mean doing nothing. It means making the enormous effort required to overcome evil with good" (80). Or, as he put it in a 1935 speech: "The only hope lies in the pacifists being better disciplined than the militarists and prepared to put up with as great hardships and dangers with a courage equal to theirs" (qtd. in Dunaway, *Hollywood*, 21). A highly disciplined, Eastern-influenced, meditative system that required great personal fortitude and stamina was precisely the methodology Huxley desired, and these traits would manifest in *Eyeless in Gaza* as the characteristic features of the novel's guru figures and the aspirations of its protagonist, Anthony Beavis, as the novel enacts a struggle to move from the pledge of peace to imagining its fruition in practice.

Pacifist Aesthetics in Fractured Time

In *Eyeless in Gaza*, pacifism and mysticism coalesce as the engines of that enormously difficult work required by the agent of active nonviolence. Anthony seeks a form of meditation derived from various threads of Catholic thought interwoven with strands of Buddhism and Hinduism, all of which will be "ends in themselves and at the same time means for realizing some of that goodness in practice"—a philosophical statement he would continue promoting throughout his activist phase (*EG*, 432). Huxley's rummaging through a variety of religious sources for political usefulness echoes other modernists' search for a religion capable of addressing the needs of a spiritually bankrupt age. Eliot, Lawrence, Yeats, and Pound all searched in different ways for a revitalized religious presence in modernity, and Huxley expresses through Anthony a similar preoccupation but foregrounds the political dimension of this search. While Eliot's "Shantih Shantih Shantih" obliquely responds to the lack of peace in Eliot's world, Huxley explicitly attends to the political possibilities inherent in religious thought. On Christmas Day 1934, Anthony Beavis writes in his journal: "The fundamental problem is practical—to work out systems of psychological exercises for all types of men and women. Catholicism has many systems of mental prayer—Ignatian, Franciscan, Liguorian, Carmelite and so on. Hinduism, Northern, Southern and Zen Buddhism also have a variety of practices. There is a great work to be done here. Collecting and collating information from all these sources" (*EG*, 431–32). The practices of various traditions may be borrowed, stripped of their specific spiritual content (such as worship of a god), and used for a multifaceted pacifist project responsive to the unique needs of individual members.

Along with methodological diversity, the centerpiece of Huxley's thought as expressed through Anthony is the valuation of means rather than ends. When he was writing *Eyeless in Gaza*, peace activism, despite its insistence on creating a nonviolent world, was for Huxley still a matter of process rather than result. World peace ceases to be simply a goal, pursued whatever way seems most effective. Most obviously, this emphasis resists the valorization of World War I as the "war to end all wars," the H. G. Wells coinage that shaped public discourse about the conflict and encouraged belief in a violent means for achieving perpetual peace. In Huxley's formulation, pacifism becomes a faith, a set of practices worthy in themselves and not undertaken simply because they are productive. Huxley's voice in this regard joins other members of the pacifist community. Max Plowman, for instance, articulates the creedal nature of peace activism in *The Faith Called Pacifism* (1936): "What now seems to be growing more and more clear is the realization that peace cannot become the reigning condition so long as the present order of values obtains. If we want peace we have got to discover new values, assert our faith in them, and order our activities in accordance with our faith" (35). The particular religious basis for pacifism upheld by Quaker and Anabaptist peace churches as well as the Christian justifications given by activists such as Sheppard and later Vera Brittain are in Huxley's model rendered universal rather than doctrines of a specific faith.

One might be tempted to see in Plowman's and Huxley's views a callow ideological retrenchment in which, instead of making a case for the pacifist position and offering a realistic solution to violence, they simplistically resort to religious fantasy. But I would argue that casting peace activism in religious terms was a way to reframe the debate about pacifism beyond what we see in Huxley's exchange with Day Lewis. Rather than being a matter of doing something versus doing nothing, peace work becomes the grounding for a set of life practices undertaken for their inherent goodness and out of a commitment to a cause beyond oneself. Huxley explained his theory of religious pacifism in a letter written late in December 1935: "I have come to the conviction that nothing can possibly work or get us out of our present state except complete pacifism of the Quaker or Buddhist kind. The implications of this are, of course, fundamentally religious . . . some simpler conception of an underlying spiritual unity, realized through the practice of meditation . . . for it is only by translating the fundamental religious ideas of human unity into political terms . . . that we can escape from destruction" (*Selected Letters*, 313–14). Thus, what appears to be personal conviction and private discipline is actually a form of political action.

Personal discipline as a mode of social transformation receives its fullest and most explicit treatment in *Ends and Means*, but *Eyeless in Gaza* demonstrates Huxley's effort to imagine the possibilities of thorough commitment to pacifist mysticism. In the novel, Dr. Miller, the physician/anthropologist/mystic who mirrors Reverend Purchas by guiding Anthony toward proper spiritual disciplines, counsels him: "When you pray in the ordinary way, you're merely rubbing yourself into yourself. You return to your own vomit, if you see what I mean. Whereas what we're all looking for is some way of getting beyond our own vomit" (*EG*, 423). In Miller's mouth, Huxley places the very critique that is so often leveled at his own mystical turn—that it was merely a retreat and an abandonment of the world's real problems in favor of some fantastical, introverted escape. Miller endorses thinking and eating like a Buddhist, telling Anthony that his diet of meat, alcohol, and cigarettes has left him with "intestines . . . ripe for fascism and nationalism" (425). The personally disciplined, monastic lifestyle is thus, paradoxically, a mode of political action. Fighting fascism begins at home—and in the bowels.

Huxley's contemporaries, and even partners in the peace movement, found this notion of politicized self-discipline ridiculous. As Plowman wrote to Geoffrey West regarding the confluence of Huxley, Heard, and Gregg, "*concern for ourselves*, for our conduct, our fidelity, our spiritual growth . . . are all concerns in the wrong direction—a back-to-the-wall direction, when we ought to be moving with initiative—a concern for spiritual perfectability when our concern ought to be with the immediate lot of others & the immediate salvation of human society.—I only know that I've felt an unconscious resistance to intensive Study Groups & all the Yogi-Bogie exercises" (*Bridge into the Future*, 578). Sheppard himself would register impatience with methods that seemed "ingrown," as Plowman put it, when at a meeting with Gregg and several PPU members, he reportedly whispered to the *New Statesman's* Kingsley Martin: "Can't you get up and tell them that we haven't time for all this intensive cultivation and that our job is to stop the next bloody war" (qtd. in Ceadel, *Pacifism in Britain*, 246). Methodological disagreement and choice words from a clergyman were reactions internal to the PPU, though the public opinion of these practices was equally suspect, raising concerns that support for the peace movement could be jeopardized by deviation from the task at hand. The popular writer Beverly Nichols, who makes several cameo appearances in Brittain's *Testament of Youth* and who for a time boosted his personal celebrity touting the slogan "peace at any price!," described the ranks of pacifists as being filled with "religious cranks, who appeared at the front door clothed in white draperies, waving banners and proclaiming that they had a Message . . . medical cranks, who believed that you could stop man fighting by altering his diet" (*Men Do Not Weep*, 10). While Huxley did not seem to recognize fully the crankish elements of his beliefs, he does show through Dr. Miller his awareness that moral discipline can appear to be little more than self-indulgence. He counters with an assertion that failing to examine oneself leaves a person susceptible to the dangerous ideologies of militaristic nationalism, and his admonition reminds us that violent desires are not merely "out there" in others but also reside within ourselves.

Although many of Huxley's views are expressed by the novel's characters, the book never devolves into a series of homilies or set of political tracts. Anthony is clearly a stand-in for Huxley in many respects, but the experimental form of the novel emphasizes the process of political awakening and the struggle to achieve a viable pacifist way of life. Huxley may have lacked a proper sense of irony or even self-awareness when it came to his mystical, pacifist politics, but the modernist form of *Eyeless in Gaza* embeds self-questioning and struggle as core aspects of Anthony's journey. Thus, criticism of heavy-handed didacticism in *Eyeless in Gaza*, as though it is one more preachy "novel of ideas," accepts too easily Anthony's conversion narrative and diary entries as the unequivocally authoritative moral answer to the questions posed by Huxley's narrative form. By contrast, I see the novel's disjointed chronology as evoking both progress and stasis and rendering Anthony's views part of an ongoing process of accepting pacifist inspiration and developing a workable pacifist orientation. The challenging form of the novel requires an active reader's struggling to synthesize Anthony's story, and the agonistic pacifist conversion is transferred into our own reading process.

Jerome McGann has praised *Eyeless in Gaza* as an underread gem in an overlooked strain of modernist writing that shies away from the mythical structures and polished artistry of canonical works such as *Ulysses*. Instead of a modernism manifested in "an ideal—or a tyranny—of the aesthetic," novels like Huxley's are, for McGann, "a form of writing where failure stalks in every word."[19] The intensely subjective text evokes Anthony's failure to fully commit to his convictions, fearing as he does at the novel's conclusion the threatening hate mail from "A Group of Patriotic Englishmen" who warn him: "If you make any more of your dirty pacifist speeches, we shall deal with you as you deserve. . . . You do not deserve this warning, but we want to behave sportingly even towards a skunk like you" (*EG*, 464). These comically mild-mannered bullies still cause Anthony great alarm, and he wonders whether he can manage to continue his peace work or whether he might retreat, as Huxley ultimately did, from the world of physical danger. Deviating from the familiar modernist turn toward Eastern mythologies, Huxley provides an idiosyncratic, self-interrogating form without a corresponding mythical order that might root his aesthetic in an identifiable tradition. *Eyeless in Gaza* does not present a reworked Buddhist, Hindu, or Christian mythology in order to reestablish some kind of ancient tradition but rather offers, in part through its experimental forms, the self in conflict seeking a discipline capable of peaceably recreating the world.

Anthony's views in any given chapter of the book are opposed or contradicted in preceding and following chapters, showing his internal development to be a series of false starts and missteps rather than a gradual accumulation of personal virtue culminating in enlightened nirvana or any other pure existential plane. For example, chapters 16 through 18 take us from June 19, 1912, to May 26, 1934, to December 8, 1926, in a succession that begins in Anthony's youthful, bourgeois naivety, passes through musings on "peace literature," and ends with the General Strike. In all of these phases we are made aware of Anthony's struggle to develop political maturity. The twenty-year-old Anthony of chapter 16 strolls with his friend Brian Foxe, using garrulousness to cover his guilt for having gotten drunk with other friends rather than keeping his promise to join

Brian at a Fabian Society meeting. Brian is a true believer in the Fabian political philosophy, and he stammeringly tells Anthony that "B-being a scholar or an artist—it's l-like purs-suing your own p-personal salvation. But there's also the k-kingdom of G-god. W-waiting to be realized" (*EG*, 93). Anthony, age twenty, doubts that Fabianism is the realization of the kingdom of God, but he has no alternative and offers instead a sophomoric stream of chatter on subjects literary, philosophical, and political. He strains to sound "interesting" to Brian, "interested in the poetry of Edward Thomas as they walked down Beaumont Street; in Bergson opposite Worcester; crossing Hythe Bridge, in the nationalization of coal mines" (157).

Much more central than politics to this phase of Anthony's life is his sexual awakening with a woman ten years his senior. Anthony goes from Brian to a romantic boat ride with Mrs. Mary Amberley, which includes a Lawrentian description of their physical intensity displaced onto the mechanics of boatmanship: "Handling his long pole with an easy mastery of which he was proud, he felt, as he watched her, exultantly strong and superior. She was a woman, he a man. He lifted his trailing punt pole and swung it forward with a movement of easy grace, of unhurried and accomplished power. Thrust it down into the mud, tightened his muscles against its resistance" (168). Two chapters later, this fervid boating is entirely replaced by Anthony's revulsion at Mary's age (she is forty-four years old in 1926) and her gauche friend, Beppo Bowles, who "popped over [to Berlin] to get away from the General Strike" and to revel in the transgressive sexuality available in Germany (175). While chapter 16 shows Anthony's insouciance, chapter 18 depicts the political shallowness among members of an avant-garde who relish any blandly fashionable transgression of middle-class values but disdain the collective politics of striking workers.

Huxley's description of his intentions with this structure is somewhat at odds with their effect on the page. Writing to Richard Meadel, the editor of *Nash's Pall Mall Magazine*, about the potential to serialize *Eyeless in Gaza*, Huxley explained that the novel includes "events in 1934 and 1935, when the character, Anthony, devotes himself to the organization of pacifism. These chapters will be intercalated throughout the book, beginning almost at the beginning, so as to form another 'melodic line' in the contrapuntal arrangement of the material—the line of achieved freedom running parallel with the lines of attempted freedom and actual enslavement traced out by the other narratives" (qtd. in Bradshaw, "Flight," 16). Counterpoint and melody are intriguing musical metaphors for a work as disjointed and dissonant as *Eyeless*, with its intercalated chapters that sustain disorientation more than harmony and struggle rather than resolution.

Overt discussion of pacifist views is sandwiched between other phases of Anthony's political growth, making pacifism a point in his journey rather than a final stop. Inserted between chapters depicting the youthful and the aging Anthony's political irresponsibility is one of his several diary entries about pacifist conversion, written as he has turned the "revolting" age of forty-four. In chapter 17, Anthony tests his vocation while presenting himself as a sage. He attacks the religious function of chauvinistic nationalism and its propensity for violence: "One of the great attractions of patriotism — it fulfills our worst wishes. In the person of our nation we are able, vicariously, to bully and cheat . . . with a feeling that we're profoundly virtuous" (*EG*, 171). The diary chapters do offer Huxley the chance to indulge in the essay form, which he favored over his novels, yet there is a tentativeness to his prose in these chapters. Anthony's views are quickly subsumed in the overall structure of the book, which shifts from May 1934 to December 1926 and highlights the casual dismissiveness of Anthony's circle toward the General Strike, the selfishness of their loves, and the bland, faux-intellectualism of their reading habits (Gibbon, Bergson, contemporary poetry, etc.). The diary form allows Huxley to present Anthony's thought as a spontaneous work in progress while he formulates his views: "Good international policies are projections of individual good intentions and benevolent wishes, and must be of the same kind as good inter-personal policies. Pacifist propaganda must be aimed at people as well as their governments; must start simultaneously at the periphery and the centre" (172). These speculations about the relationship between individual conversion and changing state policies seem half-baked, as does a later proposal that universal love is the key to international peace. Huxley proclaims the power of individual choice, but the surrounding chapters demonstrate the power of systems and even internal desires over the free will of an individual. The diary chapters do not stand out as the triumphant, definitive statement to which the other chapters humbly defer. Incidents and ideas in the novel are not merely props for Huxley's mystical social statements, and the succession of chapters creates a sense that no single proposition is entirely sufficient or dominant. The novel is unambiguously in favor of pacifism, but the formal complexity allows Anthony's pacifist awakening to emerge as a key feature in the landscape of his life rather than the sole focus of the narrative, and the onus is placed on the attentive reader to assemble these clashing fragments into a meaningful whole.

Through its fractured chronology, *Eyeless in Gaza* draws attention to a desire for unity, the demand that we see all things as being interconnected, as a basis for pacifism. A common notion among nonviolence advocates is the need to recognize the other as a full human being rather than as an idea, a means to an end, or a "legitimate" target. Huxley extends this logic into even more minute areas, suggesting that peacefulness in individual matters such as dietary and sexual habits affects larger scale politics involving governments and international conflict. The fractured chronology enhances the connection points among many of Anthony's life phases, producing an unexpected unity, and with this device, Huxley enters the time-philosophy debates that preoccupied many modernist writers and aligns himself with modernist notions of time felt as disjunction and fragmentation rather than some vital flow. The novel opens with Anthony perusing his old photo album, sourly observing that certain women's fashions so attractive at one time now seem distinctly "anti-aphrodisiac" (*EG*, 1). Though *Eyeless in Gaza* is a book of memories, these memories emerge like the snapshots in the novel's opening chapter—less nostalgic than embarrassing and distasteful. The memories build on each other not as a smooth, steady progression from one moment to the next but rather as a flurry of jagged fragments.

In this jostling chronological structure, the ideals that Huxley would preach in *Ends and Means* are undercut and criticized. Although meditation is ultimately one of Anthony's (and Huxley's) treasured practices, valuable as a political weapon in the pacifist arsenal, the idea of self-analysis receives much rough handling through the novel. Huxley puts in Anthony's mouth a scathing description of Proust: "that asthmatic seeker of lost time squatting, horribly white and flabby, with breasts almost female but fledged with long black hairs, for ever squatting in the tepid bath of his remembered past. And all the stale soap suds of countless previous washings floated around him . . . And there he sat, a pale repellent invalid, taking up spongefuls of his own thick soup and squeezing it over his face" (*EG*, 6). Anthony finds in Proust a failed Tiresias: not quite androgynous, unable to be fully enchanted, and certainly unable to be authentically visionary. In one form of contemplative modernism, self-reflection is just the sort of bad prayer Dr. Miller criticizes, a return to one's own excretions. Huxley attacks the modernist aesthetic of Bergsonian flow, preferring a splintered, satirical approach to the novel. Huxley gives us no overall blessing for contemplation, and the time structure adds to his contradictory vision of spiritual discipline.

With a straightforward chronology, *Eyeless in Gaza* might have suggested a simplistic message, in which Anthony's progression of life experiences would culminate in spiritual and political sagacity. But the disjointed narration fractures this simplistic moral and accentuates another key feature of the novel's complex expression of pacifism: the recurrent images of bloodshed. A consistent presence of violence permeates the novel and contributes to the unity of all things despite the palpable disjunction of time. In Brian Foxe's suicide, Anthony's mother's early death, the newspaper reports of young men killed in the Boer War, and many other gory moments, Anthony's life is shot through with violence that he scarcely has the resources to endure. One notable example is the famous (or notorious) "dog episode," which occurs early in the text, though its setting on August 30, 1933, makes it one of the later events of the story. Anthony and his lover, Helen, are interrupted during a tryst by the "clattering roar" of an "aeroplane" above them. Anthony curses the plane, disturbed partly by its noise and partly by its vantage point: "These damned machines! . . . They'll have a nice God's-eye view of us here . . . David and Bathsheba" (*EG*, 113). His guilty conscience is pricked, along with his irritation at being bothered during love making. But the scene takes a magical realist turn as the air is "punctuated" by "a strange yelping sound," an explosive thud a yard from where they are lying, and the sight of "a red pool at their feet [in which] lay the almost shapeless carcase of a fox terrier" (ibid.). Anthony tries to quip away his discomfort, saying, "Yet another reason for disliking dogs" and telling the blood-spattered Helen that she looks like Lady Macbeth (114). Helen, in shock and horror unmollified by Anthony's humor, flees his side and ends their affair. With an airplane unleashing carnage among civilians, we see a premonition of the bombing war to come, the great terror for Huxley and many of his contemporaries. As he wrote in *Ends and Means*, "In any future war, it is clear that [civilians] will be exposed to risks almost, if not quite, as great as those faced by the fighting men," and he suggests that this in itself should be a deterrent (*EM*, 107). The bigger social calamity of air war transfers in this scene to the personal unrest in Anthony's love life.

Though the dog incident may allude to aerial bombing, it has also been read more favorably as a quasi-religious blood sacrifice that fundamentally benefits Anthony and Helen. Seeing Helen sobbing and "in the hopeless abjection of her bloodstained nakedness," Anthony unexpectedly feels "pity stir[ring] within him and then an almost violent movement of love for this hurt and suffering woman" whom he had earlier regarded as a sexual object rather than a person (*EG*, 114). Anthony feels compassion, and Helen is shocked into self-awareness that leads her to end their affair. Susan Venter gives an especially favorable view of the dog scene, arguing that it portrays Huxley's turn away from the idiosyncratic religion of his friend D. H. Lawrence: "the death of the dog implies the symbolic death of 'the animal'—that 'mystique' of the body postulated by Lawrence," and thus the dog's death affects Anthony's and Helen's lives such that "meaningfulness replaces meaninglessness" ("The 'Dog Episode,'" 19). This scene conveys both a pacifist satire on air war and a bizarre but ultimately humanizing ritual.

The dog episode displays contradictions that resurface, even as the novel concludes in Anthony's lyrical glorification of Unity as his foundational belief: "Frenzy of evil and separation. In peace there is unity. Unity with other lives. Unity with all being. For beneath all being, beneath the countless identical but separate patterns, beneath the attractions and repulsions, lies peace. The same peace as underlies the frenzy of the mind. Dark peace, immeasurably deep" (*EG*, 471–72). He sees unity in his commitment to the political group called the Organization, to the pacifist cause, to his comrades, to Helen, his former lover who is now a friend wavering on the brink of pacifism, and even in enemy love. And unity is the term he finds to link several of the novel's striking scenes of gore: "in the drunken Mexican's pistol as in the dark dried blood on that mangled face among the rocks, the fresh blood spattered scarlet over Helen's naked body, the drops oozing from the raw contusion on Mark's knee" (467). Through the blood and violence and political mistakes of Anthony's life, he struggles to achieve a worthwhile pacifist presence. Rather than a conclusive endpoint, pacifism is a journey like monasticism, placing Anthony outside mainstream national and religious identities. As Huxley wrote during his own conversion, pacifism "entails devoted and unremitting personal service for the cause . . . peace is the by-product of a certain way of life" (qtd. in Dunaway, *Hollywood*, 22). The form of *Eyeless in Gaza*—a certain way of writing—attempts to portray that impersonal yet somehow purposeful organization of life. A disjointed yet unified life emerges through the shifts back and forth in time and our experience of Anthony's vacillating philosophy, religion, politics, and erotic loves.

Not simply didactic, *Eyeless in Gaza* evinces through every chapter an enduring struggle with personal convictions, public actions, physical desires, and intellectual pursuits. The novel's title lifts from Milton the image of Samson, blind and bound, caught in slave labor for the very tribe he was prophesied to vanquish for Israel's freedom:

> O glorious strength
> Put to the labour of a Beast, debas't
> Lower then bondslave! Promise was that I
> Should *Israel* from *Philistian* yoke deliver;
> Ask for this great Deliverer now, and find him
> Eyeless in *Gaza* at the Mill with slaves,
> Himself in bonds under *Philistian* yoke
>
> (*Complete Poems*, 443–44)

For a supposedly didactic work, Huxley's choice of title is curiously ambiguous. Thematizing bondage and sightlessness as the conditions of the protagonist would seem to contradict the enlightenment and sagelike contentment discovered by Anthony as an antidote to the slaveries of the modern world. Huxley's lifelong problems with eyesight persistently emblematized his struggles to be a successful visionary, and this ocular theme echoes in the choice of title. The Samson of Milton's chamber drama bewails his incapacity to fulfill the salvation of Israel by his hand. The novel ends with Anthony in a similar state, dedicated to a cause and persevering in his convictions but lacking any clear vision about how to act. The agony of political awakening is emphasized rather than the successful contentment of a visionary, mystical pacifism.

Pacifist Afterlife

Self-imposed exile to America marks a third phase in Huxley's political life following his early role as sardonic social critic and his rebirth as a peace activist.[20] As controversial as his mid-1930s peace work remains, his abandonment of England threatens to cast his earlier activism in a worse light, as though his inability—or even refusal—to see his idealistic and utopian convictions through to their conclusions nullifies them completely. An often repeated narrative among prominent British peace activists in the late 1930s was the public retraction of their former pacifism. Beverley Nichols, whose pacifist screed *Cry Havoc!* of 1933 had been widely admired throughout Britain, made an about-face, publishing *Men Do Not Weep* in 1941, in which he imagines an autobiographical novel called "Death of a Pacifist," which celebrates the legions of ex-pacifists in barracks "forming threes in khaki" (7). A. A. Milne would respond to his own antiwar treatise *Peace with Honour* (1934) with *War with Honour* (1940), a qualified support for the war effort. Scholars such as Martin Ceadel even speculate that Dick Sheppard, whose death in 1937 precluded his need to choose between antiwar and anti-Nazi values, would have likely joined other PPU members who turned from absolutism to pragmatism. Many pacifists resorted to "collaborative orientation" during the war, "bound by their conscientious inability to fight" but having "to admit that one side had the better cause and should not be obstructed"(*Pacifism in Britain*, 247–48).

These intense, often personally demoralizing debates about the persistence of absolute pacifism or its modification into pragmatic forms will be examined further in subsequent chapters, but Huxley poses a striking case in that his absolutism seems never to have flagged, though his actions lacked the same idealism that he had proposed in his pamphlets and essays. It should be noted, however, that Huxley's move to America was not simply a matter of fearful avoidance. His apparent intention was to return home eventually, and though his leaving in 1937 was undoubtedly inopportune for the PPU, he saw his lecture tour with Gerald Heard as carrying on the work of preaching nonviolence. These lectures and his *Encyclopaedia of Pacifism* were contentious enough to get him placed on the FBI's watch list under "Subversive Activities—General," where he would continue accumulating a file until his death in 1963

(Murray, *Huxley*, 306). But from the safety of Los Angeles, thriving as a screenwriter, he could write to Naomi Mitchison after the Munich crisis of 1938, suggesting that "in the existing circumstances, Chamberlain's choice between evils was the better one" (*Selected Letters*, 357). He was not alone in this view, of course, but it is harder to countenance an affirmation of other people's sacrifice from someone who had so much less on the table and who spoke from an aloof position of relative comfort. A return to "case-hardening" seems a justifiable diagnosis.

Unlike members of the peace movement who adjusted their pacifist views once they saw no alternative to war, projecting a sense that pacifism was limited in its effectiveness, Huxley never wavered. His turn during the war years was away from nonviolent action—not that he no longer professed a belief in the efficacy of nonviolence, but his own activism and testing of pacifist convictions through nonviolence was severely diminished. Instead of campaigning for peace or following the model of other unflagging pacifists, such as Vera Brittain, who remained in England writing peace-oriented journalism for pacifists needing guidance about how to live out their convictions during wartime, Huxley turned even more steadfastly toward imagining a rebuilt civilization after the war. He affirmed his brother Julian's pamphlet *Reconstruction and Peace* (1941) and would offer his own brief commentary on rebuilding society in *Science, Liberty, and Peace* (1946).[21] His final novel, *Island* (1962), was still part of this effort to imagine a world without violent, technocratic wreckage. The British peace movement and Huxley's activism were never again quite so full of promise as they were in 1936, which marked a high point for the antiwar struggle as well as the first major shocks to its viability. As Huxley wrote to Leonard Woolf in March that year, responding to Woolf's mischaracterization of pacifism in *The League and Abyssinia* as simply passive, the "pacifist way may not succeed; but on the other hand it might. And if it succeeded only partially, the international atmosphere wd be cleared" (*LAH*, 401). Hope for even partial fulfillment of pacifist values animated his writing, and Huxley's great novel of 1936 remains a testament to the struggle for personal and political unity through chaotic and fragmentary modernist forms, literary expression that enacts the confusing, difficult work of not just pledging but living for peace.

CHAPTER 2

Challenging Death in Storm Jameson's
Mirror in Darkness Trilogy

The utopian bent of Aldous Huxley's thinking—as in, for instance, the radicalism of his suggested social reforms—has been taken metonymically among some peace movement critics, as though far-reaching (and therefore "unrealistic") political agendas characterize the entirety of interwar peace activism. The title of Martin Ceadel's monumental work on the British peace movement from 1854 to 1945, *Semi-Detached Idealists*—a scrupulous chronicling of pacifist politics in Britain—implies that the peace movement was out of touch with reality. Even less nuanced than Ceadel are critics who characterize the efforts of the peace movement as simplistic, childish, or "intellectually primitive" (Zwerdling, *Virginia Woolf*, 286). Alex Zwerdling, portraying the PPU as infantile, observes that Beverly Nichols and A. A. Milne were antiwar propagandists "now better known for writing children's books" (ibid., 286). For evidence, Zwerdling quotes Milne's *Peace with Honour* (1934), which calls war "a Bad Thing." Zwerdling's portrayal misses the irony in Milne's comment, which occurs in the context of a humorous takedown of leading churchmen and politicians whose rhetoric boils down to war's being "Much too Much of a Good Thing."[1] More important, the charge of unrealistic immaturity obscures the variety of positions held by peace activists as well as the kinds of literary production that complemented and propelled pacifist and antiwar writing in the thirties.

Even Milne, who admittedly has a reputation secured by Pooh stories and children's verse, had far more to say about war than his decontextualized "Bad Thing" quotation might suggest. In *Peace with Honour*, he attempted to distinguish among antiwar positions based in political expediency, fear of self-endangerment, unimaginative conflict resolution, and his own sense of the immorality of killing, ultimately resolving that the best way to work for the end of war was to rethink policies that entertain "the conventional use of force to satisfy some national ambition regardless of consequences" (*Peace with Honour*, 47). As his views developed in relation to Hitler's conquests of Austria, Czechoslovakia, and Poland, he would publicly redefine his position, first in *War with Honour* (1940), a pamphlet that he described as an addendum to his previous book, writing, "If anybody reads *Peace with Honour* now, he must read it with that one word 'HITLER' scrawled across every page" (12.) In a critique of his earlier argument, which anticipates the judgment of later historians, he notes that his former views were crafted in response to the world of 1934. Attacking the "war convention" no longer applies with an adversary whose ambitions are not constrained by the territorial and political mores of the past. Intriguingly, though, Milne did not describe himself as renouncing pacifism, accepting "realism" after awakening from parochialism, or even fully repudiating *Peace with Honour*. Rather, he regarded the earlier book as a worthy contribution to antiwar arguments for an older global situation, attesting that "the very ardour of his Pacifism" was "unchanged since 1934" and "inspires his passion now for military victory" (*War with Honour*, 13). Milne would later publish another pamphlet, *War Aims Unlimited* (1941), developing his position as a convinced pacifist who nonetheless affirms the necessity of this particular war: "Through all these years Europe was living in a state of war and the fear of future wars. I wanted to end that war; and by ending it, to end the fear of all further wars. That is why I still call myself a Pacifist; . . . my only war aim is to defeat Hitler, and my only peace aim is to ensure that, with his defeat and death, the reign of war shall be ended" (24). Embracing the logic of a final war to end war becomes the mode of Milne's pragmatic pacifism, declaring this particular situation different and thus requiring a violent response to mass violence.

Milne's efforts to think through his pacifism while deciding that the war against Hitler must be fought, in contrast to Huxley's unwavering absolutism, provides a useful context for examining the fiction of this chapter's central figure: Margaret Storm Jameson. Like Huxley, Jameson insisted on thoroughgoing social reform as a necessary element for a world in which peace could be truly possible. But as Phyllis Lassner has shown, she was wary of any absolutist politics or totalizing aesthetic practices, and her concern for justice extended toward Jews and the peoples of Eastern Europe victimized by Hitler's actions.[2] When circumstances in Europe appeared no longer to offer viable nonviolent options, Jameson changed her position, much in the manner of Milne's pacifism-with-exceptions (what Ceadel calls "pacific-ism"). Scholarly interest in Jameson's writings has grown in recent years after decades of neglect, but even during this increase, critical attention has tilted toward the "European fictions" that were the hallmark of her wartime prose. By contrast, her work in the first half of the 1930s is the central focus of this chapter, which examines the relatively brief phase when her pacifism and antifascism were consonant motivators for a spate of literary, critical, and journalistic publications.

For his early, steadfast, and productive commitment to the Peace Pledge Union, Huxley remains the preeminent literary figure active in the British peace movement. But Huxley's closest rival in this study is Jameson, whose staggering productivity as a writer was matched by heroic work on behalf of refugees and a variety of peace-oriented and antifascist causes.[3] Living well, in the hermitic manner of Huxley and his protagonist Anthony Beavis, offers a compelling vision, as long as one finds contentment in an idealistic, prophetic mode spared from firsthand contact with war violence. Each of the writers in the current and subsequent chapters stayed in England and provides unique accounts of pacifism in the presence of war. Jameson, like Huxley, sometimes assumed the role of prophet, which critics including Chiara Briganti and Elizabeth Maslen show was modeled on Cassandra, prophesying doom in a Europe hurtling toward disaster.[4] Though capable of speaking unpleasant truths to others and about herself, this role was wearying, as Jameson told Rache Lovat Dickson in 1948: "I must give up prophecy—no one loved Cassandra" (qtd. in Maslen, *Life*, 353).

Though she did not claim the role, we might also see Jameson as a Diogenes, critically biting at the peace movement for its strains of hypocrisy, illogic, injustice, and wishful thinking. To understand the ways her literary production was itself activist in its orientation—a practice she firmly maintained and later came to regret—we can look to the matrix of political positions that animated her activity: the Little England movement, socialist nation-building, resistance to foreign and domestic fascism, and absolute pacifism, which she would finally, despairingly abandon during the Second World War. All of this vibrant activity was marked by a wide-ranging skepticism, emblematized by her comment that peace work in the thirties was like "children throwing sand against the wind" (*JN*, 326).

Much criticism of Jameson's work gravitates toward her two-volume memoir, *Journey from the North* (1969–1970), a lively, magisterial look into her life, writing, friendships, and politics, with special attention to the 1930s and the war years. While this memoir is stimulating for its view of the period and informative about her writing life, there is a danger of relying too heavily on her cynical, retrospective judgments, which amplified her lifelong habit of disparaging her literary efforts and regarding her political philosophies and activities as foolish and inept. As Briganti describes this tendency, Jameson "was her own worst enemy and mostly responsible herself for what happened to her critical reputation" ("Mirroring the Darkness," 72). When Jameson published *That Was Yesterday* (1932), a novel she would see as her first mature work, she included in the front matter this disclaimer: "A few sentences in this book, chiefly conversational, have been lifted with slight alterations from an earlier novel of the writer's. This earlier book was fortunately not much read: even more fortunately it was printed on quickly perishable paper. The pity is that it was printed at all"—not exactly an encouragement for the potential reader. This sarcastic approach to much of her earlier work predominates in *Journey from the North* and colors her political positions: "For some years after 1933 I lived in equivocal amity with pacifists and combative supporters of the League of Nations, adjusting my feelings, in good and bad faith, to the person I happened to be with. I swayed between the two like a tightrope walker, or a politician" (*JN*, 326). The rhetorical force of Jameson's self-assessments might lead us to hew closely to these comments about her writing and activism, which, as Jennifer Birkett has claimed, have the benefit of honesty at the expense of making "her seem duplicitous and shallow, in comparison with contemporaries who built their pacifist careers on the profession of more absolute principles" (*Margaret Storm Jameson*, 121). But taking *Journey from the North* uncritically as the final word on Jameson's efforts can obscure the prodigiousness with which she attempted a combination of literature and activism.

This chapter concentrates on the internal conflict that motivated her political thought and aesthetic practice as Jameson struggled to reconcile deeply felt antiwar and antifascist convictions. Like Milne, she abandoned her direct affiliation with peace groups, but also like him she continued to see herself in pacifist terms. Her PEN pamphlet *The End of This War* (1941) is usually read as an outright renunciation of the peace movement and declaration of her altered views about military force. But she referred to this public statement in her private correspondence as an attempt to muddle through an as-yet-unfocused understanding of her "present pacifism."[5] Rather than the waffling dilettante she sometimes portrayed herself as, or a pacifist turned realist as a political conversion narrative might suggest, Jameson can be seen as a critical pragmatist even at the peak of her involvement with pacifist organizations such as the Peace Pledge Union.

This critical pragmatism, which combines pacifist and antifascist ideals, is manifest in *The Mirror in Darkness*, a trilogy of novels written in the 1930s but focusing on the years 1918 to 1926, from the Armistice to the General Strike: *Company Parade* (1934), *Love in Winter* (1935), and *None Turn Back* (1936). Jameson believed that socialist economics and an internationally cooperative Europe led by a patriotic England was the best way to eliminate war and reform the social order. Her socialist ideas are scattered through an array of occasional essays and letters in periodicals. "Documents," a minor classic of 1930s writing published in the left-wing journal *Fact*, is one of her most sustained examinations of socialist literature.[6] In this essay, she argues that new forms and a different angle of focus are required of all socialist writers creating revolutionary literature: "The writer living in one moment of time and in one society, and perpetually conscious of another trying to break through, has been set a task which calls for special discipline and effort" ("Documents," 11–12). Revealing the emergent new society breaking forth from within the old is the necessary labor for the socialist writer, whatever the specific content of her subject matter or structure of her work. *The Mirror in Darkness* is a demonstration of this effort, an attempt at collective novelization and a major example of Jameson's efforts to write English social fiction akin to French models such as Balzac—though she was scornful of naturalists who made "drab tuppeny-ha'penny dramas" ("Documents," 13).[7]

The main character in the series, Hervey Russell, is a novelist seeking a literary form adequate to the modern condition, and while Hervey is something of an autobiographical double for Jameson, the form of the narrative contorts in ways that capture a broad swath of British society not limited to Hervey's perspective. Georg Lukács's classic reading of Balzac in *The Historical Novel* shows how the French realist produced richly detailed "types," characters whose construction demonstrates their social condition.[8] Jameson offers characters whose typicality suggests that social critique is central to her project. As she later described it, *Company Parade* is "a really good book, crowded with men, women and a child or two . . . there are ex-soldiers, industrialists, a Jewish newspaper proprietor and his family, writers, a segment of the literary *panier à crabes* of the twenties, a Marie Lloyd figure, a young Labour politician and his wife" (*JN*, 328). This rare judgment that the book is good and that "*fleuve* for *fleuve*, [the trilogy] ran faster and deeper than any flowering now, in the sixties," is quickly countered: "But what a devil of an idea to set myself up as a Balzac. I must have been mad" (329). Mad though she sometimes felt it to be, Jameson attempted in *The Mirror in Darkness* a "complete" portrayal of Britain after the First World War, showing us a range of characters debating the pressing topics of their day, but most often returning to discussions about how the war started, what its outcome produced, and what might be done to prevent a future cataclysm. Other novels by Jameson from the 1930s deal more explicitly with Fascism/Nazism and war, but none have the ambitious scope of *The Mirror in Darkness*. The few critical analyses of the trilogy have with good reason emphasized its socialist dimension and relation to Jameson's French models, her antifascist concerns, and her feminism. Less has been written about the subtler but still insistent presence of pacifist aesthetics. In writing what she hoped could be socialist literature, Jameson evokes the "structural violence" described by Johan Galtung as that force which exerts itself not by active, acute moments of disaster but through social organization that inherently damages some members of society by giving advantages to others ("Violence," 170–71). Whatever flaws in her methodology were divined by Jameson's critics and her own evaluations, *The Mirror in Darkness* still amounts to a vigorous condemnation of Britain's violent social order, reeling from one war and charging toward another. The trilogy strives through literary art to challenge the forces of death and violence that Jameson saw as the essence of the interwar era.

Life-Writing as a Challenge to Death

Mary Hervey Russell, the fictional avatar that anchors *The Mirror in Darkness*, is also part of a larger autobiographical enterprise. Though *The Mirror in Darkness* is commonly referred to as a trilogy, its origin as a proposed five- or six-book sequence, along with its close relationship with several novels written before and after the three books of the trilogy, gives it the effect of a longer project, despite Jameson's claim that she had abandoned her original scope.[9] While the other related novels are different in style and focus from the three *Mirror in Darkness* works, they still give evidence of Jameson's sweeping perspective on interwar England and, later, postwar Europe. Her first major trilogy, collectively referred to as *The Triumph of Time—The Lovely Ship* (1927), *Farewell to Youth* (1928), and *A Richer Dust* (1931)—details the life of the formidable Mary Hansyke, who creates a successful shipbuilding enterprise in the second half of the nineteenth century. In *That Was Yesterday* (1932), Jameson introduced her fictional double, Mary Hervey Russell, Mary Hansyke's granddaughter, whose awful marriage to Penn Vane gives an additional layer of personal trauma to the Great War years. *The Mirror in Darkness* followed quickly after *That Was Yesterday*, though its style is far less conventional, using collective narrative techniques indebted to Dos Passos, fused with a Balzacian sweep.[10] Though Hervey Russell remains a centerpiece and anchor in the trilogy, its canvas is larger and methods more experimental than anything in the Hansyke-Russell saga. Jameson may be right that the massive scope of her intended project was beyond her means, given the pressure she felt to publish a novel every year and sometimes several, but her talent was clearly capable of tackling large-scale works and compressing complex historical and political situations into novelistic form. In her prolific output, she would use many forms and styles to grapple with the ideas that consumed her, but several kinds of "life-writing" would be essential to her politically committed creative expression.

Like so many activists in the peace movement, Jameson's first official entrée occurred because of Dick Sheppard. In May 1936, as part of his goal of bringing women into PPU membership alongside the men who had signed the initial pledge, Sheppard invited Jameson to become a sponsor (Maslen, *Life*, 156), a designation that carried with it an expectation to publicize the PPU and attend regular meetings with other sponsors as an "informal consultative committee" (Hetherington, *Swimming*, 6). As a writer with a well-known, if not quite best-selling, literary reputation, plus a firm commitment to war prevention, Jameson was a natural fit for Sheppard's organization. Her own feelings about the PPU were somewhat mixed even from the start, and while her name remained on the letterhead for many years, she never found herself in the mainstream of the organization. She joined before her close friend Vera Brittain did, though they both initially struggled with having to adopt the absolute pacifist position of the PPU and to disengage from groups, such as the League of Nations Union, that were internationalist and opposed to war but were not pacifist hardliners. Later in the 1930s, as Jameson began disengaging from the PPU more completely, she would report to Brittain that she had always been reluctant to take part in the organization because she "could not take an active, that is speaking and committee-work part, in the Union. . . . The P.P.U. is not a thing one can go into with one foot" (qtd. in Maslen, *Life*, 206). Off-balance because of her "one footed" connection with the PPU, she found herself unable to speak out publically against positions such as the PPU's objection to Air Raid Precautions (ARP). Jameson (and Brittain) saw preparation for bomber attacks as a necessary measure for preventing greater civilian deaths, while the official position in the PPU regarded ARP measures as a concession to military solutions for the as-yet-undeclared war.[11] On these and several other matters, Jameson's pragmatic sensibilities were at odds with PPU members whose idealism or mysticism (like that of Huxley, Heard, and others) she could not countenance.

Though the PPU became the one explicitly pacifist organization with which Jameson associated, her participation with Sheppard was based on several earlier efforts toward peace activism. Some of her literary works of the 1920s have been regarded as antiwar, but her first monumental pacifist book was *No Time like the Present* (1933).[12] This volume appeared as a memoir, aligned in theme with the many "war books" that were popular in the late 1920s and early 1930s—including her husband Guy Chapman's *A Passionate Prodigality* (1933). Unlike Chapman's memoir, which includes telling moments of adulation for war experience, Jameson's pacifism was unquestionably a driving force in her narrative.[13] For Jameson, the pacifist agenda catalyzed her writing from the start, and she even told Brittain that the memoir form was just a ruse: "when I began [*No Time like the Present*]—at Whitby and with the feeling of isolation—I thought I had to trick people into reading anti-war. I don't now think it necessary but it is too late."[14] Jameson's shifting view of her audience tells us something about the prominence of war aversion in the British public during the early 1930s, and we can also glimpse Jameson's position at the crest of the wave of war books that had been captivating the public imagination. By 1933, as *No Time like the Present* was about to be published, Jameson believed that she did not need the layers of distance from war required a decade earlier. She could also think of the book as preparing the way for Brittain's *Testament of Youth* (1933), describing it to her as "a thin feeble John the Baptist blowing across the ground in front of the 'Testament.'"[15] This gesture of self-deprecation and flattery, always attentive to Brittain's sensitivities, highlights her political intentions as well. Jameson saw herself attempting what she felt Brittain had accomplished: a memoir as peace witness, told by a woman to reveal the extent of war's destruction on those who did not fight.

Jameson's first memoir functions as a kind of war memorial, sustaining memories not of glorious death but of mundane life that has been corrupted by global violence. In a striking paragraph early in her narrative, she tells of her university days, which are, like so much of her prewar life, rendered in terms of the devastation that followed. She writes: "With one exception, all the young men who were my friends in the university were killed within the next three years" (*No Time*, 61–62). Her memorial in print enumerates the "small things about them," a list of memories, such as the time that one friend "was angry with me because I could not recognise God Save the King when he whistled it for me during a competition at some professor's garden party" (62). Appearances and mannerisms too insignificant and ephemeral for notice in recorded histories are precisely the mundane things lost and forgotten in war. Official war memorials fail, Jameson says, because they cannot capture the fine trivialities rendered irretrievable by death: "The war memorial, with its long list of names, is not, as some think, a permission to forget how this boy laughed and how another liked strawberries and dancing and to read German aloud. Because it was laughter, dancing, strawberries, and the reading of books, that they laid down, and not something vague and immaterial" (ibid.). This passage highlights one of Jameson's abiding interests: the recording of small details so as to preserve in memory the lives destroyed by war. As she would theorize in "Documents," these concrete details are the essential elements in socialist fiction, which depicts not just the travails of the working classes (as in "proletarian novels") but the granular materials of a changing social world. In *No Time like the Present*, the documenting captures the societal change particular to Jameson's left-wing commitments and marshals these documents in service of her pacifist memorial. E. M. Delafield's review in the *Morning Post* criticized Jameson's book for its bifurcated structure, suggesting that though she agreed with the antiwar portions, they were all too familiar, while the personal elements were truly original: "I admire both pieces of writing: I am only puzzled in the same way that I should be puzzled by meeting a very charming and delicate *berceuse* that, in the second movement, suddenly developed a *tempo di marcia* and a corresponding theme" ("The Past or the Present?"). This problem with form would continually plague Jameson, and the feeling that her memoir perpetrated a "trick" would nag her as she sought more unified, holistic ways of espousing her political agendas through narratives like *The Mirror in Darkness*.

No Time like the Present was far less commercially successful than Brittain's *Testament of Youth*, a difference that was a persistent sore spot through the closest years of their friendship, but this antiwar treatise disguised as memoir solidified Jameson's pacifist credentials, which she further developed in the laborious editorial process for *Challenge to Death* (1934). Philip Noel-Baker and Jameson collaborated on a scheme to bring together well-known writers who might share a basic aversion to war, though not necessarily a commitment to absolute pacifism.[16] A dinner party was convened at the estate of Robert Cecil, 1st Viscount Cecil of Chelwood, who was a leading figure in the creation of the League of Nations and whose peace advocacy would earn him a Nobel Prize in 1937.[17] This gathering, in which Viscount Cecil presided with Rose Macaulay and Rebecca West on either side (Jameson later recalled a coin toss to decide who sat on his right), was the initial meeting of minds for dinner and discussion to court possible contributors to the volume that became *Challenge to Death* (*JN*, 327). Jameson's labors in producing the book were arduous and extensive. Brittain's foreword to the American edition claimed that Jameson had personally written 174 letters during the process of cajoling responses from her authors (*CTD*, ix). Catching Aldous Huxley at a key moment before his pacifist convictions had solidified, Jameson received from him a high-handed letter of refusal describing the inevitability of war and the futility of opposing it. Jameson returned with a small bit of literary revenge, having a character in *None Turn Back* say, "I can't run about with a manifesto in my pocket, it's not my rôle. Ask Huxley to do it—but he won't" (*NTB*, 22). Ever the overfunctioning laborer, Jameson ended up contributing two essays herself when her myriad request letters failed to secure an introductory contribution.

Her own essays in *Challenge to Death*, though written while intensely overworked and later criticized for derivativeness and cliché, still manifest some of the core beliefs that undergird her most committed years of pacifism.[18] The first of these essays, "The Twilight of Reason," describes the underlying causes of war, which perpetuate violence despite significant opposition to belligerent solutions. The main thrust of her essay is that the passionate mob mentality found in the emergent dictatorships of Europe signals an end to reason. Unlike the often heard pacifist appeal to reason over irrationality as a solution to the problem of war, she is dismissive of much pacifist rhetoric, especially the kind that appeals to "decency and sanity" or to revulsion over war's horrors, noting that these objections can always be overcome when violence becomes inescapable or otherwise justifiable (*CTD*, 3). Her attention to the allures of fascism foreshadows her depiction of authoritarianism in Britain from *The Mirror in Darkness* and later European fictions.

In place of zealous nationalism such as that promoted by Mussolini, in which "the national State is the highest and most complex social organism possible," Jameson advocates an international governing body (*CTD*, 13). She does not specify at this point in her life whether this body should be open to using violence for ensuring collective security, but she asserts that some new global organizational strategy must be adopted to revise the overly broad question, "Will you choose war or peace?," into its superior form, "Will you choose the sovereign independence of your country, armed to enforce its rights, or will you choose peace?" (19). In this revision of the question, Jameson joins a long line of antiwar theorists going at least as far back as Kant's writings on "Perpetual Peace" and including Jane Addams and Bertrand Russell as prominent twentieth-century advocates of supranational governance.[19] Her position in "The

Twilight of Reason" foreshadows the changing relationship she would have with League of Nations supporters who might be willing to embrace what Ceadel terms "defencist" reliance on strong military capabilities (*Thinking*, 72–100). Her desire for collaborative internationalism within the European community—albeit with England at its heart—would remain a lifelong value, expressed most forcefully in her essay "On Patriotism" (1935):

> I am a Little Englander on one side (the left—the side of the heart), and on the other I try to be a good European. Much good it will do us now to talk of Isolation, standing on the edge of a continent which can be overrun in a few hours by air. Nor can I find anything comfortable in the equally irrational fantasy of building (only for our defence) more aeroplanes than every other country is building (for its defence) . . . For ill or good England is a close part of Europe and will remain so until aeroplanes are forbidden to be built. (*Civil Journey*, 252–53)

Jameson proposes a distinctly patriotic Englishness consistent with committed participation in a cosmopolitan "idea of Europe," and the fear of a coming war with its boundary effacing technologies makes this rooted cosmopolitanism an urgent necessity.[20]

It is worth noting as well that whatever changes were afoot in Jameson's beliefs about pacifism, she selected both of her essays from *Challenge to Death* for inclusion in her collection *Civil Journey* (1939). This is not to say that her positions were unaltered during these years, but it does indicate willingness for her public persona to remain closely tied to pacifism in the late thirties. In "The Twilight of Reason," she criticizes (among many other things) the generals who dislike bloodshed but "helped by a fortunate want of imagination [can] insulate their minds from the practical consequences—which after all can be buried in quicklime—of their orders" (*CTD*, 2). Alluding to the atrophied imaginations of generals— the trait that allows them to read honor rolls as statistical abstracts rather than as individual stories of death and dismemberment—conveys her underlying conviction (anticipating Lederach) that the writer's imagination is capable of greater moral weight than the imagination of military leaders. *No Time like the Present* sought to cut through the insulation by recording and preserving the small human traits of friends who had become merely names in a casualty list. In *The Mirror in Darkness*, Jameson pursued this documenting through fiction, displaying a moral imagination spurred on by her intellectual absorption with socialism, English patriotism, internationalism, and a highly emotional revulsion against war.

Socialist Fiction against War

By focusing on *The Mirror in Darkness* rather than on a more explicitly pacifist text such as *No Time like the Present*, I seek to demonstrate that Jameson's socialist and antitotalitarian aesthetics are essential to her pacifist imagination. As she wrote in 1936 while completing *The Mirror in Darkness*, "in 1919 I imagined that it had been demonstrated to the world that war is an unmitigated disaster: I was too ignorant to understand that war remained a necessity of capitalist society . . . I thought that my own job began and ended when, as a writer, I upheld pacifism and the classless State. I was a pacifist because I hated war, and a Socialist because I hated poverty and the injustice and waste of inequality" ("Crisis," 156). The three novels of the series, in which she tried to capture the "contemporary scene" through a panoramic depiction of characters in crisis during the 1920s, constitute her most ambitious effort to critique the plutocratic, militaristic structure of British society.[21] Like many of her contemporaries in the peace movement, her diagnosis of militarist impulses in the interwar years was predicated on a model of international relations derived from the Great War, in which mismanaged allegiances and faulty diplomacy turned territorial disputes into global catastrophe. More than most, she saw the "peace" work of politicians as duplicitous, the "polite speeches of statesmen who are only too ready, in the interests of economy and as a gesture towards their own academic preference for peace in our time, to abolish arms they can do without while retaining those they have a mind to" ("About the Next War," 144). Tough-minded and allergic to hypocrisy, she was unable to applaud modest disarmament in the early 1930s, when total disarmament was her mission and goal. As she saw it, the supposed peace of the years following World War I was only the cessation of active violence, and she affirmed the metaphor of "an old and very tired Austrian professor" who "said that a man died when the will of his body to resist death began failing and its will to live was transformed gradually, by the spreading apathy of its cells, into a will to death" (ibid.). The apathetic purveyors of merely "academic" peace were a symptom of general apathy throughout Europe and a cultural death that Jameson strove to challenge in her writing. *The Mirror in Darkness* challenges death in this sense, taking the form of a social chronicle to meticulously record the debates, actions, and feelings that defined London after the war, to expose the elements that made this current peace something false. The de facto trilogy remains an under-studied example of socialist fiction of the thirties applied to an historical examination of the 1920s and the changing conditions that were shuttling England toward another war.

All three volumes of *The Mirror in Darkness*, though sharing characters and some narrative modes with the other parts, use formal experiments distinctive to each novel. The first entry in the series is most invested in a collectivist narrative point of view with many angles on postwar thoughts and feelings. The second entry shifts focus toward new notions about family life and sexuality emerging in the twenties, and its structure borrows romance novel conventions that it subverts with several subsidiary plots to reveal a maelstrom of economic power plays. The third entry, as compared with the other two, radically compresses time by narrating just a single week surrounding the General Strike of 1926, thereby making this moment of failed revolution a tragic misstep in the effort toward socialist renewal. Chiara Briganti has provided the most thorough catalogue of the many aesthetic influences on the trilogy, arguing that the broad range of economic and political concerns expressed through a constellation of narrative devices helps produce Jameson's version of the socialist "collective novel" ("Mirroring," 71). Borrowing from the dialectical cinema of Sergei Eisenstein, the social research of the Mass-Observation project, the panoramic novel (or "la simultanéité narrative," as Jameson's French models called it) and Woolf's experiments with free indirect discourse, Jameson created a capacious narrative form indebted to high modernist work of the 1920s but developing in more explicitly political directions (85). For Briganti, "rather than hindering [Jameson's] formal experimentation, political commitment fuelled it" (72). Her politically committed writing of the thirties remains illuminating through its struggle to unify and integrate her activism and fiction writing without succumbing to political dogmatism.

Calling "Bogy" in *Company Parade*

The formal sophistication of *Company Parade* has attracted critics from as far back as Graham Greene, who reviewed the first edition in the *Spectator*. Greene observed that the unfinished quality of the novel was acceptable because it introduced a series, but he discerned a more troubling incompleteness in its "mood shadowed by war, the War which is just over and the worse war which is already being prepared."[22] He advises that "her theme cannot remain indefinitely the threat of war. That would be to call 'Bogy' once too often" and presciently quips: "but I fear that unless another European war breaks out before Miss Jameson's novel reaches its conclusion, she will find it difficult to present a climax adequate to her beginning" ("Review," 634).[23] By 1936, as Jameson published the last of the *Mirror in Darkness* volumes, her attention would indeed be drawn to other means of addressing the threat of war: her dystopia about British fascism *In the Second Year* (1936), her fantasy of global annihilation *The World Ends* (as "William Lamb," 1937), and her Spanish Civil War novel *No Victory for the Soldier* (as "James Hill," 1937). But for its own sake, whatever technical challenges might exist in holding readerly interest while unfurling the storm shadow of war, *Company Parade* and its sequels offer a rich condemnation of the causes and cultural legacies of militarism.

Though he was skeptical about the first novel's form, Greene usefully notes that the unifying force of Jameson's many concerns—industry, literature, intellectualism, and more—is "the weight of this impending war" and with it "the weight of the internal war between the classes," which "grows heavier as the book proceeds" ("Review," 634). Thus, Greene's review aligns with Nancy Knowles's theory of narrative pacifism, discernible in fiction that presents social inequality in the foreground, war in the background, fragmented narration that requires active synthesis from readers, and a suggestion that art is essential for responding to conflict ("Active Pacifism," 242). Looking at just one of the many possible representative scenes, we might consider Hervey's surveying the London crowd filled with reminders of military violence, poverty, and the changing sexual mores of the postwar years: "Going on the way to the office she saw a fair tall girl, clad from head to ankle in pale blue, striding along like a man; a poor woman's little merry baby, in a frock of red velvet, and gold rings in its pierced ears; a soldier without legs or hands; and a woman and a child begging. They were figures in the front of a vast frieze, a faceless anonymous multitude, which flowed past her without stopping" (*CP*, 86). Though closely observing the society around her, Hervey cannot make sense of it except as a "frieze" and a "multitude," and her primary artistic challenge is to find a literary form that is both emotional in its particularity and important in its broadest social implications. Jameson thus stages her own aesthetic struggle in her central character. Throughout the novel, there are persistent reminders about poverty and the disproportionate wealth and power of the ruling classes and corporate bosses. In the background, the war exerts a constant pressure among the several traumatized ex-combatants and women like Hervey, who attempt to love and befriend them. The rapid shifting from one character to another demands an active reader only partly aided by the novel's precisely dated, specifically detailed chapter titles and subsections with headings such as "Philip makes plans" and "Hervey meets a minor power." Throughout the book we return, however, to Hervey, the insecure linchpin of the narrative as she strives to create art that will adequately mediate the new, disorienting, postwar world.

Company Parade offers a textbook case of these pacifist aesthetics, with the crucial reservation that throughout the novel the redemptive power of art is deeply contested. Hervey is a writer with a novel set for release in May 1919, like Jameson's own first book *The Pot Boils*, and, like *Company Parade*, a satire about pompous intellectuals. Hervey is uncertain of her own talents and is sucked into the "literary *panier à crabes*," which includes the defensive, past-her-prime Evelyn Lamb and the popular hack William Ridley (*JN*, 328). Nowhere in the novel does there emerge a community of mutually collaborative, engaged socialist writers such as Jameson theorized in "Documents," in which writers might come "into relation with their fellow-men and women" and "between them, provide the conditions, the warmth, for a new literature" (18). At best, we find by the novel's end a slightly more autonomous Hervey, willing to stand up to the embittered urgings of her colleague, the socialist-pacifist, ex-combatant David Renn. Hervey is exhausted from working on the well-meaning but failure-prone radical paper, *The Week*, and from caring about peacemaking alongside Renn's churlishness. Renn shows her photographs of the current state of Germany in 1923, full of ugliness wrought by the stringently punitive Treaty of Versailles—what Hervey thinks of as "the aegis of a dirty Peace" (CP, 324). Looking at the pictures makes her numb and more resistant to Renn's admonition that she write overtly political novels. This path, she knows, would unfailingly lead her into propaganda: "Without thinking, she had closed her ears and turned her eyes from the spectacle of Europe being driven as an ox is driven towards the next war" (325). This moment of refusing to look captures the foreboding about future war that had only deepened as Jameson composed the trilogy, and her subsequent fictions show her wrestling with the problems she expressed through Renn. Reluctant to create simplistically didactic fiction, she nonetheless wrote works such as *Europe to Let* (1940), which is full of indignation at the Munich concessions and the dangers of Nazism. With *Company Parade*, her pluralistic approach to character reflects a wide range of conflicting arguments and emotions about the state of England, the effects of war, and the future conflict ahead. That pluralism mitigates the didacticism and challenges any domineering, totalizing politics—and it gives voice to her fear that art has little hope of saving civilization.

Jameson assaults the redemptive power of art from another front by depicting capitalist cooptation of writers and the writing process. Advertising appears to be the only surefire place for creative people to obtain regular salaries. Hervey works at an advertising agency as she tries to start her fiction-writing career, and she finds herself writing copy for chemical companies selling cleaning solutions based on their success during wartime. Exacerbating his already conflicted sense of self, Renn also labors at the agency, and a subplot involves Hervey and Renn's collaboration on an ad for "Saloxide," a mix of "saline and peroxide" guaranteed to save lives during peacetime as it had in field hospitals. At an early stage of their partnership, Renn suffers a posttraumatic episode while reviewing the ad's evocation of injured men returning from combat, and "without warning, he was sick over his hands and the drawing" (CP, 86). It is as if the disgust Renn feels at his current life and work, along with the psychological damage and moral injury scarring him from the war, must be expelled, literally covering his hands just as guilt sticks to him figuratively. No mere chemical product can clean this internal mess, and the creative energies that might be employed toward this end are consumed instead by the gaping jaw of the market. This explosive scene lacks subtlety, but its crudeness matches the character Jameson is creating, a reflection of blunt views untempered by decorum or taste and offering Hervey another possible model for political engagement. While Jameson's nonfiction exhibits her outrage at anyone who profits from war violence, she conveys this position through a character too extreme to carry the weight of the entire novel, and her autobiographically inflected protagonist retains a wary distance from Renn's diatribes about war and economics. Art is not a cure or even an effective salve, and Jameson embeds self-criticism within the novel's attempted pacifist witness.

The persistent self-doubt that colors Jameson's memoirs can be found in her fiction as one technique by which she gives nuance and complexity to moments that espouse her own point of view. In *Company Parade*, Hervey reunites with her two friends, Philip and T. S., the young, politically active idealists who violated their own consciences by going to war in *That Was Yesterday*. Philip returns to civilian life radicalized by combat, committed to a matrix of values quite reminiscent of Jameson's. He looks at his friends "with a serious air" and slowly intones his platform: "Pacifist, socialist, and classicist" (*CP*, 40). Hervey recalls that Philip was always a strong supporter of workers' rights, capable of organizing his friends and the community to give time and resources for causes that provoked him, but there is something in his self-seriousness that appears ossified and naive, as though the organic commitment to local matters has become a caricature by hardening into dogma. Philip launches into a speech before his friends, and like a demagogic speaker at a rally puffs himself into an abstract ideal rather than the human being that Hervey and T. S. love. Insisting on the need for a new world order that will resurrect prewar optimism, he expounds on his positions:

> Socialist—because even to tolerate the idea of there being rich and poor is vulgar—disgusting and ill-bred . . . Pacifist—because it is always the young who die of wars, and this creates for the time an elderly experienced world, which smells *used*. And classicist—because it is your romantics who cover up wars, dictatorships, and the other nastiness with their bad sentiments. I detest romantics. Nearly as much as I used to detest our heroic civilians and the indecent women who gave away white feathers . . . Because we have survived the War, we have to keep a

channel open between us in 1914—do you remember us?—and the future. Before long something new will begin. (40)

Lost youth, the ersatz heroism of civilians, and "indecent" persecutors of suspected antipatriots—all of these tropes appear in Philip's speech and are culled almost verbatim from *No Time like the Present*. Few of these sentiments and little of its tone would be out of place in the earlier memoir, but transposed to fiction, there are several effects that undercut Philip's tirade. For one thing, Philip remains a minor character who dies later in the novel, never finding the new world for which he longs. He seems like a left-wing version of T. E. Hulme, decrying the failures of society and dividing the world into "romantic" and "classicist" sides, though (unlike Hulme) he puts the detested war promoters into the first category (*Collected Writings*, 60–61). His views are quite literally eccentric, positioned outside the central focus of the novel. Like Hervey, the reader is allowed to see a range of possible options for ending war or profiting from it, building a new society or pillaging the current one, and generating aesthetic beauty or selling out to the all-consuming fictions of the marketplace. "Pacifist, socialist, and classicist" is Philip's motto—aligned with Jameson's sympathies—but his vision is displaced and even further removed from the novel's core than the didactic strains of mystical pacifism in Huxley's *Eyeless in Gaza*. Jameson's later dismissiveness of her political stances can be discerned in this novel from 1934, used as a shading device to give gray tones to an otherwise starkly presented set of black and white convictions.

This destabilizing of her own strongest beliefs should not be taken as simple abandonment, however, because few absolutes surface preeminently in her complex form. At multiple levels of the social strata, there are instances of acute violence and a pervasive sense of structural violence. Jameson's parade of Londoners reveals physically and psychologically damaged ex-soldiers, corporate cooptation of art and domination of political dissidents, the pressures of the "bad peace" in Europe, and an overall feeling that everything has changed for the worse. Hervey sees a "soldier in leather-cuffed khaki" sitting in a restaurant, "drinking coffee and his eyes over the edge of the cup had a puzzled stare. He seemed not to know any better than she did what he was about. Behind his eyes were roads leading to trenches and the sights and sounds of that life, and he could not relate it to this nor this to anything waiting for him in the future" (*CP*, 19). This young man's ravaged psyche is mirrored in virtually every ex-combatant character in the novel, and the disconnection between war experience and postwar life finds its analogue in the culture at large.

The war has shaped—and persistent militarism continues to shape— the entire culture, not just those who have directly experienced violence. In one of the sage moments in *Company Parade*, the narrator transitions to a discussion of war profiteering through a description of the effect of warfare on the civilian population. "War ennobles few it does not kill," Jameson writes: "It happened to a great many non-combatants in the last war to suffer a loss less palpable than the loss of a son, a husband, a lover. They lost heart or decency, or only their heads. There is some natural law in this. If some quarter of a modern town or city were set apart for the legalised slaughter of human beings there would spread from it a strange infection through the rest" (*CP*, 117). This sense of a population infected by both direct and indirect experience of war permeates the *Mirror in Darkness* novels, which become a testament to the British people's effort to regain balanced perspectives—restoring hearts, heads, and decency all lost when peace was replaced by legal slaughter. It is a challenge to death when a society restores its natural reluctance to kill and its compassion for all lives. Seen in this light, Jameson's ultimate renunciation of absolute pacifism was part of her growing awareness that returning to this balanced life requires violence once political conditions have made violent solutions inevitable. In several of her later war novels, the metaphorical zone of legalized slaughter has shifted, motivated by forces that make a violent response necessary. But in the 1930s, as she reflected on the aftermaths of World War I, Jameson's imagination was fueled by her desire for a British society reforming itself for peace and life.

Romantic Casualties and "Embryo-Fascism" in *Love in Winter*

Of the three books that comprise *The Mirror in Darkness*, the first volume deals most explicitly with war's consequences in England by using an expansive cast of characters to show the vibrating aftershocks of violence. These acute feelings have dulled somewhat when Jameson returns to Hervey and her circle. At the start of *Love in Winter*, six years have elapsed since the Great War, and though the veterans are still fixated on that time, the rest of the world appears—superficially at least—to be moving on. Like *Company Parade*, Jameson's next novel employs a panoramic form and renders character actions simultaneously, attending to a range of figures in the London scene. Two interrelated narratives, however, predominate: the titular love plot involving Hervey and her cousin, Nicholas Roxby, and the unspooling web of London's nascent fascists.

These two major plotlines bear traces of the Great War past and the undeclared war to come as Jameson demonstrates how even the personal, private sphere is corrupted by militarism. Jennifer Birkett notes that in the novel "love and marriage are also a form of war," but this metaphorical relationship is not the only angle from which Jameson works, and throughout the novel war itself is a defining force in the various romantic entanglements (foreword, 14). Hervey and Nicholas's relationship repeatedly founders on the mental and emotional damage that Nicholas carries with him from his combat days. During many of their meetings, Nicholas lapses into war thoughts with Hervey, and the fundamental obstacle to their romance is the unbridgeable distance between the combatant and the civilian. Hervey notices that as Nicholas reminisces about the war, "his face became happier and smoother" and "certain names of places, Bapaume, Gommecourt, Arras, Bucquoy, had for him more than the significance of poetry" (*LIW*, 42). In moments like this, Nicholas is not troubled by anxiety, depression, or other obvious posttraumatic symptoms, but his mental state is still a problem in an otherwise flourishing relationship. As Phyllis Lassner describes it, "the war's haunting wounds and hopes cannot be assuaged by the consoling promises of passion or vocation," and Hervey and Nicholas's romance "is only a replay of the war propaganda that asked women to sublimate their power" ("On the Point," 123).

Hervey's growing love with Nicholas contrasts neatly with her awful marriage, which itself bears war scars. The wretchedness of Hervey's husband, Penn, is alluded to in *The Mirror in Darkness*, especially in *Love in Winter* as he torments Hervey throughout their divorce proceedings. But the full extent of Penn's viciousness can be seen in *That Was Yesterday*, in which he is not only self-absorbed, profligate, and unfaithful but also beats her. Penn is so vile and antagonistic to Hervey that the war does little to change her feelings about him. With Nicholas we have a far more sympathetic figure through whom Hervey enters a new level of recognition about how war divides men and women. Nicholas's memories "involved depths of an emotion into which she could not enter, by any effort, or by fasting, or by love" (*LIW*, 43). Hervey thinks of Nicholas's thoughts as "occupied territory," and "with despair she understood that the War had taken the fullness of his life and energy. Less than a whole man survived. She saw that women have more than one reason to fear war" (ibid.). What at first seems to be a story about making sense of romantic love within the looser moral codes of the modern era soon reveals itself as narrative of postwar distress in which every character struggles with his or her lack of wholeness. The recent war has turned all their memories into occupied territories.

Painful memories about things seen and done bring together the former combatants, creating what one character thinks of as "the *lingua franca* of a generation" (ibid., 124). But unlike the usual explanation for this condition, trauma has a smaller influence than does misplaced energy and ambition. Jameson's sage narrator opines:

> The least tolerable side of war is not its horror but its pleasures. There is a satisfaction in prolonged dangerous effort which is paid for—if not immediately, with one's life—with years of spiritual and bodily exhaustion. In 1924 all the War countries were filled with still-young men whose energies just carried them to the end of a normal day. Any extra effort was too much. For most, they had no idea what had happened to them. Brimming with enthusiasm, they took up ideas, they began this plan and that— and suddenly their enthusiasm vanished. Their cup was dry and empty. But why? They did not know why. (67)

In this and many other instances of her writing about the conditions of veterans, Jameson seems to be drawing on her life with Guy Chapman, the husband she loved but whose struggles with work and writing were perpetually bound by his depleted energy from combat experience.[24] The dryness and emptiness of men who ought to be vigorous and productive is a running theme throughout *Love in Winter*, and with Nicholas we see its most sympathetic version.

A less sympathetic version of the survivors' failed ambitions appears in that second major plot element, which Jameson referred to as "embryo-fascism." This term was not original with her; it appeared, for instance, in the pamphlet for the Cambridge Exhibition against War and Fascism in May 1935 that attacks Mosley's "embryo-fascist ways" and denounces his British Union of Fascists for being "zealous apprentices of German and Italian methods" (*Cambridge Exhibition*, 8).[25] The latent but growing tendency toward authoritarianism that Jameson perceived in Britain receives her fullest treatment in *In the Second Year*, but that novel's grim dystopic fantasy has roots in the more realistic *Mirror in Darkness* trilogy. Hervey's American love interest, Jess Gage, from *That Was Yesterday* returns in *Company Parade* and tells her of his business wrangling with the industrialist Thomas Harben. The two men tussle over Mexican and European oil reserves, which they each hope to cash out during "the next war," and while Gage boasts, Hervey seethes in silence, thinking that "a world torn between Gages and Harbens is in a bad way" (*LIW*, 123). She fears for her son, the inheritor of this world, and finds that "words like 'the next war' filled her with rage" (ibid.). Horrified and growing angrier at the "men who make a business of death," Hervey imagines them as parasites who "must have wars in order to live": "A swollen louse, world size, sucked the blood of all the men and women on earth. They worked, married, had children, and all the time this horror had fastened on their bodies" (ibid.). The parasitic war profiteers squabble with each other about victory spoils, unabashedly manipulate governmental regulations for personal gain, and mock the doomed League of Nations. Hervey's anger is additionally stoked by her impotence in the presence of these powerbrokers. This vision of the world's people carrying on with their ordinary lives, unaware that they are being drained, exemplifies the condition of slow violence, in which the precise causes of their diminished quality of life cannot be detected as they are leisurely killed at a distance by plutocrats who bend the world to their own advantage. As Jameson shows us Anglo-American militaristic capitalism run rampant, the consequences for future war are strongly implied. Torn between "Gages and Harbens," supposedly democratic societies are merely in a holding pattern, preparing for the next violent clash of nations.

Because of the ways this growing war played out in the years after 1935, with the threat of Nazism leaving little alternative to military defense, it can be difficult to recapture the attitudes of the time when Jameson was writing *Love in Winter*, a period when pacifism and antifascism were mutually reinforcing convictions. For many pacifists and antiwar activists, the ominous political fervor burgeoning in Italy and Germany was a prime example of the frightening results when nationalism and militarism combine—but this mixture was only an extreme form of the military dependence and national chauvinism readily witnessed in other European centers, including England. In 1933, Jane Soames's translation of Mussolini's manifesto "The Political and Social Doctrine of Fascism" became widely read among English-speaking people, published first in *Political Quarterly*, and then as an article in the New York–based magazine *The Living Age*. It was also a runaway success for the Woolfs' Hogarth Press, going into several impressions throughout the 1930s.[26] In his article, Mussolini famously denounced pacifism, declaring that "above all" Fascism "believes in neither the possibility nor the utility of perpetual peace. It thus repudiates the doctrine of pacifism . . . War alone brings up to its highest tension all human energy." Along with pacifism, he decried "all the international leagues and societies, which, as history will show, can be scattered to the winds once strong national feeling is aroused by any motive—sentimental, ideal, or practical" (237). With his language of arousing lusty nationalism and releasing "high tension" through war, Mussolini (in Soames's translation) revels in the eros of belligerent jingoism. Pacifism, in this metaphorical scheme, obstructs war's consummation. Similar passions were to be found with the BUF, but Oswald Mosley's exhortations of "Britain First" insist that Fascism is socially progressive rather than relying on emotional and libidinal attractions: "It combines the dynamic urge to change and progress with the authority, discipline and the order without which nothing great can be achieved" ("Greater Britain," 28–29). Jameson's perspicacious attack on British fascism emphasizes the corporate-industrial dimension of totalitarianism in Britain rather than merely its affective and erotic allures.

A triumvirate of crypto-fascist industrialists forms the wedge of Jameson's socialist-pacifist critique in *Love in Winter*. Thomas Harben, oldest of the three, has little interest in authoritarian politics as long as the market swerves to his will and obstacles such as legal regulation are no hindrance. His portfolio includes running a corporate shell game with majority ownership of Garton's, the shipbuilding enterprise formerly run by Hervey's grandmother Mary Hervey (née Hansyke). Harben tells his younger rival, William Gary, about his financial exploits, dodging a public inquiry into his profiting from manipulation of steamship prices during the war, and is especially proud of owning a newspaper that publishes the only Labour-affiliated journalist investigating the scheme (*LIW*, 65). Profiting from war, monopolizing several industries, and manipulating public criticism are the central ways Harben achieves his mogul status. Hammering this point, Jameson offers a scene in which Renn shows Hervey his latest creation, a satirical painting in a modernist style, allegorically rendering Thomas Harben with railways for thighs and a phallic geyser spouting oil, coal mines for feet, and hands that "were the long snouts of guns, strong and ugly, like the reddened right hand of Jupiter" (50). He calls it "Thine be the Kingdom, the Power and the Glory"— linking industry, militarism, and Christianity into one hideous monstrosity (51). Hervey is disgusted, partly by the portrayal of Harben but mostly by Renn's deterioration into obsession and bile. Though Hervey does not fully realize it, Renn has attacked the wrong part of the problem. Harben is a catalyst within an economic system thriving on war, but he is a figure of another era, not the future of what will plague Europe. Harben merely represents capitalism run amok, the logical outcome of an economy that benefits a few entrepreneurs when massive resources are mobilized for military operations. Jameson's socialist critique exposes Harben's destructive power, but unlike the party-line communist literature she resisted, her critique does not stop with an assault on unjust capital.

Harben enriches himself, but he lacks the robust ideology of the dictator in embryo, which Jameson depicts most blatantly in Julian Swan. Swan is a particularly extreme version of the British fascist manqué, murmuring at the sight of London: "What a city to sack!" (129). He thinks, "hereby I declare war on all spineless snickering intellectuals, blind-at-birth idealists, liberals, pacifists, shopkeepers" and then—"his mind leaped forward to a moment when he would stand in Trafalgar Square, with the phalanxes of his young men—as in Rome he had seen Mussolini stand, and the arms lifted, the flags, the music, the shouts of five thousand as one shout. He raised his own arm. He beckoned. A disciplined wave moved over Whitehall, and the foam of its shouting flew over the whole country, bringing hope and life where it fell. 'Ave, Julian!' After all, it was an Emperor's name" (130). Swan's attraction to Fascism could not be clearer, and Jameson's portrayal of right-wing demagoguery is so blatant that it verges on parody. Swan is obviously a villain, and his self-aggrandizing, totalitarian ambitions are disturbing, but the extremity of his views and the obviousness with which he conveys them make him cartoonish, a paper villain whose absurd grandiosity, like Mussolini's, might be deflated through mockery.

Between Harben's old-fashioned robber baron capitalism and Swan's inflatable Anglicized fascism is William Gary, the emasculated veteran who plans to acquire Harben's empire and who explains himself in a chapter of internal monologue that he imagines as a conversation with Hervey's lover, the liberal Nicholas Roxby: "I shall give the men what they want. None of them want what you would give them, ideas are nothing, responsibility is nothing, freedom is a burden; they want clean dry quarters, the rations coming up at night and divided fairly, they want security, they want coals by the side of the fireplace, and a piano for Winifred. In their minds your talk will make the noises of wind in an empty chimney. They will rather choose mine" (199). This reverie about power over unthinking masses grows in Gary's fantasy into a vision of planes, roads, and steel, all of which will emerge from his own body: "I shall sit at the centre of this, the roads and the cables will run through my brain, the aeroplanes will take off and land there; I shall be grass, scorched earth, air, water" (200). If Harben is the captain of industry and Swan the proto-dictator, Gary desires something even more: to become elemental. Like Leonard Woolf's *Quack, Quack!*, which was also published in 1935, *Love in Winter* diagnoses European fascism as a matter of savage impulses gone awry. Woolf's vision of primitive eruptions within civilized culture is belied by its goofy title, a mark of the limited seriousness with which the growing menace was perceived. Woolf describes the rise of the BUF two decades after the Great War, while England was in financial ruin and people yearned for remedy from "magic and quackery": "Instead of painting their bodies, circumcising themselves, and placing themselves under the orders of some super-medicine-man, as their ancestors of the Stone Age would have done, they vary the ritual by dressing up in black-shirts, making odd gesticulations with their right hands, and selecting Sir Oswald Mosley to fill the position previously held by a long line of kings, magicians, witch-doctors" (*Quack, Quack!*, 37).[27] The quasi-religious fervor of Mosley's supporters and their Italian and German counterparts suggest to Woolf a lurking primitivism that irrationally results from a "simple" failure to build a better, more just economy. Jameson, however, goes a step further, portraying those elemental urges not as an intrusion on an otherwise rational, modern culture, but as a manifestation of this culture's basic evil. Gary's brain is air and earth, railway and port, and an essential will to power.

With his extravagant aspirations and reservoir of anger about the war and all it took from him, Gary becomes the most compelling character in the novel. Through him Jameson identifies war damage as a fundamental motivation for the most plausible British fascism. The multifront corporate empire that Harben runs clearly has disastrous results for laborers and for anyone working to prevent future wars, but Gary finds Harben's extreme laissez-faire views insufficiently visionary, a sign of "the gulf between himself and Harben" formed by Harben's love of money as a gateway to power and by Gary's love of "power for its own sake" (LIW, 302). For Gary, the "triumphs and struggles" of the past extend to the future, "magnified to infinity"; "in this vision (if one choose to call it vision) England was no larger than a trench marked on a map, the war map laid on the table of his mind" (ibid.). Wealth and influence are enough for Harben, but Gary's "vision" is more wide ranging and is informed by his military life; the whole of England is part of a battle map in his quest for power. The primitive impulses that Leonard Woolf diagnosed in Fascism clearly apply to Swan's self-promotion, but Gary eschews mere celebrity along with mere wealth. To Gary, Harben is "after all an anarchist," a proponent of deregulation and brute force capitalism, while Gary himself has a bigger dream, to control all England by bending other men's wills into submission and twisting their desires toward his own (ibid.). The gulf between Gary and Harben is generational—the old man who sent youth into the Great War and the young ex-combatant who fought to safeguard the economic interests of the elders. Love in Winter suggests that the aggrieved survivor of the First World War is the most likely dictator; what is happening in 1935 in Germany could very well be replicated in Britain.

Instead of Swan's bullying, Mosley-like authoritarianism, the most insidious means of control emerges through Gary's manipulation, finding common ground with others and satisfying their needs in order to corrupt them. Several of the male characters Jameson introduces in the series hope to recraft the world, to build a socialist economy that cares for the poor and a nonviolent society that enables peaceable relations within and between nations. Philip from *Company Parade* is the most visionary socialist-pacifist, but after his death, several former combatants pick up pieces of his mantle: the left-wing journalist Louis Earlham, the well-intentioned Nicholas Roxby, and the idealistic but psychologically damaged David Renn. In each case, Gary appeals to shared war experience and recognition that the world they fought for is not the world that presently exists. With Earlham, Gary hopes to contain a potential threat—the socialist muckraking of Earlham's newspaper stories—and over dinner at Gary's invitation, they find themselves agreeing about many things, particularly their mutual hatred of the high-ranking officers (the "brass hats"). Gary avers: "It is even possible that you and I want the same kind of world. Without brass hats and with plenty to eat and good dry quarters for the men" (*LIW*, 125). The pact he hopes to form is instigated by shared resentment and a conviction that the masses will prefer blissful ignorance as long as their basic needs are satisfied. This same tactic—start with war-based injustices and move onto a shared sense of revolutionary objectives—is Gary's modus operandi with others, including Renn and Nicholas. Though he is unsuccessful in wooing these men, the portrayal of his corrupting influence is crucial to Jameson's socialist-pacifist critique. Gary works like Dostoevsky's Grand Inquisitor, promising satisfaction for all who cede their own will to his. He entices them with what he implies is a kinder, gentler Fascism in a British style. As Gary puts it to Nicholas, "no Englishman who is worth anything wants to splitarse about the streets in a uniform, bawling *Giovinezza* and administering castor oil to Ramsay MacDonald" (225). The flagrantly emotional, demonstrative fascism abroad has little appeal for Britons, but Gary's version is all the more sinister for being quiet, satisfying, and cushioned with a friendly smile. Like the situations in Italy and Germany, postwar grievances are a catalyst in the nascent British fascism Jameson depicts, indicating that even the war's victors have not won a viable, lasting peace.

Structurally, nothing conclusive occurs in the fascist narrative, and the love plot similarly ends in uncertainty embroidered with optimism. Popular romance novel conventions dictate that the love promised by the novel's title should be successful and that whatever evils persist in the broader society, at least the romantic coupling will be definitive and whole. Pushing into more experimental middlebrow territory, Jameson thwarts this expectation without completely rejecting the initial narrative arc. The title of the final chapter is a quotation from Heine—*Mein Herz gleicht ganz dem Meere, / Hat Sturm und Ebb' und Flut*—and the storm and tides that wash over Hervey's heart in this chapter make romance inseparable from economics (395). Part of the last chapter is an extended quarrel between Nicholas and Hervey, strained as they are by the indignities of divorce proceedings that require public airing of infidelities and "smelled too much of the keyhole" (400). Their understandably peevish former spouses launch spiteful barbs, but this annoyance is less problematic than Hervey and Nicholas's own recognition that a marriage forged from the collapse of two past relationships may be on rocky footing. These elements of the narrative explore the predicament of modern romance and effectively maintain the promise of generic conventions.

An even more insistent part of the narrative, however, is the economic *Sturm* that exacerbates the uncertainty in the novel's conclusion and reveals Jameson's interests beyond conventional romance fiction. Each of the characters wrestles with a perilous financial situation, such as Nicholas's inability to run a shop and Hervey's failure to sell her novels for a livable wage. These localized financial problems create the last prongs of plot tension, but more important than their function in the love story is their embeddedness in the broader structures of corrupt capitalism and the concomitant rise of fascism. In the last paragraph, Hervey looks out from her bedroom window into the night, pondering her mortality and the fleetingness of romantic love. She subconsciously registers the culture of death that has stalked her since *Company Parade*: "Even her young London had now died a score of times. The ghosts it had given up were three poor merry scholars, and then a harassed young wife, and then young men in an earth-coloured uniform, a boy clumsy in his airman's jacket, with shamed tears in his eyes, and then Philip who should have died sooner" (*LIW*, 407). These half-recalled memories, impressionistically rendered, are energizing for Hervey, but they offer no simple solution to the political, romantic, and economic problems repeatedly posed by the novel. Optimistic youth is gone, the most idealistic of her friends ought to have died in battle so as not to face the worse realization that no socialist-pacifist revolution is coming, and the death of her brother and other combatants has not purchased a better world—all of these factors in Hervey's mind amount to no clear-cut political agenda. Rather, she ends with a thought about her son, Richard, whom she knows could be swept up into the next war (precisely Jameson's own worry that would become reality within five years). All of Hervey's closest relationships merge in this inconclusive last paragraph. *Love in Winter* reveals and exposes the war-damaged culture that inspires fascist energies, but its jagged inconclusiveness is as close as we come to political hope. Enacting what she theorized in her essay on socialist fiction, Jameson documents the newly emergent society and leaves precise agendas up to her readers.

A Week of Crisis in *None Turn Back*

Failure is an inescapable part of any discussion of *The Mirror in Darkness*, from Jameson's declaration that she was unable to complete her full narrative scheme to the bigger problem that her desire to wage a socialist-pacifist war of words against fascism grew increasingly impossible (Feinstein, introduction, vii). This political failure correlates with aesthetic failure, as many critics regard the last official volume of the trilogy as a disappointment. Elaine Feinstein's otherwise sympathetic commentary in the Virago reprints introduces *None Turn Back* with rather weak commendation: "When Storm Jameson put *The Mirror in Darkness* to one side, many of her best novels remained to be written. . . . But readers who have followed the central characters as they grow through the first two books of this series will not be disappointed in *None Turn Back*" (ibid.). Any reader tempted to finish the series gets little more encouragement than the adage "in for a penny, in for a pound." Despite being a truncated denouement, *None Turn Back* signals Jameson's last major attempt at peace activist fiction and a manifestation of her changing views about the sort of political activity that was viable for novelists and, perhaps, for pacifists more broadly.

Despite its author's concerns, the views of later critics, and the broader political context, *None Turn Back* successfully thematizes—even embraces—the notion of failure. Jameson reduces the chronological scope she initiated in the preceding two books, concentrating all the action within a seven-day span from May 6 to 12 in 1926—the week of the failed General Strike. Many writers from across the political spectrum, including Wyndham Lewis and Ford Madox Ford, found this week to be deeply significant, a sign of Britain's inability to restructure its moribund class hierarchies.[28] In Jameson's hands, the failed strike becomes emblematic of larger failures in radical politics, and the characters in *None Turn Back* exhibit the loss of power for the pacifist left. The powerful embryo-fascists prevail over the strike, the investigative press led by Louis Earlham and Marcel Cohen is co-opted, and Hervey is incapacitated by uterine surgery—events that serve an abrupt but fitting end for a pacifist trilogy whose basic political assumptions were by 1936 greatly under siege.

In the mouth of T. S. Heywood, successful scientist and veteran of the war, Jameson puts a critique of the General Strike's timing, suggesting that it might have been more effective had it come during the Armistice. The miners, according to Heywood, "lost their chance in nineteen-nineteen. That was the last moment for a general strike—why, if the army had been sent home by regiments instead of men from this company and that, scattered groups, strangers, they would have started it themselves. The men who rule this country are too clever for you. They'll outlive everything, even their time. What is in front of us is a slow crumbling, decay, barbarism" (*NTB*, 22). Heywood's statement about the cunning destabilizing of grassroots political actions by autocrats such as Harben and Swan becomes a guiding theme in *None Turn Back*: all efforts to mobilize mass protest have been foreseen and defeated in advance. From the averted mass protests of 1919 to the failed General Strike, the history of radical politics in postwar England is one of defeat.

The surgery plotline in *None Turn Back* also evokes warfare. Before going under anesthesia, Hervey receives the advice, bizarre for twenty-first century readers, that she ought to eat a big meal. She refuses and tells the nurse: "But I thought you didn't give food to people who were going to be operated on" (250). The nurse responds: "All that has been changed . . . They discovered in the War that soldiers who had been fed beforehand did better in an operation than men who had fasted" (ibid.). Medical logic has changed as a result of anecdotal evidence drawn from military conditions, and all facets of civilian life bear signs of the intruding force of war. Surgery and debilitation compel Hervey into closer alignment with male combatants. She is removed from the action of the General Strike by this necessary medical intervention, and she becomes like a wounded veteran, sidelined by injury. This connection with combatants is solidified later when her nurse comes in the night to offer Hervey "a pair of long woollen stockings, like the thigh stockings given to soldiers during the War" (251). This close, bodily connection to combatants and their insular culture does not, however, fulfill the wish from *Company Parade* and *Love in Winter* that Hervey can somehow find her way into greater understanding with the men who haltingly and despairingly endure postwar recovery. Like them, she is sick and wounded, but unlike them she is still cut off from the cliquish realm of ex-combatants whose minds remain "occupied territory." Her surgery, referred to throughout the novel in euphemistic terms, is a hysterectomy, and like the emasculated veterans she loses her powers of generativity. Left open-ended in the novel is whether she will regain generative power through creative pursuits.

These markers on Hervey's body emblematize a British culture indelibly affected by war. By 1926 the immediacy of postwar sentiment had diminished greatly from where it was in *Company Parade*, and though fears about another future war are not absent in *None Turn Back*, the General Strike and its whiff of socialist revolution and civil war take precedence. The pacifism of *None Turn Back* is not presented through open debates among the characters but rather through Jameson's repeated depiction of violent conflict that once broached cannot be recontained.

In Jameson's portrayal, troop demobilization at the war's ending reshapes the political and economic landscape so that a major effort toward revolutionizing society and introducing just labor relations was forever curtailed. The war profiteers and other industrial drivers exert their will on the restructuring of British society so as to maintain their advantage over the laboring classes. William Gary, we are told by our sage narrator, if he "had not been castrated by a shell bursting close to him in October 1918 . . . would have married, spent his money, had children," but "as things were, he had nothing to do less deathly than make money breed" (83). Gary's war wound, in this theory, literally becomes the source of his most ravenous economic and political desires, and without the tempering effects and alternative libidinal and generative outlets of family life, his passions run toward the fanatical, with a coal mining empire that his workers "carried . . . on their stooped shoulders" (ibid.). *None Turn Back* depicts the week of the General Strike as a microcosm of what is wrong in British society, moving the focus away from sexual morality that we saw in *Love in Winter* and offering instead a critical view of unjust economic conditions in Britain. These unjust conditions are presented as the chief source of conflict among British people and a primary cause of new violence.

None Turn Back concludes with the strike's failure while Hervey recuperates. Gary converts sexual impotence into financial prowess, and Hervey's hysterectomy coincides with her desire for literary production—but we never see these results. This is a particularly crushing way for Jameson's novel sequence to peter out, our heroine incapacitated and any hope for a revitalized, socialist future in England thoroughly dashed. The disappointment in Jameson's vision is tempered somewhat by Hervey's perseverance, which Lassner reads as a "sign of mental agility and drive to self-definition" ("On the Point," 124), and Hervey's final reflections on pain's awakening her will to live conclude with assurance that she is a survivor and a Little Englander, "identifying herself with the common earth of Danesacre" (*NTB*, 319). Despite this final uplift and late glimmer of hope, the ultimate result is smashing defeat for our heroes and victory for Harben, Gary, and the other capitalist, quasi-fascists. Failure abides throughout the book at nearly every level. We know the strike will fail and that Jameson felt her series of novels had failed. On completing this volume, her attentions turned to crises throughout Europe and the first shocks to her absolute pacifism. Though campaigning for peace was still a stimulating concern, the threat of fascism and how it was being handled soon drew a bigger measure of her attention, especially after Munich. *None Turn Back* supplies a crucial bridge for Jameson's changing literary-political dreams, and through its profound evocation of personal, structural, and economic failure, the novel becomes a compelling conclusion for the trilogy.

The PPU, the PEN, and an "Armed Truce of My Devils"

The demands on Hervey's writing at the end of *Company Parade*—charged by Renn to write something more political and "useful"—were ones that Jameson clearly felt herself. In her later years, she wrote self-critically about these impulses and the works she produced while enthralled by politics, but though she grew increasingly disenchanted with activist writing, she felt a lifelong attraction to the role of the writer as a public sage. In an essay originally published in a 1949 issue of the *Vir-*

ginia Woolf Quarterly, she writes about the interwar novelists as people with "a new *mot d'ordre* . . . social significance" (*Writer's Situation*, 63). Writers were "dragged, whether they enjoyed it or not, on to platforms, and called into committee, to defend society against its enemies. Writers in Defence of Freedom, Writers' Council against War, against fascism, against being atomised, against, many of us are beginning to feel, our reason for existing" (ibid.). By 1949 she suggests that the days of activist literature are gone and that something more like *l'art pour l'art* must return. This self-critique, however, neglects some of her most compelling and visionary creative labors of the 1930s.

The novels that followed *The Mirror in Darkness* pick up her concerns about the growth of Fascism/Nazism and extend them into a broader European context that became ever more pressing after Munich. Jameson stands out among her peers in the peace movement; always the vigilant critic of politics and strategies she found wanting, her objections to appeasement were swift and decisive. She would turn against Jules Romains, the international president of PEN, after he sent a congratulatory note to two of the French negotiators at Munich (Maslen, *Life*, 199), and she would write to Brittain in late September 1938: "The Czechs are cooked, and Europe is cooked . . . It is peace, but at a price and what a price" (qtd. in ibid., 200). She was not among those who took even momentary pleasure in the Munich decision, cherishing instead friendships gained through her experiences traveling in Central Europe. Her *Europe to Let*, with its four related stories of burgeoning Fascism/Nazism and indignation at the perceived betrayal by Western powers, stands out as a clear example of her affective and intellectual commitment to people whom many British citizens seemed willing to sacrifice in order to postpone a total war. The unnamed narrator of the stories, a British man exploring several areas of Hungary, Czechoslovakia, and Austria, is told by a woman in Prague: "What extraordinary people you are. You have so many refined feelings, yet you sicken the rest of the world with your materialism and your brutal self-interest" (187). British self-interest forms one of the major motives for selling Czechoslovakia in a bargaining process from which Czechs are excluded. Also apparent in *Europe to Let* and Jameson's other European novels about the continent during wartime, such as *The Fort* (1941), *Then We Shall Hear Singing* (1942), and *Cloudless May* (1943) is her particular concern for the treatment of

Jews. Though not unique, Jameson's use of fiction to reveal the pervasive workings of continental and British antisemitism distinguishes her writings from many of her contemporaries.

Munich became for Jameson a symbolic moment of change in her politics, felt most personally during the gradual decline of her friendship with Vera Brittain, who maintained an absolutist pacifism, while Jameson turned toward a pragmatic acceptance that war had made itself necessary. There is great pathos in her letters of the late 1930s and early 1940s, in which she describes her intense anguish over her inability to reconcile her absolute hatred of war and absolute hatred of fascism, eventually resulting in what she would describe as "an armed truce of my devils."[29] But despite her feeling constricted by these forces, Jameson remained astonishingly productive, and to a certain extent this clash of values produces the energetic quality and literary sophistication of her fiction.

As an activist, Jameson eventually abandoned her sponsorship in the PPU and more deeply invested in PEN, the writers' organization that made her its president and through her leadership turned toward explicit political commitments.[30] In October 1938, she declared in PEN News her conviction that "we of the P.E.N. believe that the intellect can, and indeed must, ignore frontiers" ("Storm Jameson on the P.E.N.," 3). Instead of national self-interest, all who care for the freedom of ideas and expression must support one another. At her behest, PEN published "An Appeal to the Conscience of the World" (1940), a statement urging allied countries and all PEN centers to fight for universal free speech. Though the place of PEN and the PPU in her life might suggest conflicted values, the energies she applied to her PEN presidency had as their ultimate goal the cultivation of that peaceful, free world she had advocated throughout the 1930s. When asked to be a PEN delegate to a conference in Buenos Aires in 1936, Jameson submitted the required biographical information with a list of a dozen publications, a typically self-deprecating description as the "author of too many books," and this statement: "That's all I've done, except to work and write against war and fascism, which I shall do until forcibly prevented" (qtd. in Birkett, *Margaret Storm Jameson*, 138). Though in 1936 her résumé could still sound unconflicted about resisting the twin devils of war and fascism, her political activity with PEN throughout the war years retained a high level of interest in subverting authoritarian regimes through the nonviolent means of creating art and in her persistent aid to refugees from battle-stricken and occupied territories.

Though she modified her views about pacifism, even her pamphlet *The End of This War* (1941) shows mournfulness about the need for violent force. Her friends in the peace movement, most notably Vera Brittain, found this document hard to stomach. In Brittain's case, this had much to do with Jameson's ill-considered use of a quotation from "a well-known pacifist" whose letter she quotes: "I admit that not to fight Hitler would have meant great difficulties and many compromises of the Munich type . . . but these compromises were slow affairs. Each one would have taken *time*, and even Hitler is not immortal" (12). Outlasting Hitler by making diplomatic concessions becomes in Jameson's essay the prime example of facile and naive beliefs. That Brittain gave consent to the use of this quotation, flippantly suggesting that letters like this were dashed off and were deliberately occasional rather than broad program-matic statements, did little to stave off the offense she took at its handling or to halt the crumbling of their friendship.[31] Jameson's rhetoric in the pamphlet is as powerful as ever, though the use of Brittain's comment as well as jabs at Isherwood and Auden for leaving Europe were late addi-tions that she eventually regretted. She presented this pamphlet as a way to come clean, to write honestly about her opinions regarding war with Germany: "During these years of acquiescence, was there a time when it would have been possible to negotiate with Hitler on a common basis of interest in saving European civilisation from disruption? I no longer believe there was. For a time I did. I think I was wrong" (ibid.). But *The End of this War* is also full of elegiac moments in which Jameson dem-onstrates how clearly she abhors war—even this unfortunately necessary kind required to stop the greater violence threatened by Nazism: "We know what bitterness, despair, and extreme horror war brings. We know it is the blind enemy of our minds, hopes, and ideals. But it is not their far-sighted deliberate enemy" (26). She has no illusions that war will be good; rather, she cannot see another solution for the problem of the "deliberate enemy," the unreasonable, nonnegotiable imperialism of the German state. She abandons pacifism—defined in this document as submission to Hitler and acceptance of global Nazi rule—and adopts a position closer to the pacific-ist desire for all war to end while believing that no purely diplomatic solution is possible in the present conflict.[32] As she put it in her private correspondence, "I am becoming convinced that there is more good to be done in talking and writing about a just and hopeful peace than by trying directly to end the war" (qtd. in Maslen, *Life*, 237). By 1941, Jameson's pacifism simply seems defeated by the war at hand.

Her last novel-length treatment of her *Mirror in Darkness* protagonist would revisit in a deeply autobiographical fashion the years leading into the war and its effect on her psyche. In *The Journal of Mary Hervey Russell* (1945), a highly experimental fictionalized diary that explicitly fuses Jameson's personal narrative with Hervey's, she returns to life-writing as a challenge to death, investigating through her fictional self the agonizing choice between her twin devils:

> I have not chosen between my pacifism and my dislike of a tyrant—which is older in me than many a fear . . . This is really the moment of decision . . . Is there a way to hold these evils in the mind, and accepting the guilt of both live quietly in the mortal silence below them—and free of an agony pressing always on the same nerve? . . . There must be. But I know already that my lack of patience will not take me so deep—when the moment to choose comes, between my submission to the evil of war and the evil of Dachau, I shall cho[o]se, blindly, the first. (*Journal*, 85–86)

Writing several years after she made this decision, after her falling out with the peace movement proper and with her pacifist friends, she returns to this choice between war and fascism not with certainty and triumphant clarity but as a matter of blind hope that the righteousness of saving innocents outweighs the unrighteousness of killing others. At the stasis point of her political commitments, she would demonstrate a model for activist fiction and the great desire for a world in which economic justice, international collaboration, and pacifist flourishing were not incompatible. Integrity in these conflicted matters was Jameson's most potent challenge to death.

CHAPTER 3

Narrating Veteran-Pacifism in Siegfried Sassoon's *Memoirs of George Sherston*

Though Aldous Huxley and Storm Jameson were deeply involved peace activists and antifascists, they were civilians without firsthand combat experience. Among the many antiwar writers who had gone through the horrors of the battlefield—soldiers, of course, but also nurses, chaplains, journalists, and others—speaking out against war took the form of prophetic witness, converting traumatic experiences into testimony for the uninitiated. Siegfried Sassoon, whose semifictional prose is the focus of this chapter, was a direct participant in the First World War. He was a renowned soldier, a notoriously good killer, and a devastated recollector of this military service for the duration of his life. Even a cursory sketch of his biography reveals him to be a mass of contradictions: an heir to land and fortune who was also briefly a socialist, a distinctly English gentleman descended from a royal Jewish family rooted in Baghdad (the Sassoons purportedly could trace their lineage to King David), a multisport athlete and man of action absorbed with reading and writing poetry, a homosexual whose stated "antipathy for women" did not preclude marrying Hester Gatty and having a son, and, most intriguingly for my purposes, a decorated war hero nicknamed "Mad Jack" for his reckless, daring trench raids, who renounced war and accepted the label "pacifist"—even while returning to combat.[1]

Dominic Hibberd once called Sassoon "fearsomely well documented," and his several biographers have wrestled with his many incompatible traits, which are only partly explained by sequential changing of attitudes over time.[2] A progression may be discerned from his beginning the war as a gung-ho idealist and becoming by 1917 a disillusioned, shell-shocked resister. His resistance turned to shame and boredom while recuperating at Craiglockhart hospital, which he left voluntarily, rejoining the battle-field a guilt-stricken combatant until he was invalided out by friendly fire near the war's end. After the war, Sassoon experienced his greatest literary celebrity along with his formal participation in the peace move-ment, which included several public appearances reading his war poetry for the Peace Pledge Union. With the onset of the Second World War his connection to peace work diminished, and he resumed writing patriotic poetry on behalf of the troops. Nevertheless, he would hold a lifelong hatred of war, and the Great War in particular, which would inform his ultimate conversion to a conservative Roman Catholicism. This life narrative became Sassoon's greatest source of literary material during his five decades following the Great War, and the most interesting and perplexing parts of his identity are the ones not so easily reconciled by chronology.

Critics have mined Sassoon's poetry for its reflections of his changing attitudes to war, its antagonistic relationship with modernism, and its ethos of masculinity and male friendship.[3] Relatively less attention has been paid, however, to the prose works he began publishing in 1928 dur-ing the boom in "war books" a decade after the Armistice.[4] This is not to say that Sassoon's prose works are necessarily less read, but they are often used to bolster an understanding of his poetry, a privileging of the poems over his prose that Sassoon hoped would someday be reversed. As he wrote to the critic Michael Thorpe, "I am a firm believer in the Memoirs; and am inclined to think that the war poems (the significant and success-ful ones) will end up as mere appendices to the matured humanity of the Memoirs" (*LTC*, 14).

Novels such as Remarque's *All Quiet on the Western Front* (1929) and Hemingway's *A Farewell to Arms* (1929) were highly successful alongside self-described memoirs such as Graves's *Goodbye to All That* (1929) and Blunden's *Undertones of War* (1928). Superficially, Sassoon's *Memoirs of a Fox-Hunting Man* (1928) seems just another title in this constel-lation, albeit a bit funnier and more fixated on the idyllic prewar age. This book, however, and its companion volumes, *Memoirs of an Infan-*

try Officer (1930) and *Sherston's Progress* (1936), are far more complex than they might first appear, and they enact in creative form some of the contradictions so beguiling in Sassoon's personal life. Placing *The Complete Memoirs of George Sherston* in the same "genre" as *Goodbye to All That* elides the classification difficulty that marks any conversation about Sassoon's books. Many critics select from a variety of terms, calling the Sherston narratives "memoir," "autobiography," and "novels," or some hybrid, such as "fictional autobiography." Hybridity in generic terminology is required for acknowledging that Sassoon's prose, like his life, defies uniform classification.

This problem with genre goes beyond minor concerns with prose mechanics or critical labels. What for some critics are signs of artistic failure in the Sherston books are in my view better understood as formal experimentation, enacting at the structural level of the works some of the conflicts essential to their political meanings. I admit that this requires some amount of reading against what we know about Sassoon's stated intentions. In spite of that, the frequently rehearsed criticisms of the trilogy are not themselves dependent on what Sassoon believed about his project; rather, they concentrate on several formal problems that supposedly mar the cohesiveness of the complete work. Many critics have argued that Sassoon cut out too much of himself from Sherston, limiting the believability of his heroism, which ultimately lurches to a halt in the poorly conceived final volume. I contend instead that the formal experimentation in the *Memoirs* is inseparable from their function as peace activist writing. Regardless of what Sassoon believed himself to be attempting aesthetically, the published books bear aspects of experimental forms familiar to modernist writing, a mode that Sassoon deliberately positioned himself against in his poetry. These experiments include his intrusive narrative voice, ruptured chronology, inclusion of seemingly extraliterary material such as diaries, and a consistently dialectical structuring of ideas, events, and characters. Like Huxley and Jameson, Sassoon combined his antiwar convictions with sophisticated literary artistry to produce an active peace witness in prose.

As early as 1936, Sassoon described his post-factum intentions for the *Memoirs* by calling them "propaganda for peace" (qtd. in Caesar, *Taking It*, 106), and late in his life he expressed this same goal in a letter affirming Michael Thorpe's take on the first Sherston book: "You have admirably indicated the value of Sherston's story as a 'human document,' and a work of innocently insidious anti-war propaganda, more effective than outspoken indignation" (*LTC*, 14). Subsequent critics have been less apt to follow Sassoon's interpretation of his books. This chapter seeks, however, to recover that "insidious" core of the Sherston narratives through analyzing their pacifist aesthetics. More than his often discussed poems written during the First World War, Sassoon's prose works are a subtle enactment of his peace activist writing—not propaganda as he described them, but complex and deeply ambivalent literary creations that enact a conflicted and finally doomed witnessing for peace.

One important caveat: Sassoon's deep ambivalence about war in general, and even about the Great War, raises questions about the accuracy of including him in a study of literary writers involved with the British peace movement. Robert Hemmings, in his sensitive study of Sassoon's works of the Second World War and after, emphatically states: "Sassoon was never a pacifist" (*Modern Nostalgia*, 85). Put like this, I would agree—as long as we define "pacifist" in Martin Ceadel's strict sense of the word, as "absolute pacifism" of the kind promoted by Anabaptist and Quaker peace churches. To read Sassoon is to enter a process of discerning which among his various, often contradictory statements and attitudes about himself and his work are the ones we should privilege. When Sassoon says of a book as complicated as *Memoirs of a Fox-Hunting Man* that it is "anti-war propaganda," the false note has less to do with inaccuracy than with oversimplification. Likewise, absolutist claims that Sassoon's works are not at all antiwar seem similarly faulty. Sassoon's lifelong ambivalence makes claims of absolutism about him indefensible. But it is also clear that for a period from roughly 1917 to 1937, Sassoon felt great animosity toward war conditions and even, at times, to war itself. In this period he lent his name, prestige, and creative energies to what Charles Chatfield calls "peace advocacy" by publicly demonstrating against war—even if absolute pacifism was not his unequivocal stance.[5] Instead of ironing out the wrinkles of Sassoon's complex life, writing, and life-writing, I intend to demonstrate how these complexities and ambivalences contribute to the literary richness of his particular moral imagination and peace witness, revealing the significant limits of elitist individualism in a society geared toward producing war.

Living on the Veteran-Pacifist Hyphen

Sassoon's fame as an ambivalent war protestor shows up in many accounts from the period, including a cameo appearance in Storm Jameson's *That Was Yesterday* (1932). The protagonist Hervey Russell receives a letter from her friend Philip, who has just been fighting "in the hell of the Somme," and he tells her about meeting up with their friend T. S. Heywood, who reports that "there's a Captain Sassoon, some name like that, of the Royal Welch Fusiliers, trying to get the truth over in England. He means well, but he'll be back here before long. Like the rest of us, *he won't be able to keep away*. And he won't get the truth over" (242–43, emphasis in original). The palimpsestic structure of this report is part of the point: stories about Sassoon are rippling out across the battlefields to the home front and back. His celebrity persona is cast both as prophetic truth-teller and guilty archcombatant. A similar effect occurs in the more commonly cited depiction of Sassoon from Robert Graves's *Goodbye to All That*. Despite Sassoon's claims of misrepresentation, Graves's version was essential for publicizing Sassoon as both "Mad Jack" and a traumatized war protester manipulated by peace activists. Graves memorably describes Sassoon by a contrast with his own soldierly persona: "I had never been such a fire-eater as he—the number of Germans whom I killed or caused to be killed could hardly be compared with his wholesale slaughter. In fact, Siegfried's unconquerable idealism changed direction with his environment: he varied between happy warrior and bitter pacifist" (*Goodbye*, 275).

This notion of Sassoon's bipolar vacillation between "happy warrior and bitter pacifist" remains a staple for interpreting his internal conflicts. The dualism in Sassoon's identity and its expression in the Sherston trilogy is characterized most prominently by Paul Fussell, whose seminal work, *The Great War and Modern Memory* (1975), includes a section on "the binary vision of Siegfried Sassoon" (90). Many subsequent critics who have engaged Fussell's attention to binaries counter the specifics of his conclusions or elaborate on those dualities without seriously challenging his theory.[6] An especially sophisticated inheritor of Fussell's view is David Williams, whose analysis of the "ontological doubling" in the *Memoirs* offers a replacement for Fussell's ironic binary (*Media, Memory*, 153).[7] As Williams argues, "in the formal doubling of a man variously identified as George Sherston and Siegfried Sassoon, we follow the process by which such temporal and ontological doublings of the self converge on an 'intermediate version of myself,' literally a self located in the space *between* differing media and among all these doubled texts" (ibid., 156–57). Williams provides something largely lacking with other critical inheritors of Fussell's "binary" Sassoon: recognition of the multiplicity and transiency of Sassoon/Sherston's selves, which produce identity through their very changeableness.

Though an insightful rethinking of Fussell's argument, Williams's reading does not describe fully enough the conflict inherent in this multiplicity. Rather than Fussell's "binary vision," which suggests merely the existence of two poles at once, I would argue that dialecticism provides a better sense of the struggle that is essential to Sherston's doubled ontology. This dialectic is not the Fichtean focus on "synthesizing" opposing forces, but rather emerges in a more Hegelian version, which Fredric Jameson describes as "the irrevocable antagonism between the twin (and entwined) forces in question: they are never reconciled, never fold back into one another in some ultimate reconciliation and identity" (*Antinomies*, 11). Instead of unity through synthesis, we find unity "as antagonism, the unity of attraction and repulsion, the unity of struggle" (ibid., 7). Throughout the *Memoirs* Sherston states his views or describes a scene, and immediately, sometimes within the same paragraph or even sentence, emphatically states its opposite. This battle of irreconcilable forces gives the entire work much of its energy and covers a vast range of topoi, but it is especially felt in the dialectical relationship between warrior and pacifist that dogs Sherston throughout the trilogy.

To take just one of these moments, whose superabundance makes it possible to choose almost at random, we might consider the scene of Sherston's first encounter with war violence, a scene that is more akin to Sassoon's grotesque war poems than to Sherston's typically chaste representations.

> I noticed an English soldier lying by the road with a horribly smashed head; soon such sights would be too frequent to attract attention, but this first one was perceptibly unpleasant. At the risk of being thought squeamish or even unsoldierly, I still main-

tain that an ordinary human being has a right to be momentarily horrified by a mangled body seen on an afternoon walk, although people with sound common sense can always refute me by saying that life is full of gruesome sights and violent catastrophes. But I am no believer in wild denunciations of the War; I am merely describing my own experiences of it; and in 1917 I was only beginning to learn that life, for the majority of the population, is an unlovely struggle against unfair odds, culminating in a cheap funeral. (CMGS, 424)

The passage shifts abruptly, clause by clause, through Sherston's reactions to the sight and what he thinks these mean for himself and for the competing values of the army and peacemakers. The final compound sentence moves from a resistance to pacifism to a seemingly apolitical gesture of individual reportage to a connection with the narrator's present-day reflection on his awakening recognition that social conditions have worsened, not improved, because of the war. This sentence demonstrates the constant effort to say everything in the course of a single utterance, to hold together several conflicting views—war denunciation is too extreme, but nascent socialism may respond to economic injustice that war perpetuates.

This passage may fit the dialectical model almost too well in that its explicit mention of class struggle binds it so perfectly to Jameson's Marxian understanding of the history of social forms. But the passage's whiplash oscillation among competing ideas, culminating in condemnation of the entire social order in which war is but an extreme case, demonstrates the mode that Sassoon uses throughout the trilogy. These shifts are not disingenuous nor do they merely create a grand irony as Fussell sees it. No part of this dialectical description can be completely discredited, from the horrific imagery that should be spurned by ordinary humans to the recognition that conditioning makes these sights less troublesome, or from the resistance to denouncing war to the contention that an unjust economic system supports violent conflict. Sherston's displayed ambivalence is vital to the dialectic, to the agonistic life on the hyphen of veteran-pacifism, and to the possibility of peace witness expressed through conflict. The hybrid term "veteran-pacifist" is especially apt if we acknowledge that

Sassoon spent much of his life living in the hyphen between these conflicted selves, attaining for a time in the mid-1930s his strongest identity as an activist writer.

The Making of an "Anti-War" Poet

On July 14, 1935, the inchoate Peace Pledge Union held Dr. Sheppard's Peace Demonstration, a large rally at the Royal Albert Hall with speeches by Edmund Blunden, the theologian Maude Royden (called in the program "the greatest woman preacher of our times"), and retired Brigadier-General Frank Crozier. Complementing this roster were poetry readings by Sassoon. As was often the case in the PPU's early years under Sheppard, the secularity of this event was tenuous. The program for the rally was clearly modeled on a Christian liturgy, complete with an offering collection and hymn singing ("Turn Back, O Man"; "When Wilt Thou Save the People"; "O God, Our Help in Ages Past"; and "Abide with Me"). The program's cover displayed a drawing by Arthur Wragg titled "Weep Not for Me but for Yourselves," showing a semicruciform Tommy in his tin hat hoisted onto a memorial inscribed with "The Glorious Dead" while a sponge on a spear is angled toward his mouth.[8] This dark image filled with Christological allusions, like the order of service itself, imbues the demonstration with religious significance. Sassoon's readings fit this liturgical pattern, replacing Scripture lessons with antiwar verse. Many participants at this rally noted that Sassoon's part was deeply memorable. Sheppard himself wrote to Sassoon's wife that the reading of "Aftermath," which begins with the famous line "Have you forgotten yet?" (*CP 1908–56*, 118), was "one of the most impressive things I have ever heard" (qtd. in Egremont, *Siegfried Sassoon*, 396). At this landmark event, and in many subsequent rallies and demonstrations, Sassoon would play the role of unofficial poet laureate for the PPU, a position that emulated sainthood.

While for some PPU sponsors, their only true activity in the organization was lending their names to the official letterhead, Sassoon was considerably more active. He never felt comfortable as a public speaker, but his poetry readings remained a constant part of his peace activism, and their effect on his audiences ensured his luminary status.[9] In a letter to Storm Jameson, Vera Brittain expressed a reaction typical for Sassoon's listeners, reporting that along with much of the audience, his reading caused her nose to redden and eyes to dampen: "Forgive this outburst. At Bristol I had one of the most moving experiences of my life in hearing Siegfried Sassoon read his poems aloud. He read them without eloquence or drama, but his gentle, diffident voice and manner only added to the effect. I'd quoted and read them to audiences so often—and to hear him read them himself—'Have you Forgotten Yet?' and others almost as well-known—was quite overwhelming."[10] In Brittain's description, these poems from the war had acquired a talismanic quality, heralds of a desire for peace made all the more potent by Sassoon's unaffected manner. His work routinely appeared in pacifist settings, where his persona conferred gravitas. In Julian Bell's anthology *We Did Not Fight* (1935), for instance, the frontispiece was Sassoon's "Asking for It," which ends with "the needlessness of shedding human blood" from one who personally knew much about killing. Throughout the thirties, his combination of literary and pacifist celebrity would remain a powerful fixture in PPU campaigns.

Though it was certainly his most prominent political commitment, Sassoon's work with the PPU was not his first attempt at peace activism. At the end of the war, somewhat adrift when no longer a soldier in wartime, he was briefly involved with the British branch of the socialist antiwar organization *Clarté*, alongside Bertrand Russell, H. G. Wells, and Bernard Shaw.[11] The French leader of *Clarté* was Henri Barbusse, author of the antiwar trench novel *Under Fire* (1916), which Sassoon had greatly admired. In his typical nonconformist and self-deprecating fashion, Sassoon left the organization, later saying that he never had "the ghost of a notion what it was all about" (*Siegfried's Journey*, 252). This short-lived commitment might seem like pure dilettantism, but its basis was his visceral desire for a peaceable world. In January 1920, Sassoon conducted his peace advocacy by touring the United States, spending several months reading his poems and proclaiming a gospel of disenchantment to audiences far less war-scarred than those in Europe. This tour, which Paul Moeyes describes as the capstone of his soldier-poet phase, was the last gesture of independent political action before his reinvention with the PPU.[12]

Sassoon's persona of "soldier-poet against war" was predicated on the name he made for himself during the war. His well-known protest letter, sometimes printed with the title "Finished with the War: A Soldier's Declaration" (1917), was originally distributed to public figures he deemed sympathetic, including Arnold Bennett, Thomas Hardy, Ottoline Morrell, and Bertrand Russell, as well as to his commanding officer Colonel Jones Williams, along with a letter explaining his regretful refusal to report for military duties (Wilson, *Siegfried Sassoon: Soldier, Poet*, 239). Another recipient was H. B. Lees-Smith, a pacifist and Labour Party member of Parliament, who read the declaration aloud in the House of Commons, and the incident, along with a transcript of the declaration, was reported in the *Times*, which extensively broadened its audience.

This protest has been the subject of much scholarly analysis, usually centering on the specific arguments that Sassoon made, its derivativeness from Bertrand Russell and H. W. Massingham's counsel, his manipulation by "opportunistic pacifists" such as Russell and Morrell, and the legitimacy of shell shock as his motivation. Historians tend to agree that peace in July 1917 would have been impossible through diplomatic negotiation because Germany effectively had the upper hand and Britain was for all intents and purposes engaged in a defensive war. Sassoon's views, as Max Egremont describes them, were "muddled" and "startlingly naïve" (*Siegfried Sassoon*, 145). Negotiation for peace was Russell's particular contribution to the letter, which corroborates suggestions by critics (and by Sassoon himself) that some of his arguments were learned from others rather than arising from his own beliefs.[13] But whatever the reasons behind what he came to call his "independent action," whether emotional fatigue or seduction by political entrepreneurs, his protest catapulted the fame he had already achieved in combat and literature, and this celebrity augmented his emblematic status as a war resister. Like many such events, emblems are largely immune to factuality.

This entire episode, which became a major source for Sassoon's later reflective writings, was in many respects a matter of image making and public relations. Sassoon's refusal to show up for duty at the appointed time and the publication of his antiwar statement were obviously acts of insubordination subject to court-martial and standard punishments. That he did not face these expected outcomes has everything to do with his established fame, his position as a decorated war hero, and his budding reputation as a poet and war commentator. The government and army effectively waged a media battle with Sassoon, silencing him with an insanity diagnosis that significantly curtailed his efforts. Sassoon's persistent revising of his life story, from his diaries to the Sherston trilogy to his later autobiographical trilogy, was all an attempt to manage his contested self-image.

Before his major protest, Sassoon's pacifist identity had been cultivated in the *Cambridge Magazine*, which published many of his poems and became a significant reference point for his antiwar credentials. Under the editorship of C. K. Ogden, the magazine ran from 1912 to 1922, and at its peak during the war years, it was sharply criticized for being pacifist and antipatriotic. On November 14, 1914, Ogden published an English translation of "Above the Battle," an antiwar polemic by Romain Rolland, along with a preface praising Rolland as "the intellectual voice of pacifism in Europe" (Brockington, *Above the Battlefield*, 63). In response, the *Morning Post* condemned the *Cambridge Magazine* as "a subtle and powerful instrument of Pacifist suggestions" and denounced its contributors as "perversely clever persons" (qtd. in ibid., 63). Numbered among the perverse and clever were Shaw, Hardy, and Sassoon. So dangerous was the periodical's reputation that Sassoon's psychiatrist and mentor W. H. R. Rivers observed in his dream diaries that he felt guilty for reading it because of its bad influence on military men like himself (Ashplant, *Fractured*, 176–77). Among its provocations was printing excerpts from foreign newspapers—including German ones—without framing them as reports about the enemy. On April 29, 1916, Sassoon published his first poem in the *Cambridge Magazine*—"The Redeemer"—which Jean Moorcroft Wilson describes as "the beginning of Sassoon's public recognition as a poet determined not to glorify war" (*Siegfried Sassoon: Soldier, Poet*, 154). Sassoon would continue submitting poems to Ogden throughout the war, even after receiving the wound that ended his active service (Egremont, *Siegfried Sassoon*, 214).[14] Sassoon's writings appeared in several journals, including more conservative publications, such as the *Westminster Gazette*, but the consistency of his association with the *Cambridge Magazine* augmented his poetry's reception as writing against war. As Sarah Cole claims, "Sassoon, perhaps more than any of the other famous soldier-poets, consistently hammers away, in poem after poem, on the troubling consequences of enchanting violence. His poetry works feverishly to expose and ironize the conventional discourses that glorify and romanticize war" (*Violet Hour*, 63). Bravely fighting and then protesting the war, hammering away in verse against enchanted violence, and exposing the disastrous romanticizing of military life—these are the signature traits of Sassoon's pacifist persona.

Just as scholars have challenged the emblematic nature of his war protest for obscuring his inner conflicts and thoroughgoing ambivalence, the "antiwar" dimension of his poems has been called into question. Brian Bond's influential essay "British 'Anti-War' Writers and Their Critics" polemicizes against historians who have too easily accepted Fussell's depiction of the Great War as a time of disillusionment. Though Bond affirms Fussell's skills as a literary critic, he finds his archival work misleading because it emphasizes sensitive, literate men of a single social class who do not represent the majority experience of the war. Bond concludes that using trench poetry to shape historiography creates a tautology, which then frames poetical analysis. All of this misguided work too readily accepts the thesis that most combatants and most war poetry were at root antiwar. Bond approvingly cites Adrian Caesar's *Taking It Like a Man: Suffering, Sexuality, and the War Poets*, the work of literary analysis that has gone furthest in arguing that trench poets have been mistakenly seen as writing against war.[15] In Caesar's view, Sassoon and other trench poets were corrupted by an educational system steeped in a repressive Christianity that bestowed warped ideas about sexual immorality and redemptive suffering. Sassoon, according to Caesar, is misunderstood more egregiously than his peers because the point of his poetry is that "the war affords peace and 'freedom' from the boredom and the tribulations of civilian life. [Sassoon's] implicit failures in both love and art will be made good by the war; by making sacrifices and being sacrificed. The will to suffer is quite clear" (*Taking It*, 69). Thus, what initially appears to be antiwar writing is really a reflection of Christian-style sacrifice made possible only by war, a source of religiously inspired masochism. The trench poems—even when they seem to be antiwar satires—in fact reveal that war is greatly desired by the speaker. Even more troubling to Caesar are poems such as "Fight to a Finish," which demonstrate "the violence of Sassoon's rage" (92). This poem in particular, with its fantasy of returning troops slaughtering a welcome home parade along with the press corps and then marching toward Parliament, leads Caesar to conclude: "We should not, I think, praise poems like this. Not only is the relish of violence distasteful, but the obviously undemocratic sentiments are chilling" (ibid.). Not merely not a pacifist, then, Sassoon may even betray signs of exuberant, quasi-psychotic militarism.[16]

Though such criticism is a valuable reminder that the simplistic "anti-war" label needs to be interrogated and qualified, this does not diminish the importance of Sassoon's early public reception for establishing his famous antiwar persona. As T. G. Ashplant observes, Sassoon's articulation of the excessive cost of the war in human terms was, for many of his admirers, precisely the grounding on which an overall pacifist case could be made.[17] The strong emotional allure that Sheppard, Brittain, and others find in his poems comes from the way his poetry can, at its best, cry out against the injustice, irrationality, and inexplicable suffering in wartime. Critics who discover a hidden core of violent sentiment within Sassoon's supposed pacifism are not planting evidence, but they do risk replacing the guise of a simplistic pacifist with that of an equally simplistic happy warrior.

Sassoon's cry for justice might at times be quite strident, but taking his poems as a dispassionately articulated political agenda misses their point. Reading "Fight to a Finish," for instance, as a fascist, genocidal fantasy neglects the poem's satirical edge, which wields ultraviolence as a reductio ad absurdum. To fight to a finish, as the belligerent politicians and military leaders demand, would mean to kill everyone involved in war making and produce the false peace of total annihilation. Sassoon believed that his irony would not be lost, writing to Ottoline Morrell that the poem is "fairly effective in its way" and encouraging her to consider it alongside poems such as "Death's Brotherhood," which she had enjoyed (*Diaries, 1915–1918*, 193). Morrell, who was among his greatest supporters from the absolute pacifist camp, was an early audience for his antiwar persona, a sign that even his most bitterly accusatory work functioned as a public performance rather than strategic policy.

That the "public protest" dimension of his persona was especially famous during his work in the PPU does not mean that he accepted the role without his typical ambivalence. Even while bringing audiences to tears through his somber readings, he privately mocked his persona and the supposed effectiveness of peace rallies. In one of the many humorous exchanges he had with Max Beerbohm, Sassoon described his first PPU appearance, which Sheppard had so admired, writing that "General

Goering hasn't yet wired 'Gratters,' but no doubt he is grateful" (*Letters to Max*, 31–32). He continues: "I reappear at the Albert Hall to ask 8500 people if they have 'forgotten yet' in stentorian tones" and recounts his private performance for his wife of "Everyone Sang" in the pompous voice of Major Paget, a gentleman officer whom Sassoon had known, while explaining that the large crowd gathered in Birmingham was "quite a beano of Quakers" (ibid.). Despite his mixed feelings, Sassoon became an emblem of the antiwar ex-combatant, and he used his celebrity and the antiwar strain in his poems to advocate for peace, regardless of internal conflicts over both halves of his veteran-pacifism.

Sherston's "Innocently Insidious Anti-War Propaganda"

If there is anything that we might find consistent about Sassoon, it is his rebellious streak, governed by reluctance to be fully revolutionary. The social class from which he came, the faith tradition that he left and then reclaimed, the literary establishment in both its popular and avant-garde forms, the homosexual subculture as well as conventional heterosexual marriage and child-rearing—all of these social institutions and movements constituted Sassoon's life, and his frequent actions against them seem motivated by contrarianism and an outsider's sensibility, but not from a need for radical, systemic change. He never held to any absolute for long, and even his famous war protest bears traces of equivocation.

Thus, it should be clear that Sassoon's late description of his Sherston books is suggestive rather than precisely accurate. To read *The Memoirs of George Sherston* as "propaganda" takes one sliver of Sassoon's complex persona—a particularly sly and cheeky one at that—and uses it to represent all of Sassoon. Rather than reducing the *Memoirs* to simple propaganda, I wish to show how the complicated dialectics of these works do in fact make them "innocently insidious" in their peace advocacy, while acknowledging that a range of contradictory views about war are sustained by the texts. The *Memoirs* is replete with historical invention, fictionalization, and omission, and they are marked throughout by a self-conscious, self-referential style that clearly separates them from any simple reportage or reminiscence. The style of the *Memoirs* is persistently dialectical, creating fruitful as well as frustrating tensions across many topics, including home versus trench life, the thrill of warfare versus abhorrence of violence, and the self-conscious constructedness of the narrative versus mimetic realism. In sum, both militarism and pacifism appear simultaneously horrible and fascinating. Through Sherston, Sassoon exposes a tension between the confessional mode of autobiography and the author's persistent withholding of information. This simultaneous extension and withdrawing of the self as well as the construction of multiple selves through narration are guiding formal devices in the *Memoirs*, generating a metacommentary that qualifies, undermines, and enriches the narrative.

This complicated relationship between genuine memoir and experimental fiction has been described most aptly by Max Saunders in *Self Impression*, his theorization of "autobiografiction." Saunders considers Sassoon's writings in an explication of Storm Jameson's theory of the difference between autobiography and novels: compared to Graves's *Goodbye to All That*, "a more dynamic shifting between fiction and autobiography can be seen in Sassoon's *Memoirs of an Infantry Officer*. When texts do this as substantially as Sassoon's *Memoirs*, the shifting back and forth between autobiography and fiction constitutes autobiografiction" (*Self Impression*, 163). The very awkwardness of the term "autobiografiction" is partly what makes it so compelling for describing the *Memoirs*. Sassoon's prose works resist easy containment and categorization, and in so doing manifest at the formal level the many contradictions of Sassoon's ideological commitments.

The contradictoriness of the trilogy has been a target for criticism of Sherston the character and the works overall. Introducing his abridgement of the *Memoirs*, Paul Fussell notes: "One reason that Sherston learns so slowly is that his character is so inconsistent and unfixed" (xvii), a view that captures Sherston's flightiness and the strange sense that we are missing key pieces of his character. But much in the way that Huxley used fractured chronology to render the pacifist conversion as a perpetual struggle in *Eyeless in Gaza*, Sassoon adopts multiple selves that are not fully abandoned when a new guise, persona, or role becomes dominant. Sassoon thus maintains the sense that the peace activist Sherston is politically effective precisely because he is still a soldier, and the soldiering Sherston who leaves Slateford War Hospital to rejoin his brothers-in-arms does so with the assurance that this war is wrong and must end. The combatant and the enemy of war never achieve simple, stable resolution.

The deceptively simple narrative arc of the trilogy has allowed for a range of interpretations as spiritual autobiography, literary mourning, modern nostalgia, or evocations of the gentlemanly ethos.[18] What many of these readings of the *Memoirs* share is the underlying conviction that Sassoon's prose exists primarily as self-diagnosis or some kind of individualized personal therapy. Sassoon's writings certainly encourage this perspective, and not just in the persistent autobiography of his prose. "Autognosis," an undated poetical fragment from (presumably) 1921, begins: "To know Myself—this fragment of to-day— / To pluck the unconscious causes of unrest / From self-deceiving nature" (*Diaries, 1920–1922*, 47). Introspection and self-knowledge would seem to be Sassoon's lasting obsessions, from his early poetry to his frequent raids on his own life story with special attention to the prewar years of the "old century," the trials of wartime, and the immediate postwar life of literary success.

Though I would not completely deny the therapeutic function of the Sherston trilogy, especially given Sassoon's own suggestions about self-knowledge as a key feature of his work, I think that overemphasizing his inward focus threatens to obscure the broader political implications of the books. Formalist critics have disparaged the trilogy's incongruities and inconsistencies as technical failures born of Sassoon's inexperience with fiction, but these deviations from conventional prose narration are vital to its political suggestiveness. Sassoon's peace activist literature shares with that of Huxley and Jameson the exposure of militarist values in the most seemingly peaceful parts of English society, but his unique contribution comes from his fixation on the impossible reconciliation of the veteran-pacifist dialectic.

Sherston, Volume One: Memoirs of a Fox-Hunting Man

In critical analyses of the *Memoirs*, surprisingly little has been written about the self-consciousness of Sassoon's form. The formalist-cum-biographical readings of critics including Thorpe, Sternlicht, and Moeyes focus on Sassoon's failure to achieve unity, plausibility, a coherent plot, and a consistent tone, but these essentially New Critical objections to the structure of the works neglect how supposed imperfections lead to the most interesting textures and help generate understated political activism. In *Memoirs of a Fox-Hunting Man*, Sherston's narration establishes a dialectical relationship between the tell-all, confessional mode of autobiography and his fictionalization, replete with overt, deliberate, and sometimes coy withholdings of information. At the end of the first chapter, for instance, Sherston narrates this Proustian moment: "And now, as I look up from my writing, these memories also seem like reflections in a glass, reflections which are becoming more and more easy to distinguish. Sitting here, alone with my slowly moving thoughts, I rediscover many little details, known only to myself, details otherwise dead and forgotten with all who shared that time; and I am inclined to loiter among them as long as possible" (CMGS, 11). His self-consciousness is acute enough to record the feeling of being alone in thought and to note the pace at which these thoughts travel. Loitering among the minor details of his life gives Sherston a Proustian quality that shows artistic polish. He meditates about meditations rather than revealing the specific "little details" over which he ruminates. Those withheld details gesture toward the many aspects of Sassoon's life that Sherston will not divulge in the remaining 650 pages—foremost among the omissions being sexuality, poetry, family, and military prowess. This comment from the end of the first chapter is one of a great many like it in which the narrative voice intrudes to comment on his process in order to seem more open, honest, and straightforward, while actually being more guarded, encoded, and imaginative. Superficial honesty thus disguises actual concealment.

This division between utterance and revelation places the reader in a precarious relationship with the text. Our expectations that memoir can give personal insight with broader application, reveal subtleties of character, or at least serve up juicy gossip are all confounded by Sherston's voice. What some critics have objected to as the all-too-limited construction of Sherston—Sassoon's creation of a character with most of his own most interesting traits cut away—is in this light the means by which the reader is kept off balance, prevented from knowing too much and invited to question the limitations of Sherston's point of view. Sherston tells us of his growing interest in riding and hunting through a visit to the Ringwell Hunt Point-to-Point Races which makes him aware of the conflict between the "red-coated fraternity" of foxhunters and the farmers whose need for fences obstructs the hunters' chase across "England's green and pleasant land" (CMGS, 93). While Sherston does not appear utterly clueless in this scene, his comments expose small forms of ignorance and prejudice as well as an authorial voice behind his own, presumably more aware than Sherston that his vision of English perfection echoes Blake's *Jerusalem* and the debates about enclosure that raged throughout English history. In confessing to the reader his newfound learning, Sherston upholds the promise of the memoir form, but in subtly revealing Sherston's class-bound myopia, Sassoon constructs a point of view that demands an active reader.

The so-called insidious quality of Sassoon's prose arises most apparently in this combative relationship between narrator and reader. Our desire to *know* is thwarted by the narrator's refusal to fully divulge. More than just a casual literary device, this technique establishes the grounding for veteran-pacifist narration in which the combat experience of the narrator distances him from the inexperienced (civilian) reader. Evelyn Cobley has argued that these formal constructs ultimately reveal that First World War memoirs and autobiographical novels are in fact less "antiwar" than they sometimes seem, and she finds in them "the source of a certain ideological complicity with the war" (*Representing War*, 17).[19] While Cobley's deconstructivist reading helpfully adds to the ambivalence already so prominent in Sassoon's writings, her argument does not negate the persistence of antiwar forms that emerge, for instance, in the ways that peacetime society sublimates war violence and encourages its continuation. The scene at the races offers a prime example of the retrospective intrusion of war into the idyllic English life of the fox-hunter. Sherston records in full the final paragraph of a speech given by the Master of Hounds to the farmers, huntsmen, and puppy walkers, in which he praises their collaboration, commends Ringwell as the greatest hunt because of its shared land use, and ends with a request "to do everything in their power to eliminate the most dangerous enemy of the hunting-man — he meant barbed wire" (95). There is no explicit mention of this final statement's resonance in the postwar world, where barbed wire conjures memories of the trenches.

Sherston's reporting of the master's speech has several layers of narratorial complexity that make the "barbed wire" comment stand out. Somewhat bizarrely, Sherston imagines himself as a reporter for the *Southern Daily News* and tentatively tells us, "I should probably have reported the conclusion of his speech in something very like the following paragraph" (95). The tentativeness of Sassoon's word choice ("I should probably," "something very like") and the odd shift into reporting for a regional paper construct the haphazard and amateurish style typical of Sherston, as if he is not quite sure how best to tell his own story. His switching for a moment into newspaper-speak produces an intertextual playfulness akin to the shifting generic fragments in well-known modernist texts. Less radical and demanding for casual readers than the formal shifts in works such as *Ulysses*, the *Memoirs* still employs unconventional, antirealist techniques and self-consciousness about form. The mention of barbed wire is a clarification for imaginary readers of his imaginary article and accentuates the already vexed relationship between Sherston's readers and his fictional autobiography. Much has been made of the binary structure of *Memoirs of a Fox-Hunting Man* and its pointed juxtaposition between idyllic prewar England and the destructiveness of wartime, but the intrusion of barbed wire on the world of the hunt is more than just an ironic reference to a civilian instrument that will later become weaponized. It is for readers in 1928 an indication that the tools of war were already present in the "green and pleasant lands."

Barbed wire in the foxhunting lands is one of many moments in which Sherston's narration indirectly reveals structural violence in prewar English society. In peacetime England, George's friend Stephen returns to the barbed wire theme, expressing his biggest daily concern about "a double-distilled blighter who's wired up all his fences . . . the same ugly-mugged sweep who persuaded the Guv'nor to get me trained as a chartered accountant!" (120). Stephen's displeasure with the state of hunting life and his accountancy job leads him to consider a career in the army, revealing his striking naivety and obliviousness to imperialist exploitation: "If only he could get into the Gunners he'd be happy. His elder brother Jack was in the Gunners, and was expecting to be moved from India to Ireland. And Ireland, apparently, was a fox-hunting Elysium" (121). Stephen's attraction to the gunners has little to do with grand ideals of serving king and country and fits more neatly with the allure of the military as a "great adventure": the best way out of a boring job is to join the armed forces.[20] Even more telling is the uninvestigated assumption that the military's purpose is to control and subdue its colonial possessions. Stephen resolves to discuss this career move with Colonel Hesmon, a retired widower whose life of country leisure appears enviable to both Stephen and Sherston. Hesmon is a lector at Hoadley Church, which Sherston attends with his aunt, and Sherston recalls: "Colonel Hesmon's wizened face and bushy grey eyebrows appeared above the shiny brass eagle to read the First Lesson," which comes from the fifth chapter of Isaiah and speaks of God's "lifting up an ensign to the nations" to call them to battle (125). This reading, made idealistic and distant through the prose of the King James Bible, is endowed with martial significance by its lector. The colonel, however, is no seasoned combatant, and we learn that he has been retired for twenty years: "the Boer War arrived seven years too late for him, and the gist of the matter was that he'd never seen any active service" (128). With the figure of this colonel turned churchman and sportsman, Sassoon once again gives prewar peacetime a militarized aura. His satire is complicated by the sense that Colonel Hesmon is not sinister or belligerent but rather outdated and inexperienced, but the critique of structural violence is still detectable. In the hunt, commerce, and the church—all spheres of respectable, gentlemanly, peacetime England—the supposedly idyllic world before the war unfolds in dialectical struggle with violent, imperialist, and militaristic ideologies that will open the way for the coming global conflict.

Early on, Sherston's narration in *Memoirs of a Fox-Hunting Man* buries present-day views about war under the whimsical flow of his story, but the first real intrusion of his antiwar position emerges in the next-to-last part of the book, "In the Army." He notes his peers' and his own feelings about the need for war at its onset, in contrast to their current, blanket disapproval: "the War was inevitable and justifiable. Courage remained a virtue. And that exploitation of courage, if I may be allowed to say a thing so obvious, was the essential tragedy of the War, which, as everyone now agrees, was a crime against humanity" (230). In the space of a few sentences, Sherston gives a miniature survey of the war's emotional logic, from widespread belief in its necessity and righteousness to the tragic exploitation of youthful courage to agreement about the war's basic criminality. The seasoned, cynical combatant who is worldly wise and ashamed of his naive younger self hovers about the trilogy, revealing himself only occasionally, but he perceptibly influences the narrative perspective.

Sherston's conflicted multiple selves develop through the trilogy, manifesting through formal play a pacifist critique of British liberal identity. Confining himself to Sherston the sportsman in *Memoirs of a Fox-*

Hunting Man, Sassoon creates a parallel between the stereotypical leisure-class life of golf, cricket, steeple chase, foxhunting, etc.—deeply serious about frivolity—and the deluded earnestness of his entry into war first as a yeoman and then an infantry officer on the Western Front. Both of these versions of himself contain an inflated notion of English patriotism and both promise disastrous consequences for Sherston and the generation of men around him. Virginia Woolf's depiction of Septimus Warren Smith as a man who "went to France to save an England which consisted almost entirely of Shakespeare's plays and Miss Isabel Pole in a green dress" (*Mrs. Dalloway*, 84) conveys one of the ways men entered the military life for reasons that seem inadequate to the demands placed on them. Sherston goes to war to fight for an England consisting almost entirely of athletic games, prize vegetables, tea parties, and fine livestock. While the real Sassoon might at least have been able to add Shakespeare's plays to the list (along with his other literary heroes and his own creative pursuits), Sherston remains truncated, and his idealistic plunge into war is thus even more foolish. Maintaining his dialecticism, Sassoon's narrator seems genuinely nostalgic about the prewar world of plentiful foxes and its "sporting Elysium," but immediately following his paean to sporting England, Sherston explains his clearly erroneous (and thus ironic) view that this world produced a "comfortable feeling that here was something which no political upheaval could interrupt" (203–4). The only incursion on his privileged life that Sherston seems aware of is that made by "those damned socialists who want to stop us hunting," and he dismisses his friend Denis's concern about a potential German attack (204). In an achronological aside, Sherston finally admits that he would have "been astonished if I'd been told that socialists opposed conscription as violently as many fox-hunting men supported the convention of soldiering" (204). This stepping outside the chronological frame signals to the reader some distance between Sherston's narrative position and the self he describes, and it raises the specter of alternative modes of social and economic arrangement that might prevent militaristic policies such as conscription. The war imposes itself on the text, though no mention is made of his later service. Instead, the reader holds together this image of naive Sherston railing against socialists whose views might have saved him along with foreknowledge of the approaching war. Paul K. Saint-Amour has argued that "in the immediate wake of the First World War, the dread of another massive conflict saturated Anglo-European imagination, amounting to a proleptic mass traumatization, a *pre*-traumatic stress syndrome" (*Tense Future*, 7–8). In the *Memoirs*, the anticipatory feeling created by Sherston's narratorial asides "insidiously" undercuts the idyllic England that appears on the surface to be the book's subject, and that anticipation resonates with an even more anxious anticipation of another war as Sassoon completes the trilogy.

Sherston, Volume Two: Memoirs of an Infantry Officer

More than either of the other volumes in the trilogy, *Memoirs of an Infantry Officer* makes explicit the agon within the veteran-pacifist dialectic. This second volume includes Sassoon's most sustained description of combatant life as well as his fictionalized account of the protest that secured his pacifist fame. Late in the book, he describes a scene in which Thornton Tyrrell, the fictional stand-in for Bertrand Russell, introduces Sherston to members of pacifist groups such as the "Stop the War Committee" and the "No Conscription Fellowship": "Among them was an intellectual conscientious objector (lately released after a successful hunger-strike). Also a genial veteran Socialist (recognizable by his red tie and soft grey hat) who grasped my hand with rugged good wishes. One and all, they welcomed me to the Anti-War Movement, but I couldn't quite believe that I had been assimilated. The reason for this feeling was their antipathy to everyone in a uniform. I was still wearing mine, and somehow I was unable to dislike being a Flintshire Fusilier" (482–83). Sherston's identity as a fusilier in military garb is both the chief source of his authority and the wedge between him and the other pacifists. Without his military service—accomplished with distinction and aplomb—his antiwar protest would lack much of its rhetorical weight. But Sherston senses an underlying distaste for soldiers among these civilians, and he experiences the awkward incompatibility of his split selves; the warrior-pacifist and soldier-civilian hyphenations cut across his mixed loyalties. He concludes that "the man who had really endured the War at its worst was everlastingly differentiated from everyone except his fellow soldiers" (482–83). While *Memoirs of a Fox-Hunting Man* bifurcates the prewar sporting life from the wartime troubles, *Memoirs of an Infantry Officer* adopts a similarly bifurcated structure, with the soldiering life divided from the pacifist protest. But just as the first Sherston volume showed how the prewar idyll was shot through with proleptic war violence, the apparent binary of the second book is in fact structured with similar alterity. Many of the wartime experiences at the beginning of this second volume reveal pacifist sympathies, and the peace protest is ironized and even fundamentally challenged by the allure of fighting.

At the height of his military service, Sherston intuits that war is horrific and not worth whatever goals it purportedly achieves. Purely military objectives aside, militarist ideology assures fighting men "that war is caused not by moral or political mistakes but by man's laudable drive to achieve his full potential" (Ceadel, *Thinking*, 21). Core to this belief in the improving effects of war is an understanding of the battlefield as the ultimate testing ground for courage. Sassoon returns to this alluring ideology repeatedly in his writings, and bravery also rates highly in his fictional avatar's hierarchy of virtues. The experience of warfare facilitates Sherston's yearning for courageous feats, suffusing the war with elements that have caused some critics to question the authenticity of Sassoon's antiwar claims. But in addition to the moments in which Sherston thrills to the tests of battle, there are times when the modern military organization undermines its supposedly beneficial dimension by revealing the cowardice and sadism inherent in belligerence as well as the deeper courage of nonviolence. A major whom Sherston encounters has an obsessive hatred for conscientious objectors, sending one "well-educated man" to a labor camp and tying "some humble inarticulate wretch who refused to march" to a wagon and dragging him through the street (402–3). As the major recounts the second exploit, he says, "After a few hundred yards he cried enough, and afterwards turned out to be quite a decent soldier. Made good, was killed in the trenches" (403). Sherston offers little direct commentary about the major, only noting that these tales of abusing COs were accompanied with a grim smile. He concludes this episode: "I hadn't formed any opinion about Conscientious Objectors, but I couldn't help thinking that they must be braver men than some I'd seen wearing uniforms in safe places and taking salutes from genuine soldiers" (ibid.). Though not an outright attack on the major, this comment casts aspersions at his rank, the genuineness of his soldierly identity, and his guaranteed safety. The conscientious objector is superior because he openly wages nonviolent struggle at great personal risk and under incredible duress to change his position. Before Sherston comes to any firm conclusions about the role of conscientious objection in his own life, he admires the soldierly bravery of others taking this stance.

This scene with the major is particularly noteworthy for peace activist literature because it does not just criticize disenchanted violence or nasty living conditions but critiques the brutality of all military service. The major has become sadistic—or at least is fostered in his sadism—by having COs to torture, and he is particularly aroused by the poor, voiceless, uneducated man he abuses into service. The major decides the value of this man's life and death in a combat zone, where he is killed for minimal strategic gain. Sherston's interpretive coda shifts us from the current structures of the military to the supposed virtues of military life, virtues that Sherston fully shares and wishes were part of the modern army. Bravery, he thinks, might be better found in a conscientious objector than a general. This moment along the way to Sherston's protest offers perhaps the best insight into his own antiwar motives.

The sadistic major is one of many instances in this volume of the *Memoirs* in which modern army practice fails to live up to militarist ideals. Another commanding officer, "a massive sandy-haired Highland Major," gives field-training lectures to new recruits about proper use of the bayonet—a scene familiar from Sassoon's poem "The Kiss" (289). The violent rhetoric of the lecture combines sporting terminology with a maniacal fixation on killing: "Remember that every Boche you fellows kill is a point scored to our side; every Boche you kill brings victory one minute nearer and shortens the war by one minute. Kill them! Kill them! There's only one good Boche, and that's a dead one!" (290). Whatever controversy remains in interpreting Sassoon's original intention with "The Kiss"—satirical cynicism or romantic bloodlust—Sherston's version of this training session is anything but laudatory.[21] In its fictional form, this lecture is devastating both to the heroic vision of military life that Sherston upholds and to the private, contemplative spaces he seeks to preserve. After leaving the lecture for the comfort of a pastoral retreat, he heads "up the hill to my favourite sanctuary, a wood of hazels and beeches . . . Peace was there in the twilight of that prophetic foreign spring" (ibid.). The peace that Sherston describes is a private, romantic peace found in nature, a sanctuary redolent with Hulme's sense of "spilt religion" (*Collected Writings*, 62). But this peace is not disconnected from the peace desired through the cessation of global war. Killing one's way to victory, "winning" the war with each death, has no appeal for Sherston. The peace that he seeks in the wooded sanctuary is contaminated by the major's violent rhetoric, another dialectical instance in which trying to sustain one emotion proves impossible without its opposite. In the sanctuary, the voice "batters" Sherston's brain, a set of gory phrases reported without any additional commentary: "'Stick him between the eyes, in the throat, in the chest.' 'Don't waste good steel. Six inches are enough. What's the use of a foot of steel sticking out at the back of a man's neck? Three inches will do for him; when he coughs, go and look for another'" (ibid., 290). Even in his most peaceful space, the war's violence intrudes, effectively making no place peaceful. Sassoon shows us through Sherston that the modern military is such a deeply flawed system that it cannot produce the good ends that warfare seeks in optimal circumstances. Sherston's criticism thus advances a version of "just war absolutism," the quasi-pacifist view that maintains that war could conceivably be undertaken righteously, but modern conditions prohibit that possibility.[22]

Modern war may be incapable of living up to the heroic ideals of militarist ideology, but antiwar protest can appear in the *Memoirs* as an equally hopeless, ineffectual exercise. Adrian Caesar is especially condemnatory of Sassoon's portrayal of his famous protest: "It is crucial to assert that the trilogy does not represent 'propaganda for peace' much less an expression of pacifism. The books have been taken by subsequent critics as being 'anti-war,' and yet much of them celebrates the event . . . It is a very conservative conclusion, made even more so by the repeated implication that individual protest with regard to international politics is both futile and wrong headed" (*Taking It*, 107). Conservative and antipacifist, the *Memoirs*, in this reading, condones the failure of Sherston's protest and the futility of individual action.[23]

Caesar's criticism instructively reads against the grain of any oversimplified acceptance of Sassoon's "bitter pacifist" side. Reading the protest scene as plainly "wrong headed," however, rather bluntly obscures its more nuanced political message regarding peace activism. It is Sherston's individualism that Sassoon skewers, not war protests in general. Sherston's encounter with the medical board, which at the urging of David Cromlech (the fictionalized Robert Graves) declares Sherston psychologically unfit rather than insubordinate and deserving of a court-martial, underscores the ineptitude of his protest. Rather than a swift and stern confrontation with Sherston that might have spurred him toward more grandiose actions, the officers in charge of his case foil his contentiousness with kindness. As Sherston puts it, "I wished I could have a talk with Tyrrell. But even he wasn't infallible, for in all of our discussions about my plan of campaign he had never foreseen that my senior officers would treat me with this kindly tolerance which was so difficult to endure" (*CMGS*, 508). The military organization is not only capable of squashing internal dissent through force, it surprisingly displays its adaptability by using gentler, less combustible means. Sherston tells us: "Nothing would induce them to court martial me. It had all been arranged with some big bug at the War Office in the last day or two . . . So that was the end of my grand gesture. I ought to have known that the blighters would do me down somehow, I thought, scowling heavily at the sea" (512). His lack of intellectual ability comes increasingly to look like a liability for the sort of protest he is staging, but even more problematic—and more revealing for the book's peace advocacy—is the way we are shown that Sherston's highly individualized action based in no small part on his personal desires for glory and martyrdom are insufficient bases for resisting a robust and supple military organization supported and endorsed by an entire culture.

The army's deft handling of dissidence combines with the overwhelming inevitability of war, too vast and implacable for any solitary person to dismantle. Sherston describes "the indeterminate tragedy" of the summer's end, which moves "with agony on agony, toward the autumn" leaving him "powerless against unhappiness so huge." He continues: "I couldn't alter European history, or order the artillery to stop firing. I could stare at the War as I stared at the sultry sky, longing for life and freedom and vaguely altruistic about my fellow-victims. But a second-lieutenant could attempt nothing—except to satisfy his superior officers"(360–61). Throughout his military life, he is by disposition and by intellect incapable of mounting the pacifist counterattack so deeply desired by one part of his conflicted nature, and he concludes: "Armageddon was too immense for my solitary understanding" (361).

Going even further, Sassoon shows us that militarism pervades all of Sherston's cultural background. He has an epiphany while surveying

Butley, remembering stories from his childhood, such as "the burning of the old Bull Inn," the closest his sleepy village has come to grand catastrophes that fill English history and produce the national mythos (493). Butley holds memories of uniformed volunteers drilling for the Boer War, but little in its cultural ethos allows comprehension of the mass slaughter Sherston has witnessed. Their lack of combatant experience means they will also lack comprehension of his pacifist convictions: "They would tap their foreheads and sympathetically assume that I'd seen more of the fighting than was good for me" (494). Sherston's epiphany occurs with his realization that an entire social realm is firmly established in opposition to his protest, and that no one from his home will be "convinced" by his statement, no matter how well his arguments are supported by logic and lucidity.

Sherston's so-called independent action against the war is not, in fact, completely solitary, but the pacifist community he presents lacks a concentrated strategic network. At best, we see aloof intellectuals or cranks such as Maccamble, the quirky PhD who is "chock-full of ideas and adumbrations" and loses favor quickly with Sherston for disdaining soldiers and disparaging Rivers (532).[24] Sherston lacks the full-bodied mentorship and support for his peace advocacy that Anthony Beavis's community provides in *Eyeless in Gaza*, and, instead, his main supporter is Rivers, an agent of the military enterprise. That individual peace actions are ineffectual is an important point in Sassoon's critique. Military might— abundant, manipulative, overpowering—goes deeper than any single person can choose his way out of. Within the structure of the book, Sherston's failure to achieve a court-martial and its concomitant martyrdom is fully recognized as the result of a military system too powerful, well coordinated, and sly for an ordinary individual like Sherston to defeat. Rather than being fundamentally antipacifist, this insistence on the superiority of military powers that be is consistent with a mode of pacifist aesthetics found elsewhere in the trilogy; that is, the exposure of social and political structures that are powerfully built against peace. Inherent in this revelation is a criticism of the peace work and war prevention activism Sassoon was conducting while writing the *Memoirs*. His autobiografiction against war remains a testament to peace but also a reminder that protests—even grandly celebrated ones—may fail in their primary objectives. By critiquing the systemic violence of Sherston's world, Sassoon makes his defeated protest more complex and aesthetically rich than an individual's martyrdom for the pacifist cause.

Sherston, Volume Three: Sherston's Progress

In her influential account of the relationship between war and bodily pain, Elaine Scarry has claimed a close kinship between war and torture, the conduct of each necessitating injury and the condition of combatants becoming, uniquely, "frozen in a permanent act of participation" (*Body in Pain*, 62). As combatants injure others and/or become injured, they strive for mastery: "the winning issue or ideology achieves for a time the force and status of material 'fact' by the sheer material weight of the multitudes of damaged and opened human bodies" (ibid.). Scarry's theory puts into corporeal terms the problem that engrosses Sassoon throughout the trilogy and especially in its final volume. That is, the act of autobiografictional narration—telling one's own story on one's own terms and with one's own style—consistently reminds us that Sherston's participation in war's economy of injury is permanent. The third Sherston book, his so-called progress, has frequently been criticized as Sassoon's weakest entry in the series, a tired addendum that limps across the promised finish line with perfunctory obligation rather than élan. But seen as a manifestation of "permanent participation," the stagnation that derives from the inescapable condition of war, *Sherston's Progress* should not be dismissed as a mere formal failure but embraced as a dynamic work signifying the precarious state of the peace movement in 1936.

To trace this linkage between the formal fractures of the final Sherston novel and the state of Sassoon's peace work, we might begin with the most powerful official voice of the war effort: the army psychiatrist W. H. R. Rivers. Because Rivers died in 1922, Sassoon decided not to change his name, and the influence of this figure on both the author and his fictional self cannot be overstated. Rivers's level-headedness and the persuasiveness of his arguments and encouragements to return to battle have led critics to posit that the real moral weight of the narrative rests on Rivers and his distinctly promilitary stance. In light of this moral center, Alex Zwerdling suggests: "For a serious pacifist Sassoon's war trilogy makes very unsatisfactory reading" (*Real World*, 298). Supporting this view is the obvious affection with which Rivers is portrayed, and the sense that among all the father-mentor-guru figures Sherston acquires (such as his commanding officers or Tyrrell and the pacifists), only Rivers is invariably noble. Describing Rivers's method, Sherston explains: "As an R.A.M.C. officer, he was bound to oppose my 'pacifist tendency,' but his arguments were always indirect" (CMGS, 521). Rivers is calm and patient, just as Tyrrell had been before, and in confronting this presence, Sherston's "independent action" acquires an unfavorable light: "the weak point about my 'protest' had been that it was evoked by personal feeling. It was an emotional idea based on my war experience and stimulated by the acquisition of points of view which I accepted uncritically. My intellect was not an ice-cold one. It was, so to speak, suffering from trench fever" (ibid.). Rivers's simple, powerful rejoinder to Sherston's objections is that the war must go on or at this point England and its allies would have to concede a "victory for Pan-Germanism and nullify all the sacrifices we had made" (522). Sherston is ill matched with this kind of pressure, coming with such deep ethos and conveyed with quietude that more emotive appeals would have shattered. It has been argued that the historical Rivers was far more conflicted about his role at Craiglockhart and that Sassoon's presence greatly complicated Rivers's feelings, but the Sherston version upholds the preeminence of the older man and emphasizes Sassoon's doubts about pacifist activism.[25]

One problem, however, with taking Rivers as the moral core of the book is that the dialectical structure persists in *Sherston's Progress*. After the tumultuous back and forth over Sherston's pacifism and antipacifism, his petulant cutting of a medical board exam and penitent restoration of mental health and commanding officer status, the section ends with condemnation of the war. Sherston sympathetically (though disgustedly) views Slateford by daylight and concludes: "Shell-shock. How many a brief bombardment had its long-delayed after-effect in the minds of these survivors, many of whom had looked at their companions and laughed while inferno did its best to destroy them. Not then was their evil hour, but now; now, in the sweating suffocation of nightmare, in paralysis of limbs, in the stammering of dislocated speech" (557). The travesty of these damaged bodies is surpassed only by their damaged virtues, which shell shock had exploded through acts "sanctioned and glorified by the Churches," thereby mocking their sacrifice and the "civilization" to which "these soldiers had been martyred" (ibid.). Sherston proclaims that "it remained for civilization to prove that their martyrdom wasn't a dirty swindle" (ibid.). Though he frequently feels hampered by a "lack of intellect" when arguing about war, his final paragraph of the section mounts his most forceful attempt to articulate his position. The best men, egged on by institutions such as the church and a flimsy appeal to save "civilization," find themselves permanently injured by the combat violence inflicted on them and, perhaps more disastrously, by their own violence toward others. "They, who in the name of righteousness had been sent out to maim and slaughter their fellow-men," are martyrs to an unworthy creed (ibid.). For the men at Slateford, it is not just their bodies that have been sacrificed but their minds, personalities, and morals. This summation goes beyond the classic war-is-hell thinking of the enlightened soldier who might detest battle conditions while accepting their basic necessity; war and its effects are portrayed as irredeemable, at least within a society that abuses the men and their military ethos. The "Rivers" section concludes on this note, which does not necessarily make it definitive of Sherston's constantly shifting views; rather, it reinforces antagonism with Rivers as a vital force in the dialectic

In spite of Sassoon's obvious affection for Rivers, their final meeting provides no real solution in the novel, and Sherston's return to combat registers hopelessness and inevitability. The anemic ending of the book, which many critics have attributed to a lack of narrative thrust or thematic cohesion or simply to authorial fatigue, might also be read as a matter of identity failure and an atrophied moral imagination. The last few paragraphs give some suggestion that the return of Rivers is the way toward a new life more rich and full than its alternatives: the shallow prewar life Sherston had once enjoyed or the military life that was exhilarating but iniquitous and destructive to body and soul. But Sherston's declaration of newfound fulfillment in Rivers remains merely platitudinous: "it is only from the inmost silences of the heart that we know the world for what it is, and ourselves for what the world has made us" (656). A return to individualism and reflectiveness is all Sherston (and perhaps Sassoon) can muster, and from this view readers have been quick to take their cue that the entirety of the *Memoirs* is a matter of therapeutic self-discovery.

While I would not discount the trilogy's invocation of self-discovery as a goal, it must be noted that very little has been discovered. Adrian

Caesar's claim that the books ultimately show us how war has improved and enriched Sherston takes one strand of the narrator's oscillating convictions and reads it as primary. Just as plausible is seeing Sherston as a broken survivor with little to return home to except the prospect of decades of self-searching, anger, and regret. His belief that he would be better off "in France where I could at least escape from the war by being in it" sustains the bitter irony that vigorous activity and suffering in wretched conditions are not redemptive but palliative, exactly the sort of opiate needed to get through a life otherwise plagued by memories of things seen and done (654).

Rather than just being therapeutic, the *Memoirs* stages its own version of conflicted protest. This protest emerges even through the diary sections that critics have singled out as Sassoon's biggest aesthetic failure in the trilogy, an indication of his waning creativity.[26] This objection to the diaries fundamentally mistakes their experimental quality and assumes too easily that they are straightforward transcriptions rather than reinventions in novelized form.[27] While completing *Sherston's Progress*, Sassoon wrote to Edmund Blunden: "I am doing all the Palestine and France part in diary form, amplifying my war diary with cunning and adroitness, and the effect is most lifelike and intense. Too much simple humanity in it, though, to please the advanced intellectuals! Howlings will attend it— from Bloomsbury" (*SLSB*, 130). Ever maintaining his combative stance toward the literary elite, Sassoon suggests his formal playfulness and reluctance to be accepted by experimental artists. More important than formalism tout court, however, is the effect of the diaries, which allow us even more direct access to Sherston's vacillations than his first person prose. Supporting the idea that war is finally beneficial, Sherston records on May 3: "I begin to see that the War has re-made me and done away with a lot of my ideas that were no good. So I am really better for it, in spite of scowling bitterly at it" (607). But on the next page, his entry from May 4 criticizes fellow officers as "a sample of the human folly which can accept war as an inevitable and useful element in the routine of life"— and his vacillating continues as he cites Tolstoy on loving despite suffering, and then feels absolved from this virtue since none of these officers would read Tolstoy (608). The nature of Sherston's antiwar protest, revealed most intensely by the diaries, is one of deep internal conflict. Taking note of his moment-to-moment feelings may produce some kind of therapeutic relief, but little calm can be detected in the diaries and their jagged, antagonistic form. Sherston describes this antagonism, felt particularly acutely when returning to the war from Slateford: "Nevertheless, there I was, a living antithesis to the gloomier entries in my diary, and a physical retraction of my last year's protest against the 'political errors and insincerities for which the fighting men were being sacrificed.' But our inconsistencies are often what make us most interesting, and it is possible that, in my zeal to construct these memoirs carefully, I have eliminated too many of my own self-contradictions" (636). In a work replete with contradictions, his last comment is something of a joke, though with this statement Sassoon subtly acknowledges the many aspects of his personality that were indeed withheld from Sherston. Through the immediacy of the diary form, which in Sassoon's hands becomes one more way to both reveal and conceal himself, we see in fictional form his mind at work and intimations of a tragic ending.

The god-in-the-machine appearance of Rivers at the trilogy's conclusion only short-circuits the tragedy; it does not reverse it. Just before Rivers arrives, Sherston feels his mind to be muddled, and he angrily poses the deliberately absurd view that he "had learned but one thing from being a soldier—that if we continue to accept war as a social institution we must also recognize that the Prussian system is the best, and Prussian militarism must be taught to children in schools" (655). He imagines this sort of education, which would stamp out all questioning and focus entirely on the exacting forms of military science—a fantasy that was being realized throughout Europe by the time this final volume was published in 1936.[28] These last few pages fully retain the dialectical structure we have seen throughout the trilogy as Sherston's most extreme and contemporarily relevant antiwar rage is quenched by the gentle appearance of the sensible military man Rivers. However, the vapidness of the conclusion's supposed panacea, the subtle reminder that "Prussian" militarism is again rising, and the depiction of Sherston as still damaged and far from recovery are features that together exhibit the costs and consequences of veteran-pacifism. Unlike Sassoon's short, satirical poems, which, in Max Egremont's memorable description, are "javelin-like" verses that conclude in a "knock-out blow," his *Memoirs of George Sherston* strives for the quieter, less confrontational approach to indicting the war machine he cannot escape (*Some Desperate Glory*, 121).

Sherston's desire for a world free from war but full of adventure hangs on too shaky a foundation. His only options seem to be returning to the doldrums of the gentleman's life made bearable by sport and sustained by neoromantic naturalism, or fighting for glory and comradeship in a war whose premises he disbelieves to protect a society he largely despises. The life that Sherston has to live in the context he is given precludes a fully pacifist imagination, dooming him instead to living forever in the dialectical tension between veteran-pacifism.

Ambivalence Retained

Huxley showed us that individual struggle is the way of a pacifist life and Jameson that collective social action is needed for the international revolution against war. In Sassoon, we find an exposure of society as structured toward militarism through an individual who can find no other options. To some extent with Huxley and very much with Jameson, we find writers whose fiction attends to history at the granular level, showing how it felt for certain kinds of people to understand their age as a period of crisis building toward war. Sassoon's prose, as many readers have noted, continually escapes into the past, treading and retreading the parts of his own life that comprise his identity. Nostalgia is one way to conceive this process, as Robert Hemmings has done, to give freshness to Sassoon's life story around the Second World War. But the nostalgic lens is limiting if it excludes the distinctly political use of Sassoon's perennial backwards glance.

His second trilogy of autobiographical works, which covers many of the same years as the Sherston books but without quite so much fictional cover, self-consciously positions these "official" memoirs as efforts toward peacemaking. *The Old Century and Seven More Years* (1938) focuses on Sassoon's youth until 1907, the years of fox hunting and idyllic England cast in rosy hues for the expressed purpose of happier ruminations while the present day drew closer to another war. As he later reflected on *The Old Century*: "I wrote it for mental release from Hitler and Mussolini — (and the war that seemed to me almost a certainty.) And designed it as an anodyne for my fellow sufferers" (*LTC*, 20). Virginia Woolf, for one, relished the anodyne properties of Sassoon's prose, recording in her diary on September 22, 1938, that she read him at bedtime (*D*, 5:173).[29] Sassoon can reasonably be accused of narcissism, a pitfall for any memoirist but one he chanced more flagrantly than most through repeated literary self-examination. Involvement in the PPU specifically and the peace movement more broadly was a crucial time when he briefly turned outward.

While writing *The Memoirs of George Sherston*, Sassoon composed several poems capitalizing on that outward turn toward peace activism. His collection *The Road to Ruin* (1933), though lacking many of the shock tactics that make the earlier trench poems so memorable, shows an increased effort to expand his canvas by getting behind the immediate war conditions and satirizing the ideological foundations of war and its continued place in so-called peacetime.[30] Rather than the brutalities of trench conditions, we have speculative histories such as "News from the War-After-Next," in which an "Anti-Christ in Europe" is chosen as "War Dictator"—an image resonant with the rising tide of authoritarianism swelling throughout the continent—and the response of those committed to destroying this Antichrist is to "inaugurate / A super-savage Mammonistic State" (*CP 1908–56*, 203). The target is broader, the turn at the poem's ending less sharp, and the edge of the satire blunted, but despite these technical flaws, it is worthwhile noting that the object of the satire has been enlarged. The forces mounting throughout Europe in this poem are the raging, belligerent demigods of totalitarianism, and the only powers rising in opposition seem equally totalitarian. Sassoon's argument in the poem is consistent with the views of many peace activists during the rise of Hitler: that Nazism was obviously disastrous, but the methods used by supposedly democratic powers to defeat Nazism were only the flipside of an authoritarian coin.

This turn to external events and the growing menace of Fascism/Nazism can also be found in his poems collected as *Rhymed Ruminations* (1940). At a high point of his involvement with the PPU, Sassoon wrote "A Prayer from 1936" specifically for the PPU rally on November 27, 1936, in response to the Italian invasion of Abyssinia. Though titled a "prayer," this poem more specifically raises lament, naming the palpable grief and hopeless impotency of well-meaning British people. It begins: "We are souls in hell; who hear no gradual music / Advancing on the air," and, instead, speaker and audience are those "who listen for hope and hear but / The tyrant and the politician talking" (*CP 1908–56*, 250). Jean Moorcroft Wilson has said of "A Prayer from 1936" that it was "not one of Sassoon's most effective anti-war poems" but despite its aesthetic short-comings, it gives evidence of "the strength of his pacifist commitment as late as November 1936" (*Siegfried Sassoon: The Journey*, 291). Like the poems in *The Road to Ruin*, this "Prayer" lacks the specificity of Sassoon's trench poetry, though its title vaguely alludes to Italian imperialism, but the clearly grief-stricken attitude of the speaker moves us away from the sardonic bite of those earlier works and into another space where sorrow over the escalation of violence gathers into lamentation.

By spring 1937, Sassoon could no longer accept his membership in the PPU, and like many others—though somewhat ahead of most—he terminated his position in despair over preventing another war. Parting ways with the PPU was not a simplistic volte-face endorsement of violence, or, as we have seen with Storm Jameson, a particularly attentive concern for people suffering under Nazism, but rather signals his increased pessimism about peace rallies and his role as an ex-soldier, poet-prophet. When asked by Rosamond Lehmann if his name could be read during a meeting organized by the Association of Writers for Intellectual Liberty, he grouchily responded: "Of course you can 'read out my name' in Queen's Hall, if it does anyone any good!—which I doubt—to hear the name of an obsolete amateur writer who dislikes *all* forms of political activity" (qtd. in Wilson, *Siegfried Sassoon: The Journey*, 473n6). Irritability notwithstanding, his personal connection to Dick Sheppard remained deep. During the years when Sheppard was alive and at the forefront of the movement, he became one of the several older men Sassoon relied on for comfort and guidance. Their relationship was close enough that Sassoon had Sheppard christen his son George at St. Martin-in-the-Fields (ibid., 298). Like many people who were or had been involved in the peace movement, the loss of Dick Sheppard was a severe blow. Sassoon wrote to Blunden: "Your letter was opportune, as it arrived when I'd just cut out D. Sheppard's obituary notice and slipped it between the pages of Foster's Perennial Calendar with a heavy sigh for all his (and my) hopes of Peace. Heavy sighs are all I can afford to allow myself at my age when these events attack the emotions" (*SLSB*, 178). Under great emotional fatigue for his personal and political loss, this posture of lamentation would carry Sassoon through the next war.

The final volume of his second trilogy, *Siegfried's Journey* (1945), alludes to the "progress" metaphor from the third Sherston book, and its literal referent is the US tour that effectively completed his soldier-poet days. Sassoon's biographers have shown how evasive this last autobiography is, especially with regard to matters of sexuality, which appear in *Siegfried's Journey* as oblique references to spending time with Oscar Wilde's companion Robbie Ross and the actor Ivor Novello, with whom Sassoon was romantically involved. Mining this book for historical accuracy requires a good deal of caution, but once again in Sassoon's writings, the factual record is less important than his self-presentation. There is persistent name-dropping—it would seem that the postwar years found Sassoon always lunching with people such as Thomas Hardy, doing readings with W. B. Yeats, or in political meetings with Bernard Shaw—which situates Sassoon among the literary elite, though always as a sheepish guest and mostly among those whose reputations were secure by the late nineteenth century rather than with the modernist vanguard. Just as prominent is Sassoon's explicit political claims for his poetry tour. Sharing a stage with Yeats in New York, he is awed by the elder poet's image—"a statuesque and remotely gracious demeanor, aided by his commanding inches and eyeglasses with a black ribbon"—and he describes himself as doing "my ineffectual best to imitate him, incapable of even asking myself whether this was an appropriate kick-off to my career as a minor prophet denouncing war" (*Siegfried's Journey*, 262–63). This moment bears many of the signature traits of Sassoon's prose: contrasting himself unfavorably with a literary icon at his most iconic (Yeats, aloof and bespectacled, complete with black ribbon), self-consciousness about class, appearance, and construction of a self-image (aping Yeats is better than any attempted "authenticity"), and a general dismissiveness about political convictions. However ironic and self-deprecating, even in 1945 Sassoon nevertheless remarkably offers for public consumption a version of his younger self as a nascent antiwar prophet. *Siegfried's Journey* is stuffed with details about his political idealism, such as giving speeches on behalf of a Labour candidate to promote socialism, which might rid the world of war. These descriptions are tinged with irony, but they are not thoroughly renounced, and much as Sassoon turned in 1938 to the seemingly Edenic years of *The Old Century* before the First World War, he reflects in 1945 on a time when his political ideals still carried some weight, for others and for himself.

Sassoon would continue morphing into new identities, remaining ambivalent and conflicted even in his Catholic conversion. But he would still grapple with the persona formed during his years of military service, and would tell Michael Thorpe in the late 1960s: "My renown as a W[ar] P[oet] has now become a positive burden to me, which makes your kind recognition of the later poems specially valuable to me. But my detestation of that war remains as active as ever, and it returns to me at times as an almost morbid obsession. The experience is quite inescapable, and there is an awful fascination about it" (*LTC*, 14). Sassoon is bound by a "morbid obsession" with war, yet he admits that detestation combines with fascination. This deep ambivalence about war and its relation to his identity exerted a lifelong hold over his writings, and his peace advocacy, though sometimes self-indulgent or self-aggrandizing, reveals a means of resisting war from within the conflicted source of the veteran-pacifist condition.

CHAPTER 4

Tending the Ruins in Rose Macaulay's *And No Man's Wit*

While the previous authors in this study each produced fictions propelled by the urgency of war prevention and fraught with the problematic combination of antiwar polemic and literary complexity, Rose Macaulay's literary production through the years leading into World War II separates her somewhat from other peace movement literati. Much of her 1930s fiction lacks any explicit pacifist agenda, even though her stature as a public intellectual and antiwar activist grew considerably throughout this decade. Novels such as *Going Abroad* (1934) and *I Would Be Private* (1937) are usually seen as lesser entries in her expansive oeuvre, and, this judgment aside, they are unquestionably less invested in matters of war and peacemaking than her works from other periods in her long literary career.[1] Two works have been especially important in discussions of Macaulay's war fiction: her World War I pacifist conversion novel, *Non-Combatants and Others* (1916), and her postwar novel about life in London's bombsites, *The World My Wilderness* (1950). While these novels are well deserving of the critical attention they have received, this chapter shifts our focus toward Macaulay's writing during the 1930s, which witnessed the growth of her activism, discouragement at its ineffectiveness, and culmination in her despair-filled Spanish Civil War novel *And No Man's Wit* (1940).

Written mostly during 1939 into the beginning of 1940, *And No Man's Wit* offers a compelling expression of pacifism in crisis, and as such registers a perceptible mood within much of the peace movement at this time. While Hitler was the most obvious and perhaps most decisive factor in the eventual decline of peace groups, the biggest initial challenge to pacifist values came from Franco and the events of the Spanish Civil War. Spain put to the test arguments about workable nonviolent options for repelling fascist aggression, and this growing uncertainty and doubt haunt Macaulay's novel. She was a vigorous campaigner against war from a platform of widely read journalism in numerous periodicals and her sponsorship in the Peace Pledge Union. Though she remained sympathetic to pacifism for the rest of her life, the late 1930s and early 1940s saw a modification of her absolutism. *And No Man's Wit* signals this change not as a sharp reversal but through its unsettling attempt to dwell fully in a state of political ruins, suggesting this move as the most responsible place for the activist at a loss for nonviolent alternatives.

This absorbing but neglected work marks a crucial turning point for Macaulay, exchanging the lightly farcical tenor of her previous two novels for the lush and darkly political mode of her occasional fictions of the next decade. The novel's primary theme is failure—the failure of nonviolence to prevent war, the failure of war to secure lasting peace, and a growing anxiety about the impotence of creative expression facing brutal force. Completing the book was arduous, strained by writing under the threat of war, and she would admit: "I am dead sick of my novel but must push on . . . rent must be paid, alas, and these intimidating taxes. So I put down words, enjoying none of them" (qtd. in Smith, *Rose Macaulay*, 151–52). Escaping into fanciful writing about animals and mythical creatures was her wish, but she forged ahead despite personal and political failures around her. As Jane Emery aptly describes the novel, it was written "at the end of [Macaulay's] public activity in the peace movement and her private pursuit of enchanting oddity in myth and legend" and it attempts to "encompass both the viewpoints of a political world and the mysteries of a magical one" (ibid., 245).

This uneasy combination of the magical and political is but one of the novel's many aspects that generates its fragmentary and internally conflicted form, turning middlebrow conventions toward explicitly political ends. Its plot suggests several literary subgenres, including adventure stories, mysteries, political thrillers, and the dialogical "novel of ideas," but nearly all are discarded or incompletely realized. Flirting with genre throughout the novel does not quite morph into self-conscious metafiction but rather exemplifies the bridge between middlebrow and modernist styles. Though Macaulay has been an important figure in middlebrow scholarship, critics rarely mention her writing in relation to the peace movement.[2] *And No Man's Wit*, however, appropriates middlebrow styles toward a complicated and ambivalent peace witness that is doubtful—even despairing—of both pacifism and military force.

And No Man's Wit, which Alice Crawford calls "an anguished signing off" (*Paradise Pursued*, 130), is a profoundly transitional work, emerging as Macaulay's writing entered a distinctly new phase, her political beliefs and public activism began changing, and the peace movement itself headed into divisiveness and decline. As she wrote the novel through 1939 into the beginning of 1940, she disengaged herself from the PPU, lent her driving skills and Morris Minor (nicknamed "Elk") to the war effort as a volunteer ambulance driver, and challenged anyone who believed that Hitler could be stopped without warfare. (A letter from September 1940 anticipates dinner with John Middleton Murry, "a pacifist who says stop the war," and she schemes to "get out of him his alternative to war or surrender, if he has one" but concedes: "he is too snakey to be pinned down" [*LTS*, 110]). But she would also continuously associate herself with pacifism, even writing to Father Hamilton Johnson in 1951 that she was going to a lecture by Charles Raven, the former military chaplain turned founder member of the PPU and outspoken Christian pacifist, saying: "He is a pacifist. I think I am too" (*Letters to a Friend*, 72).

Her Spanish Civil War novel would be the last she published for ten years, after a highly prolific earlier career, and its bleakness makes it consistent with the mournful, elegiac fictions that followed—her short story "Miss Anstruther's Letters" (1942) and novel *The World My Wilderness* (1950). The death of her longtime lover, Gerald O'Donovan, and destruction of her possessions during the Blitz—most pointedly her personal and family library, letters from her lover, and research for a never completed literary bestiary—create additional layers of grief and trauma in these later works.[3] The turn toward personal and political brokenness, however, was already underway in *And No Man's Wit*. She was a great enthusiast for ruins, well before the Luftwaffe created what Beryl Pong calls the "urban unmapping" of London, and the many metaphorical and even hermeneutical uses she makes of ruins in her later writings are prefigured in *And No Man's Wit* ("Archeology," 92). Hers is not the optimistic, utopian vision of Huxley imagining a better world to come but rather a dwelling in the wrecked and broken parts of civilization, grieving what is lost and refusing to simply replace this loss with future-directed hopefulness. As she wrote to Virginia Woolf, who had recently read *And No Man's Wit*, "This war is thoroughly demoralizing . . . (a) sleepy (b) mentally disintegrated' as a result of it" (qtd. in Crawford, *Paradise Pursued*, 139).[4] Macaulay's fiction turns from the social critique that was central for prewar activist literature into a mournful, lamenting attention to ruins that extend across literal and symbolic levels. Absolute pacifism had been for her a matter of saving civilization against the barbarism of warfare and militarist ideologies. In accepting this war, she believed that near annihilation of civilization was better than certain, total annihilation under Nazism. But this nearly annihilated condition is not cause for rejoicing, and unlike Storm Jameson, whose hearty political presence remained intact after giving up her absolutist pacifism, Macaulay's war fiction seems as devastated as the physical ruins around her. In tracing Macaulay's progression from PPU activist to caretaker of ruins, I argue that her fiction suggests an alternative to the peace witnesses we have seen so far, an effort to live in wreckage and failure, uncomfortably accepting neither a utopian pacifism nor a salvific militarism.

"Trying to Shout above the Storm"

Like many of her generation, the First World War was greatly responsible for Rose Macaulay's conversion to pacifism. Working for a few months as a Voluntary Aid Detachment nurse in Great Shelford and witnessing the results of combat altered her perspective, and, as Sarah LeFanu writes, "tore into shreds the romantic veil through which she had viewed the fighting in Europe" (*Rose Macaulay*, 7). Her extremely popular, patriotic war poem of 1914, "Many Sisters to Many Brothers," voices a yearning for trench life denied to her because of her gender: "Oh, it's you that have the luck, out there in blood and muck" (qtd. in ibid., 105). She concludes that combatant men are lucky, while "for me . . . a war is poor fun." For half a year, beginning in May 1915, she witnessed more blood than her poetry had imagined, and she vented her feelings in the satirical, antiwar and overtly deromanticizing novel *Non-Combatants and Others*.[5] Published in spring 1916, her novel expresses anger at the tragedy of the war and, implicitly, at the death of her friend Rupert Brooke, while mocking the idealism of militarists and pacifists alike. The protagonist, Alix Sandomir, undergoes a pacifist conversion, experiencing personal and ideological losses that turn her into what Jane Emery calls a "surrogate mourner" for Macaulay (ibid., 149). Mourning and peace activism are intertwined in much of Macaulay's antiwar writing, but her tone just as often achieves a sharp, combative quality through its satire. The staunchest pacifist in the novel is Alix's mother, Daphne, whose uncompromising views are satirized as overly romantic. Watching her mother at an antiwar meeting, she finds herself "glad Daphne had a sense of humour, and didn't rant or sentimentalise. She could talk of the part to be played by women in the construction of permanent peace without calling them the guardians of the race or the custodians of life" (Non-Combatants, 180). The novel mocks sentimental feminist pacifism with almost as much vigor as it does militarist ideologies. Even Alix's convictions are presented with a measure of ironic distance, rendering her pacifist journey both earnest and naive. Alix tells her brother, Nicholas: "As I can't be fighting in the war, I've got to be fighting against it. Otherwise it's like a ghastly nightmare, swallowing one up. This society of mother's mayn't be doing much, but it's *trying* to fight war; it's working against it in the best ways it can think of. So I shall join it" (195). But undercutting her credibility, she adds, "Christianity, so far as I can understand it, is working against war too; must be, obviously. So I shall join the Church" (195). Nicholas observes skeptically that Alix will find that these pacifist and Christian institutions require certain "things to believe, you know" and that she will "have to believe them—some of them, anyhow" (196). Alix's commitment to an idea of peacemaking goes little further than her belief that she must be antiwar since she is one of the titular noncombatants, and both pacifism and religious faith are more convincing as generalized abstractions than as political or theological propositions. This scene between Alix and Nicholas sounds like a conclusion, but another chapter follows it, set on New Year's Eve, 1915, when the many confused characters of the novel celebrate an uncertain new beginning that Patrick Collier describes as a "pronounced pastiche of characters each locked in the cell of his or her own experience" (Modernism on Fleet Street, 144). The fragmentary ending suggests that "the novel is anything but assured at the viability of its own solution" to the problem of war despite Alix's emerging political clarity (ibid., 146). The internal criticism of pacifism expressed by this novel, however, seemed to matter less in its public reception than Macaulay's having produced during wartime fiction that seriously, if not uncritically, examined peace activism. It was a poor seller on its initial release, and one reviewer spoke for the general attitude by attacking the book for being insufficiently patriotic and "belittling those who fight" (qtd. in Emery, *Rose Macaulay*, 155). The novel did, however, secure Macaulay's place as an outspoken pacifist, even though this label did not account for her internal conflicts, and prepared the way for her later public role in the peace movement.

Following the war and throughout the 1920s, Macaulay produced a string of successful novels and became a regular among the Bloomsbury circles, sustaining a long if somewhat rivalrous and uneasy friendship with Virginia Woolf.[6] Her combination of popular success plus pacifist reputation led to her becoming one of the first female sponsors in the Peace Pledge Union. Macaulay's involvement with the PPU was brief but intense, caught in what she called Dick Sheppard's "white-hot enthusiasm," which swept the more cautious and timid and skeptical along with him" (qtd. in Scott, *Dick Sheppard*, 226). She was enchanted by his charismatic yet humble personality and his belief that "pacifism was an ardent adventure. It was a crusade. It might not work yet, he would admit, but it was worth a throw, worth taking a chance on" (ibid.). For eighteen months her campaigning against war on behalf of the PPU was prodigious. She used the platform of her literary celebrity to publish opinion pieces and public letters in the nation's most read venues as well as the PPU's official publication, *Peace News*. She also played a prominent role in the effort to get Sheppard elected rector of Glasgow University, running as a peace candidate against a field including Winston Churchill. For her part, Macaulay's celebrity generated much excitement among students in Glasgow, and a group of undergraduates campaigning against Sheppard tried to kidnap her on arrival and pelted her with wadded paper.[7] Despite this activity for Sheppard and the PPU, Macaulay was always a restless critic and uncomfortable with holding the party line, even though she agreed with the core values of the PPU and their antiwar stance. As Storm Jameson memorialized her, "Anatole France might have cast her for one of his rebellious angels, detached, searching, amused" (qtd. in Emery, *Rose Macaulay*, 206). The "detached" and "searching" aspects of her personality provided her with critical distance even when she was fully participating in the PPU. Macaulay wrote many essays for periodicals, including the *Listener*, the *Spectator, Horizon*, the *New Statesman and Nation*, and *Time and Tide*, and her large body of journalism demonstrates what Constance Babington Smith described as Macaulay's "great relish for argument and intellectual controversy, especially if the issues were ethical ones."[8] She could be pugnacious and unafraid of conflict, writing editorial columns defending pacifism in mainstream periodicals and biting criticisms of pacifist attitudes in *Peace News*.

Her "great relish for argument" was much on display during her time as a PPU sponsor, particularly in an article she wrote for *Time and Tide* in 1937, which was reprinted as one of the PPU's "open letters." This series, which included pamphlets such as Richard Bland's *An Open Letter to Men of Conscription Age and Their Parents*, presented topics designed to spark public discussion on difficult issues. Macaulay's *An Open Letter to a Non-Pacifist* takes head-on a series of objections to pacifism, beginning with a persuasive critique of the ways pacifism is defined narrowly or erroneously by nonpacifists who proclaim its implausibility. The straw man pacifisms that Macaulay attacks include three types: (1) the refusal to kill any human or nonhuman, (2) accepting only absolute passive resistance against oppression, and (3) believing that no fighting is worthwhile (OL, 1). Confining pacifism to these three varieties, as her nonpacifist interlocutor does, alleviates the need to dispute more robust versions; in anticipation of later pacifist typologies such as John Howard Yoder's *Nevertheless*, Macaulay contends that there are many more kinds of pacifism than her opponent's "three main brands."

With her characteristic punchiness, she dispenses with the first brand altogether, calling it a "mania [with] some other technical name, which I forget" (OL, 1). Likewise, she forcefully challenges the assumption that pacifism is synonymous with passivity, advancing a strain of thought that we have seen in Gerald Heard's writing on the "new pacifism" and also in the essays of Aldous Huxley, whose influence on her thinking can be strongly felt in this period. In June 1936, as Macaulay was beginning her PPU service, she encouraged her sister Jean to become "a full member of the Brotherhood" by joining with Dick Sheppard, whom she had recently met and found greatly compelling (LTS, 76).[9] Sheppard had admitted to her that in his own thinking, the biggest challenge for pacifism was what to do about "the bully who is attacking and killing the weaker power," but he encouraged her to look at a pamphlet describing "something called non-violent resistance" (ibid.). This letter indicates the freshness of these ideas within Macaulay's thought, and she alerts her sister to an enclosed pamphlet by Huxley on nonviolence that she encourages her to read. When writing her *Open Letter* in 1937, she had taken nonviolence much closer to heart, and she echoes Huxley in asserting that "coercion" of certain types is well within the bounds of pacifism and that a revolutionary utopianism underpins the active dimension of the pacifist vision: "But it is, of course, the pacifist's contention that the more civilised and pacific conditions of life which he is, on the positive side, bent on bringing about, and which include fairer economic distribution, and education in anti-nationalism and international understanding, as well as the relaxing of the tension of fear and hate which the disarming of even one great country in the name of civilisation should begin, will make attack less likely, not more, make aggressively-minded, war-like States less nervous, indignant, and inclined to pounce" (*OL*, 5). Her premise is that the best bulwark against international militarism is a fully civilized Britain that has abandoned the archaic and tribalistic practice of warfare, just as it has already progressed beyond other "barbarities of past ages . . . of slavery, of legal torture, of the burning of heretics and witches, of public floggings, brandings, pillories" (8). This utopian view, she concedes, is a "gamble" and may be assessable only in a "long run" perspective, but like A. A. Milne, she sees pacifism as a worthwhile gamble because the convention of war is so clearly flawed, and like Huxley, Jameson, Sassoon, and Woolf, she conceives of this long-term process as bound up with changes in international relations and the economy.

The troubling point that grew increasingly more vexing for her as the war with Hitler became unavoidable was her uncertainty about the effectiveness of the nonviolent action she learned about from Huxley and Sheppard. In 1936, shortly after becoming a PPU sponsor, she admitted being swayed by Gilbert Murray's assertion that increased armaments was the surest route to lasting peace, telling him "I am haunted by your saying that you thought the advocates of complete pacifism here were doing harm; it is a fearful thought, that I often have" (qtd. in Smith, *Macaulay*, 140). She would in the same year write about the Abyssinian crisis, telling her sister Jean that their brother "suggests that everyone should draw lots, and the shortest would have to shoot the Duce. I quite agree . . . I don't believe anything else can now stop this business" (*LTS*, 66). She half-jokingly offers herself, saying that she might be made an "Abyssinian saint" and have a statue erected for her tyrannicide.

These moments of questioning absolute pacifism and the effectiveness of nonviolence never quite left her, though her arguments in the *Open Letter* are still forthrightly in favor of pacifism. One element of the essay, however, has often been misconstrued by critics looking to demonstrate the inconsistency of her views. She writes with obvious impatience in response to her opponent's supposition that violence is equivalent across all settings, declaring: "Speaking for myself, if some one were to attack and try to rob or injure me, or if I saw him attacking some weaker person, I should endeavour by all means (though probably unsuccessfully) to knock him down" (*OL*, 3). This statement of her convictions is an amusing handling of the classic puzzler supposed to stymie pacifists: "What would you do if someone tried to hurt one of your loved ones?"[10] Expressing a view shared by many subsequent readers, Babington Smith takes this belligerent moment as a sign of the "vacillating nature of Rose's pacifism" (*Macaulay*, 140). However, this judgment relies too heavily on a rigid conception of pacifism, similar to the kind Macaulay attacks throughout her *Open Letter*. Her argument provides a clear example of the way pacifism includes a range of positions rather than a fixed point at one end of a spectrum in the use of force. While the Huxley/Heard/Gregg strain in the PPU was undoubtedly disinclined toward individual physical violence within a broader political pacifism, more pragmatic voices in the peace movement formulated situational approaches to reducing violence. Prefiguring recent work by strategists such as Rory Miller and Gene Sharp, the first systematic academic treatment of achieving political goals nonviolently was Clarence Marsh Case's *Non-Violent Coercion: A Study in Methods of Social Pressure* (1923), in which Case critiques pacifist reluctance to use force of any kind and for conflating personal and collective nonviolence: "there is a marked tendency for peace advocates to assume that what is true of *personal* non-resistance is likewise true of group non-resistance, which does not necessarily follow. The result is that many true friends of peace are hanging back from the movement to enforce peace by means of world organization. This failure . . . is rooted in the erroneous opinion, held by such friends of peace, that Christian non-resistance requires the rejection of physical force under all circumstances in human affairs" (7).[11] Though I am not contending that Macaualy's *Open Letter* has anything like the scholarly and theoretical rigor of Case's massive book, her distinction between personal and political violence as well as her recognition that violence can be "scaled"—knocking down the aggressor rather than killing him—is perfectly consistent within the spectrum of pacifist positions. And, as we will see, this problematic relationship between individual and collective nonviolent action became a point of debate within *And No Man's Wit*.

Though some of the specific arguments she presented in her *Open Letter* grew less persuasive to her—particularly her claim that civilized behavior could be a bulwark against foreign aggression—and though she would formally separate herself from the PPU, Macaulay continued wrestling with her essay's underlying questions. As Emery claims, "the eight pages of the pamphlet set forth concerns which were to dominate her thought for the rest of her life: Is there hope that civilization will win out over the barbarism that has periodically overrun it throughout history? Can we reasonably believe that . . . humanity can progress morally?" (*Rose Macaulay*, 250). These questions, and particularly the problematic dichotomy of "civilization versus barbarism," become the crux of Macaulay's intellectual and political thought in her several books following the *Open Letter*.

She further developed this concern about English social regression in her essay "Aping the Barbarians," included in the collection *Let Us Honour Peace* (1937), published by Richard Cobden-Sanderson along with contributions by PPU dignitaries such as Dick Sheppard, Charles Raven, Vera Brittain, and Gerald Heard. With an echo of Leonard Woolf's diagnosis from *Quack, Quack!* that the deepest form of primitive barbarism was to be found among the neopagan worshippers of Mussolini and Hitler, Macaulay writes that "A nation at war is a nation dragooned into acceptance of the Fascist state" ("Aping," 14). By going to war with an "uncivilized" aggressor like the fascist nations, England and all its peaceminded, democratic citizens will enter a "sinister suicide pact, all set to kill the thing they love. Wars to end war only give war a fresh lease of life" (15). Among those beloved things threatened by war is the English language itself. In her Hogarth Press pamphlet *Catchwords and Claptrap* (1926), she anticipated Orwell's celebrated "Politics and the English

Language" (1946) by claiming that political discourse mangles English with a "tendency to magnify" that emerges during "wars, revolutions, and other general human troubles," leading politicians into "slip-shod cant and invective" (*Hogarth Essays*, 117–18). She later credits Huxley for criticizing wartime euphemisms, such as "resisting the enemy" and engaging in "self-defense," when we mean things much more disastrous and bloody (*OL*, 8). Respectable talk of war, she argues, gives this "lunatic civilization destroyer" an "added danger, since it entraps the good, and is haloed by their honourable intentions ("Aping," 15). When we "let decent people themselves accept [war]," she writes, "it begins to wear a plausibly sanctimonious air, as if a cannibal orgy were to be attended by bishops and got up to look like a church service" (ibid.). Refusing to sanctify military violence through measured language and euphemism, and refusing to participate in brinksmanship and the "vicious circle" of "acting like savages because other people do" is central to her antiwar mission (ibid., 16). With these essays, Macaulay pins her hopes for peace on a civilizing impulse capable of rising above belligerent nations—a hope that becomes increasingly shaky with the mounting aggressions throughout Europe.

The last book-length work she completed during her time with the PPU, explicitly devoted to peace activism in defense of civilization, was *All in a Maze* (1938), an anthology of "prose and verse" compiled by Daniel George [Bunting] "with some assistance" (as the title page demurely puts it) "from Rose Macaulay." Macaulay's introduction to the volume is a brisk, witty, and sarcastic overview of the history of Western thought about war since the Greeks. Her paragraphs on Christianity offer several digs at Saints Augustine and Aquinas, who justified war in keeping with the newly imperial scope of their religion, while noting that in her own age, the "'unfortunate' early Christian view [that is, pacifism] seems, in fact, to be increasingly edging in again, religion joining hands with good sense and humanity to protest against the long-drawn-out English adventure in France" (*All in a Maze*, 9). After surveying the types of opposition and affirmation one finds in the varied writings on war, she tells us that "we arrive at the frightful period 1914–1918, of which we have made a scrapbook by itself, which may be omitted by the squeamish, though those interested in human nature will find here matter for study . . . The maze has thickened to an intolerable sad mess and we are all lost in it" (14).

This sense of being lost in a maze since the Great War offers a metaphorical, formal concept for the condition of perpetual war. From the midst of this maze, Macaulay and George's anthology seeks to be a testament for peace, demonstrating the wealth of antiwar sentiment throughout Western history like a stockpile of evidence for the breadth and consistency of pacifism over and against the commonly held view that all of history is a procession of wars, their precursors, and their aftermaths.

As it happens, *All in a Maze* was criticized by her publisher for seeming too much like an apology for appeasement, and Macaulay's postscript dubiously insists that an "ignoble peace," however bad, is better than war (16). She would eventually distance herself from this claim, but its central dilemma consumed much of her thinking and writing for many years: how can one live with the costs of an impossible choice between ignoble peace and barbaric war? Macaulay's love of collecting is on display in her peace anthology and other works, such as *The Minor Pleasures of Life* (1934) and *Personal Pleasures* (1936), which become virtual storehouses of things she valued, standing as evidence of the civilization she wished to defend from collapsing into war. Building up collections as material witnesses to civilization and arguing for pacifism while nationalist militarisms escalate became increasingly futile, but even at the height of her peace activist days, the feeling of futility was never completely absent. While completing *All in a Maze* and surveying centuries of antiwar writing, she wrote to her coeditor: "It's like trying to shout above the storm, or stem Niagara with bare hands, or like frail human voices among a jungle of wild beasts" (qtd. in Emery, *Rose Macaulay*, 254). The weather, water, and animals are natural conditions, unstoppable because they are not susceptible to arguments or art, intellect or emotions. War, it seemed to Macaulay in 1938, imposes itself as one of these forces of nature, continually decried throughout human history and perennially emerging as normative rather than aberrational. Much like Jameson's description of peace work as akin to children "throwing sand against the wind," Macaulay sought metaphors of futility to capture the experience of resisting insurmountable forces (*JN*, 326).

Though the minutes of the PPU meetings record her official resignation from membership on March 14, 1938, Macaulay continued to debate committed members about their stances toward the war, Nazi Germany, and British foreign policies.[12] As late as October 1939, Macaulay was still campaigning against war, as Virginia Woolf discovered when she found Macaulay that month in a full-throated antiwar rant. Angelica Bell later described this scene: "Rose Macaulay was screeching in the London Library, holding up passers-by with questions about L[eonard Woolf]'s views on the war, until V[irginia] had to draw her aside . . . she is all for peace" (Lee, *Virginia Woolf*, 679). Woolf's run-in with Macaulay, though potentially exaggerated in the retelling, still reveals Macaulay's vigorous engagement in war debates—a vigor she expressed just as fully when criticizing other pacifists. As the war progressed, the PPU struggled with public perception that their pacifism was really collusion with Hitler. Indeed, it became known that Aryan supremacist groups such as the Nordic League, as well as members of (or sympathizers with) the British Union of Fascists, used the PPU as cover for pro-Nazi agitation.[13] Nazism, as Macaulay saw it, was corrupting honest peace work, and critical debate within the PPU was essential for maintaining the fight against war without enabling enemy aggressions. "Damn the Nazis," she wrote, "they are persecuting us all, befuddling our minds and dominating our imaginations and making pacifism impossibly difficult" (qtd. in Smith, *Macaulay*, 145). In the spirit of this debate, and with an effort toward clarifying the pacifist imagination, Macaulay wrote two provocative essays in May 1939 for *Peace News* under their "Speaking Personally" heading, in which she claims: "Occasionally, when reading some letters in *Peace News*, I (and others) half think we have got hold of the *Blackshirt* by mistake" (qtd. in Brittain, "Letter").[14] Though this comment has often been taken out of context as proof that the PPU and the BUF had become synonymous in the late 1930s, Macaulay's criticisms were directed at PPU leaders, pressing them [to get their house in order. Hangers-on with pro-Nazi sympathies were distracting from the true aims and intentions of the organization's official policies, she argues, and the PPU's willingness to accept support from all comers has had a deleterious effect. This charge provoked a series of responses, including letters from Vera Brittain, who endorsed Macaulay's criticisms, calling them "a friendly warning" and a valid critique from a sympathetic voice rather than slander from a hostile opponent (ibid.). Tenaciously pursuing this debate, Macaulay responded to Brittain's defense of building connections across national boundaries, asking pointedly whether a pacifist might be inadvertently strengthening Nazism in "betraying its victims by apparent condonation of cruelty"

(Macaulay, "Letter"). Her unresolved quandary was this: "Where to draw the fine line between friendliness to a nation and apparent excusal of the behaviour of their government—that is the question; and it is one that can and should be discussed by pacifists. Perhaps other pacifists feel clearer about it than I do" ("Letter," 9). Noticeable in this exchange is her effort to keep pushing a pacifist group toward better thinking and actions, regarding herself as a pacifist though unable to commit to PPU membership, and believing that more deeply engaged dialogue within a political group is indispensable to its success. Her essays and letters in *Peace News* did indeed propel the debate, which continued in its pages for many months, and that argumentative spirit was a fixture during the height of her antiwar activism.

The shift in Macaulay's politics was motivated by her belief that Hitler was an even greater threat to civilization than war, but her accepting the need for this particular war did not lead her to conclude that violence would restore civilization whole and intact. The fiction she produced between 1940 and 1950 gives evidence of a torturous, even traumatized struggle to come to grips with the failure of pacifist war prevention efforts and the hopelessness of a world in which violent conflict is more chronic and endemic than any recourse to "civilization" can overcome. But the competing forces of civilization and barbarism remained the central preoccupation of her fiction, and through this dichotomous framework she explored her feelings of social, political, and personal failure.

Spain as a "Challenge to Pacifism"

Civilization versus political ruins—in her *Open Letter*, Macaulay proclaimed: "The situation seems urgent" because "if civilization, even such as it is, is to go under hatred and lies, blown to bits by crashing hordes of bombing planes, as it is even now being blown to bits in Spain, it is going to be pretty difficult to put the pieces together again" (OL, 8). For some members of the conflict, the destruction seemed liberating, as the anarchist Buenaventura Durruti boasted, "We are not afraid of ruins, we are going to inherit the earth. The bourgeoisie may blast and ruin their world . . . But we carry a new world in our hearts."[15] That redemptive view of war cannot be found in Macaulay's writings about Spain. Instead,

Spain is the testing grounds for what is coming, and Macaulay fears that "Culture will be gone, barbarism will reign" (8).

For many in the British peace movement, the Spanish Civil War presented the first major obstacle to maintaining an absolute pacifism. George Orwell, who had been a signatory of the PPU's pledge in 1936, found in Spain later that year that his pacifism was no longer tenable.[16] As Stanly Weintraub observes, "suddenly Spain made the pacifist stance seem obsolete. Writing and fighting had become, for many, inseparable" (*Last Great Cause*, 9). Before the Spanish war, the Italian invasion of Abyssinia had galvanized Huxley and others, calling forth a wave of arguments about how to deal nonviolently with an aggressor state. But this event, disturbing though it was, could still be understood within the framework inherited from World War I, the nineteenth-century model of territorial disputes shaped by imperialism. Richard Overy has also shown that Italy's conquest (like Japan's attack on China) was perceived as "[taking] place in distant and exotic locations" and "not on Europe's doorstep, as was Spain" that presented "the contest between democratic civilization and fascism" ("Saving Civilization," 188). Spain was something else, not just because it was an internal conflict but because the combatant forces were at war over ideologies that had been creeping into Europe throughout the interwar period and were strong portents of the war to come. The new era of total war was officially inaugurated in Spain, and along with this devastation a host of competing viewpoints made the Spanish Civil War an event bigger and more significant than just an intranational power struggle.[17]

For anyone involved in the peace movement, the war in Spain became a test case for articulating the moral or rational basis of pacifism and for applying theories of nonviolence in an instance of active military violence and ideologically driven aggression. Debates were fierce within peace organizations about official policies that might best respond to the war. In 1936 Herbert Runham Brown, who spent two years in prison during the First World War for his refusal to fight or even to do alternative service and who later became the first secretary of the WRI, published *Spain: A Challenge to Pacifism*, a pamphlet in which he admitted to wavering in his hardliner position: "War resisters are as much opposed to tyranny and injustice as they are to war and violence and it is possible that some in the hot blood of their indignation might find it difficult to restrain themselves from taking up arms, but on cooler reflection with their previous training, I have little doubt but that they would refrain. If they did not, at least their error would be more pardonable than if they had betrayed their principles by accepting the cold blooded preparations for the slaughter as in an international war" (6). Brown goes on to say that he would have no problem supplying food for the people, even though he knows that this would support the violent effort. He notes that he might be seen as inconsistent, but he quips: "I have yet to learn that consistency is an absolute virtue" (ibid., 7). For an activist such as Brown, a staunch defender of pacifism who had suffered imprisonment and personal threats for his beliefs, to admit that some inconsistency might result from his compassion for fighting men suggests how deeply this challenge penetrated.[18]

For its own part, the PPU initially responded to the Spanish Civil War much as Brown did, with Huxley's pamphlet *Pacifism and Civil War* (1936) even naming Brown's essay as the best resource for PPU members to consider (*Peace and Philosophy*, 37). Putting the situation in terms of its "challenge to pacifism" is open to criticism for remaining coldly intellectual, as if the death and suffering of this war were secondary to theoretical debates about how much assistance pacifists could entertain. But the core problem for Brown and others was that commitment to abstract ideas like peace, liberty, and civilization were conflicting with deep-seated revulsion to violence and close attachments to living people. Huxley's PPU pamphlet precisely identified the dilemma, but his implicit solution required an impossible turning back of the clock: "Once civil war has broken out it is extremely difficult for pacifists to do anything effective to stop the fighting or mitigate its horrors. Cures have little hope of being successful; the pacifist must concentrate above all on prevention" (36).

The literary intelligentsia was, broadly speaking, on the side of the Republicans — or at least opposed to the Francoist dictatorship and Fascist insurgency. The *Left Review* survey published as *Authors Take Sides on the Spanish War* (1937) shows the responses (or deliberate silences from the likes of James Joyce and Virginia Woolf) of two hundred writers to the query: "Are you for, or against, the legal government and people of Republican Spain? Are you for, or against, Franco and Fascism? For it is impossible any longer to take no side." That final demand—none may remain truly neutral—seemed to many writers the essence of the war in Spain. Despite the obvious survey bias inherent in the *Left Review*'s solicitation and categorization of the responses into "For the Government," "Against the Government," or "Neutral?," it remains an important record of attitudes toward the incipient war among several peace activist writers we have considered thus far.[19]

Improvisation with an effort toward changing or qualifying the polarized terms characterizes many of the responses, even when sympathies are squarely located among the champions of freedom, antifascism, and antimilitarism. Vera Brittain, contentiously categorized as "Neutral?," wrote: "As an uncompromising pacifist, I hold war to be a crime against humanity, whoever fights it and against whomever it is fought. I believe in liberty, democracy, free thought and free speech. I detest Fascism and all that it stands for, but I do not believe that we shall destroy it by fighting it" (Cunningham, *Spanish Front*, 229). In Brittain's attempt to circumvent the binary logic of the questionnaire, she explicitly names the underlying ideologies that she supports (liberty, democracy, etc.) and rejects (fascism and its concomitants), but just as clearly opposes warfare as a solution to this conflict. Huxley, though placed in favor of the Republicans, similarly attempts to change the terms of the discussion: "My sympathies are, of course, with the Government side, especially the Anarchists . . . As for 'taking sides'—the choice, it seems to me, is no longer between two users of violence, two systems of dictatorship . . . The choice now is between militarism and pacifism. To me, the necessity of pacifism seems absolutely clear" (54). Though not wishing to be mistaken for someone unsupportive of the warriors against fascism, Huxley shares with Brittain the basic view that violent responses to militant forces will only reproduce the violence inherent in those detested ideologies. Peace can only be achieved through peaceful means.

In Storm Jameson's response to the question, we can find a separation from Huxley and Brittain, naming even more forcefully than they the horrific nature of war but signaling her equally great hatred for Fascism: "This hideous war, which is murdering Spain and may let war loose again over the whole of Europe, is the deliberate act of the two Fascist dictators, and avowed by them as such. It is an act they will not hesitate to repeat. Civilisation, the civilisation of the mind and the heart, is threatened with utter ruin by this doctrine which exalts violence and uses incendiary bombs to fight ideas. For any writer to support it is plain treachery and worse, if there is anything worse" (226–27). Jameson's answer, in keeping with her writings of the late 1930s, shows the "twin devils" of war and Fascism in deadlock, and she vents her frustration and anger with particular vehemence at writers who might support Francoist violence. Also noteworthy is her use of two terms central to Rose Macaulay's thinking during these years: civilization and ruins. Fascism, with its repression through violence, makes ruination the only possible future for the civilized world. Though Jameson does not explicitly propose armed struggle as a strategy for preserving civilization, she noticeably does not turn the discussion—as Huxley and Brittain do—toward pacifism.

Differing from her peace movement peers, Macaulay's response was considerably terser: "Against Franco" (227). Rather than change the debate by emending the question, her brevity makes clear her basic view and avoids the entanglements of any suggestion about strategy or policy. The divisiveness of the Spanish conflict was a significant reminder that the common ground for peace activists—hatred of war and desire for its prevention—was a smaller space than was needed for large-scale unified action. As Macaulay would later describe this period in her historical survey *Life among the English* (1942), "the Spanish *pronunciamiento* split the British public; the fashionable continental tour was to government or rebel Spain, according to the tourist's political colour" (46–47). Even bourgeois tourism reflected political partisanship, and inconsistency within peace groups presented a troubling lack of organized response to a war that was all too eerily predicting the next.

British and American writers of all political stripes were drawn to Spain for its emblematic possibilities, as recent scholarship has shown.[20] Gayle Rogers and Patrick R. Query demonstrate that an array of British writers, including Stephen Spender, Graham Greene, and Evelyn Waugh, enacted "projects that aimed to 'speak' for Spain . . . through channeling foreign voices" (Rogers, *New Spain*, 164) and made of the civil war a "political workshop for Europe . . . in which the increasingly urgent questions of tradition and modernity, continuity and difference, order and freedom were contested on the ground, as well as in literature" (Query, *Ritual and the Idea*, 139). Lurking in many of these writers' speaking-for-Spain projects were problematic forms of racialist paternalism, Anglocentrism, and political, commercial, or creative opportunism, though these problems are much less pronounced in Rose Macaulay's foray into Spanish Civil War fiction. Though to some extent Macaulay does use Spain as a canvas for projecting her own personal and political problems, her novel rejects the didacticism that colored other attempts to enlist Spain for causes such as "the last-ditch stand of Christian civilization" or "the battle of social progress against entrenched interests of reaction and fascism" (Patterson, *Guernica*, 5).

In Macaulay's approach to her material, Spain becomes an opportunity to think through her own internal debates about peace and war; and, remarkably, her novel even troubles the civilization/barbarism binary she so heavily favored. When invoking this binary, she sometimes indulged her least savory moments of condescending racialism, as when she accuses men at war of being "like savage Hottentots, like murdering savages, like the barbarous beastly Indians and the cruel atrocious Spaniards of whom the Elizabethan pirate navigators, with rather smug disapproval, relate" (*OL*, 6). But this revulsion at the savagery of belligerents, not to mention her view of "atrocious" Spaniards, largely dissipated when she wrote *And No Man's Wit*, which adopts instead a mournful tone and a structure that accommodates a wide range of voices across the spectrum of political, racial, and gendered difference.

Middlebrow Fiction and Political Ruins

As the few critics who have attended to this neglected novel point out, *And No Man's Wit* has since its publication been overshadowed by other works, most notably Hemingway's blockbuster *For Whom the Bell Tolls* (which was also published in 1940), and fallen into obscurity like so many war-themed novels by women—even among academic readers best positioned to recover these works.[21] Even scholars who otherwise champion Macaulay's fiction often rate *And No Man's Wit* lower in her achievements than other novels. "It is a trudge," writes Sarah LeFanu (*Rose Macaulay*, 224), and Alice Crawford calls it "structurally unwieldy" and "a dreary book that tries to tackle the decade's political menaces head-on, yet gives the impression of knowing that the task is too great" (*Paradise Pursued*, 130).

What these complaints about the novel's structure and dark tone neglect is how well it conveys a sense of impasse, anguish, and failure. It also offers a sophisticated example of middlebrow fiction crafted for unmistakably political purposes with a plot that evokes elements of mystery, adventure, travelogue, and political thriller genres. The shrewd and redoubtable Dr. Kate Marlowe (a surrogate of sorts for Macaulay herself) goes to Spain searching for her son Guy, who has disappeared while fighting against Franco with the International Brigades. For two-thirds of the novel, this quest and the puzzlement over Guy's disappearance creates a narrative hook on which Macaulay hangs a great many scenes of conversation between the English liberal Dr. Marlowe and a host of characters taking various positions within the conflict. Jane Emery describes how successfully *And No Man's Wit* marshals Macaulay's "seemingly disparate findings . . . her detailed review of Spanish history and politics, her anti-war activism, her intermittent despair about humanity's inhumanity, her admiration for strong women, her love of bathing, her delight in travel, her engrossing study of strange, imaginary creatures, her belief in the loyalty of friendship, and her private guilt" (*Rose Macaulay*, 258). These many fascinations, fixations, pleasures, and pains emerge through the persistently embattled conversations that fill most of the book's pages. Structural unwieldiness is an understandable formalist criticism, but it relies too heavily on expectations about easily achieved, satisfying answers to the difficult questions the novel raises as well as an insistence on generic coherence and wholeness that the novel openly rejects.

One consequence of fresh scholarly energy around middlebrow writing is the recognition that easily digestible conventionality, the purview of low and middlebrow work, and avant-garde formal and ideological complexity, the realm of high modernism, are no longer impermeable domains. Melissa Sullivan has argued that Macaulay's "successful positioning of herself as a reputable and popular public intellectual" was a major factor in her middlebrow status, combining popular journalistic writings with engaging but not noticeably experimental fiction ("A Middlebrow Dame Commander," 168). *And No Man's Wit* thus appears as an exceptional case in her oeuvre in which she explored in fiction the peace activist dimension of her public intellectualism while testing the middlebrow readership's threshold for formal experimentation. This boundary crossing, as recent studies have shown, was more common than the stereotypical "middlebrow" label allows, and indeed, as Lassner, Rea, and Brassard note, the "recent outpouring of critical examinations of the middlebrow in turn allows re-examinations of modernism and shows that the terms themselves are contingent and indeterminate, and often fade into one another" ("Reading Sideways," 7).

With Macaulay's novel, the cross-pollination between middlebrow and modernist aesthetics emerges as familiar generic tropes raise readers' expectations only to leave them unfulfilled or constrained by insoluble political problems. Everything seems to be in ruins, even the fractured narrative form, which gives us a broken mystery plotline that flirts with but does not fully mutate into a political debate novel such as D. H. Lawrence's *Kangaroo* (1923) or a thriller à la Graham Greene. By using the search for Guy as a narrative hook—a romantic hero mysteriously lost in combat sought by his detective-like mother and attractive fiancée—Macaulay gives an alluring structure to what would otherwise be just a string of debates among characters with differing positions on the war in Spain and the state of politics in Europe. Once Guy finally turns up, however, the narrative loses its primary impetus, the MacGuffin that gave the plot its forward momentum, and the remainder of the novel emphasizes the lack of direction, clarity, and meaning that become its overall agenda. Guy's appearance is anticlimactic, emerging from shadows to reveal himself to Ramón, his old friend and now his mother's guide, and to inform him that he is no longer imprisoned in Burgos, having killed a prison guard and escaped into the hills with a group of gitanos (ANMW, 236–37). For several more chapters, Ramón allows Dr. Marlowe to pursue dead leads in hopes of finding Guy, but he finally buckles and tells her a version of what he knows. This revelation to Marlowe, even more than the particular argumentative stalemates within chapters, causes a collapse in the narrative tension and registers a bigger sensation of failure for her quest, the romantic plotlines, and even for the antifascist forces and the political future of Europe. The parables, mythical writing, historical debates, and genre fiction resist any easy synthesis that could suggest a totalizing discourse. *And No Man's Wit* even avoids the modernist impulse to "shore up fragments against ruins" that emerges later in Macaulay's work, when she brings the incantations of *The Waste Land* to the bombed-out rubble of *The World My Wilderness*. Instead, the novel enacts through its collapsing genres and intractable debates a sense of politics in ruins.

With *And No Man's Wit*, the confusion goes far deeper than *For Whom the Bell Tolls* or Orwell's *Homage to Catalonia* (1938). Though Hemingway and Orwell convey the political and moral ambiguities of the Spanish War, they share a projection of plainspoken, ruggedly masculine superiority over the material, as if their narrators could straighten everything out were they simply given the power to do so. Stan Smith has persuasively argued that the structural complexity of *And No Man's Wit* suggests a broader concern with the problems of history and the creation of national identities as Europe plunges into war. For Smith, "it is precisely the stratified confusion and incoherence of national consciousness which this novel takes as its central thematic," and "as Macaulay represents it, Spain with its fissiparous separatisms, is a world that's all in pieces, unlikely to be welded together by Franco's centralising grip" ("The Answer," 21, 23). Smith's analysis perceptively makes connections between the formal chaos of the novel and its larger concerns about Spanish (and broadly European) history, the role of the strong, liberal woman in engaging muddled political conflicts, and the capacity for and limits of resistance to Franco. These concerns culminate for Smith in "a world that is beyond ideological reclamation, that cannot be made to fit any of our faiths and factions, where the answer is not what we expect at all but something at once sour and bracing in its uncompromising difference" (ibid., 33). The bitter ending of the novel thus rebuffs the myriad competing claims of Spain's contentious warring parties, rising fascist militarism around Europe, and even the appeals of family and tradition.

A spectrum of views about the necessity and morality of warfare forms a current within many of the novel's debates, and there is no obvious victor among the narrative's various positions. Little certainty is achieved through these conversations, and in preventing any side to gain conversational victory, Macaulay avoids didacticism. Gone is the humorous satire of *Non-Combatants and Others*, and instead the characters are stymied in the face of active violence. Peace is greatly desired but seemingly unattainable. Thus, *And No Man's Wit* predicts the immersion in ruins that will consume Macaulay's imagination for many years to come. All of the debates in the book enact that ruined form, since they essentially go nowhere. Every ideological position appears dysfunctional, but no fixed point enables straightforward satire and the conflicts achieve no satisfying dialectical synthesis. One common strategy for novelists eschewing polemic in favor of fiction is to generate sympathies even for characters espousing positions certain readers might find repugnant. To some extent, Macaulay embraces this strategy, leading us to understand Ramón's motives while rejecting his opportunistic Francoism, but she never allows sympathy for individual characters to trump the pervading sense of political disarray and ideological devastation.

At one extreme is the fantastical and highly idealized pacifism of Ellen, Guy's erstwhile fiancée, who is quiet, aloof, and—we eventually learn—part mermaid. This surrealistic flourish has for some readers been the novel's only redeeming element, a "refreshing streak of fantasy," but Ellen also presents one of the clearest challenges to Macaulay's fragile pacifist values (Smith, *Macaulay*, 147).[22] Ellen dislikes the aridity of Spain and finds opportunities for bathing, exhibiting a strangeness that places her above the political fray. In a meeting about Guy with the "marquesa vieja," grandmother of Ramón and one of the "anti-Republicans of the old régime in feudal Aragón," Ellen is challenged: "Guy is a rather wicked young man, not so? He did not ought to join that impertinent brigade that formed itself to fight against Spaniards in Spain. Don't you agree, my child?" (ANMW, 94, 104). Ellen murmurs "I don't like any fighting," and the marquesa retorts, "Ah, you are pacifist. In Spain we don't have that" (104). Dr. Marlowe intervenes, saying "Ellen knows *nothing* of politics," and the conversation turns to the sea and Ellen's desire to swim at the Basque coast, much to the chagrin of her intended mother-in-law. For Stan Smith, this depiction of Ellen is Macaulay's renunciation of an impractical, "personal pacifism," and though this reading helpfully counters critics who find in Ellen the potential for redemption through fantasy, I would point out that Ellen is not merely discredited or satirized ("The Answer," 32). After all, the character is infused with her author's own great love of mythical creatures and water: "vaguely ichthyous and mer," was occasionally Macaulay's self-description (LeFanu, *Dreaming of Rose*, 24). Ellen, in the end, fails to fully reclaim her mythical ancestry and dies in a drowning accident, a casualty of the harshly realist world that cannot sustain her. Ellen thus embodies the predicament for antiwar values in Spain. Any version of pacifism that floats too ethereally above the conflict cannot affect its outcome, even if that magical separation is far more desirable and valuable than the blood-soaked reality it avoids. Yet the war also makes impossible the peace it hopes to defend.

While Ellen's character suggests a deeply idealized peace witness, rendered both compelling and implausible, Macaulay also includes direct commentary on her former peace organizations. Describing how easily one can become friends with people whose political views are atrocious, Dr. Marlowe's younger son Hugh explains his friendship with a Portuguese Fascist: "he wasn't a bad kind of man. I rather liked him, except when he talked Fascist—then we all treated him as a ghost and pretended he wasn't there till he stopped; that's a very useful technique invented by a man who belonged to the Peace Pledge Union; he called it non-violent resistance, and tried to put it across us that it would work on a mass scale on the enemy. That's where those people can't see straight, but it really does work with individuals" (ANMW, 10). Macaulay's growing interest in nonviolence, which we have traced from her initial meeting with Dick Sheppard to her espousal of Huxleyan concepts in her *Open Letter to a Non-Pacifist*, reaches a climax in this description (presumably referring to Richard Gregg's *The Power of Non-Violence*), which she places in the mouth of the intellectual communist Hugh. Mass- scale nonviolence is rejected in this speech, with a curious inversion of Macaulay's own claims in her *Open Letter*, which were more hopeful about stopping international aggression and accepted small- scale violence when facing personal attacks. With Hugh, nonviolence is a useful tool for keeping conversations civil with otherwise agreeable people whose political beliefs incline toward ranting. At the macro level, however, the novel gives little hope for nonviolent action.

Even Dr. Marlowe, who in many respects functions as the fixed center in a welter of moral ambiguities, becomes at last an expression of pacifism in crisis. Her liberal idealism is challenged by the Spanish conflict's imperviousness to her will, her charms, her intellect, or her demands for justice. On learning that the search for Guy is over and that he will not be returning with them, Dr. Marlowe decides to leave Spain, fearing the onset of a full-blown European war. Hugh is disappointed by the news of the recently announced Nazi-Soviet Pact, and he sadly reflects that Stalin "sees which way the wind is blowing. If we had meant business, meant a real anti-Fascist war for democracy, he'd have backed us up. He's shown contempt for us; and rightly. It's the wrong war" (*ANMW*, 287). Dr. Marlowe replies: "All wars are probably the wrong wars" (ibid.). Her "probably" signals a trace of doubt, and she continues explaining why she is uneasy with the term "pacifist":

> Oh, what does one mean by pacifist? I think war is horrible and cruel and grotesque, of course, and belongs to the dark ages as much as the rack and thumbscrew do. But if you ask me, is nothing worse, I think it's worse to let more and more people be tortured and enslaved without protest—I mean effective protest. On the other hand, *is* war the only way to stop it, and have we tried all the others? Of course we haven't. You see, I don't know what I think; one's altogether confused. It would be simpler if one could be wholly pacifist. But the pacifists don't seem to have alternative ways to suggest of stopping the Nazis. And they *are* sometimes very silly. (287–88)

This speech adopts a voice very much like Macaulay's essays: thoughtful, punchy, complicated, and brutally honest. Echoes of her *Open Letter* remain in the charge that war is an outdated barbarism, but the questions about nonviolent alternatives posed at the end of her pamphlet now take over Marlowe's thoughts, and the shortcomings of particular peace activists are seen as even more ridiculous. The bind seems to be that war is nearly the worst thing possible, but no viable alternative can be found, and so a return to the "dark ages" is what we are in for—that, and a need to dwell in confusion.

But Dr. Marlowe does not have the last word, and her exit from the novel allows the final scene to consider another debate about the coming war with the three former Oxonians—Guy, Armand, and Ramón—arguing about value of fighting. Their English, French, and Spanish nationalities give them unique voices in a microcosm of the international conflict that is brewing. For Ramón, Francoism is a means to an end, preserving the oligarchy from which he benefits, and he rejects Armand's charge that he must "as a loyal Franquisto, back Monsieur Hitler" (339). Instead, he claims, he will "back none of you," carrying the attitude "of a detached philosopher, musing over the follies of mankind in the Bar

Basque" (ibid.). Armand proclaims himself on the side of France, not as "a patriote barbare, or marching about singing the 'Marseillaise,'" but still embracing French nationalism against foreign invasion (342). Guy rejects both of these paths, saying that he would "rather have a war of ideologies—a disagreeable word, I call them doxies myself," though he concedes that this particular national war is as close as one can get to fighting an ideology (ibid.). The argumentative weight seems tilted toward Guy's views, a suggestion that fighting against corrupt ideologies would be the best solution, but this idealistic view of war is also revealed as hopeless. As Armand counters, war cannot "defeat totalitarianism," it can only "defeat Germany, and kill several million Germans, French, and British . . . it can't kill opinions or cure a disease" (347). Even the most appealing and justifiable parts of the coming war are tainted with failure and confusion.

Though the novel ends with threats of ruination and worse things to come, a flicker of possibility lights its last moments. Guy finds that the hatred he had felt for Ramón has evaporated, but around them "the world was acid and sour with hate, fat with greed, yellow with the triumph of the strong and the rich" (351). Alongside this image, the narrator declares: "The answer would appear to be a lemon" (ibid.). Despite the "nuisance coming tomorrow," however, there is modest reassurance from momentary peaceable togetherness: "Still, here they sat and talked, three friends together in the Bar Basque (ibid.). Conversations such as these are not much to go on, rather far from a vision of renewal or redemption, but they suggest the civilized living that Macaulay desired so greatly and a mode of staying close to the ruins without unwarranted optimism or total despair.

Aerial Bombardment and "Ruins on the Brain"

Macaulay's focus in *And No Man's Wit* is on political gridlock in Spain rather than the now iconic images of aerial bombardment, but new ruins made by bombs would become a consuming passion that was equally painful and pleasurable for her in the years after publishing this novel. In her art criticism/travelogue *Pleasure of Ruins* (1953), she would conclude with "A Note on New Ruins," observing that they "are for a time stark and bare, vegetationless and creatureless; blackened and torn, they smell of fire and mortality" (*Pleasure*, 453). That mortal smell haunts her even as she relishes their aesthetic pleasures, and the inescapable feeling of death that lurks in the bombsites becomes her fixation, as she observes in a self-mocking comment about her series of books on ruined places: "People will begin to think I have ruins on the brain" (*Dearest Jean*, 215n1). Ruins became for her a sign of the end of civilization, but also a place to dwell, a kind of in-between space within the civilization/barbarism binary.

Her essay "Consolations of the War," written in January 1941 as a morale booster for the war-stricken readers of the *Listener*, surveys the "rather melancholy consolations" of living through the Blitz, and she returns to guiding themes of civilization versus barbarism in claiming that her earlier predictions about warfare in the middle 1930s were now coming true. This war is "a grotesquely barbarous, uncivilized, inhumane and crazy way of life to have had forced on us by a set of gangsters who are making us use their own weapons and practise their own horrid incivilities—as if we were jungle savages like themselves instead of twentieth-century men and women who had hoped war to be for ever outlawed" ("Consolations," 549). The "fresh ruins" caused by this war tempt her with purely aesthetic appeal, but the neoromantic impulse fades and she bluntly states: "Ruin is indiscriminate and stupid" (550). Six months later, the Luftwaffe bombed Luxborough House, destroying her flat and all her possessions, and the trauma of this event plus the anguish over her lover, who was confined to his deathbed was registered in her short story "Miss Anstruther's Letters," originally published in Storm Jameson's anthology *London Calling: A Salute to America* (1942). This story is shaded with guilt and anxiety and blurred by a traumatic haze, and its key features are the descriptions of ash and ruin, the direct results of war, and a subtle plea for the end of mass bombing.

Returning to Spain in 1947 as part of her research for the travelogue *Fabled Shore* (1949), she reported to her cousin other scenes of war ruins: "The destruction of the civil war in Catalonia is sad; old Gothic churches burnt down by anarchists all over the place. Some are empty shells; some are already rebuilt or nearly so—but what is the use of that?" (*Dearest Jean*, 206). There is little pleasure for her in these ruins, and no sign of coming redemption. Even the idea that churches are being rebuilt seems to her not a sign of hope but of pointless activity. In light of failed pacifism and persistent reminders of civilization's decline, she held her course with attention and thoughtfulness, expressed through writing and action, to care for and tend the ruins.

CHAPTER 5

Thinking as Fighting in Virginia
Woolf's *The Years* and *Three Guineas*

The other writers in this study were clearly identified with the peace movement, making many of their most important contributions to antiwar activism under the auspices of the Peace Pledge Union. With Virginia Woolf, it may seem that we are encountering another case altogether: a person who refused to join organizations even if she valued their objectives. Though conventional wisdom has mostly moved beyond the view of Woolf as a disengaged aesthete—even mentioning this portrayal of her in Quentin Bell's and Leonard Woolf's later reflections has become something of a critical cliché—it is still not commonly accepted that her political engagement went further than her occasional lectures and words on a page, notwithstanding their provocative and committed energies.[1] Gone is the image Forster spurned, the "the Invalid Lady of Bloomsbury" (*Virginia Woolf*, 3), but even Jane Marcus, a fierce opponent of that image and longstanding champion of Woolf's triune values of "pacifism, feminism, socialism," can bluntly assert: "Woolf was not an activist."[2]

Marcus explains this judgment in a way that justifies her central contention; Woolf was not an activist so long as we define "activist" as someone working in the mode of the suffragette movement that Woolf witnessed but did not (militantly and bodily) join.[3] Street corner demonstrations, broken windows, imprisonment, and hunger strikes were not a part of her political record, and the embracing of *A Room of One's Own* (1929) and *Three Guineas* (1938) as crucial texts of feminist activism later in the twentieth century rests a bit uneasily with their author's reluctance to employ physical demonstration in her own praxis. As she stated in her diary in May 1940, testing a thought she would later articulate in published writing and lectures: "This idea struck me: the army is the body: I am the brain. Thinking is my fighting" (D, 5:285). At the time of this comment, during the ill-ease of the "long 1939," when the Blitz had not begun and the "phoney war" was still underway, Woolf recorded in this same entry a range of fraught emotions and conversations.[4] Leonard, to his wife's chagrin, announced his plan to join the Local Defence Volunteers (later the Home Guard) in case of invasion but eventually decided against this, and their conversation turned to shared suicide amid the background reports of Germany's conquest in the Netherlands. Self-inflicted death rather than either submission or physical retaliation while Europe's Low Countries fall to Hitler—this thought establishes Woolf's "striking idea," put into military language, that she must fight using her mind.

Plotting suicide instead of determining some other, more overtly defiant course, and refashioning combat as a mental activity have been among the more controversial of Woolf's positions, both in her own lifetime and for later readers. Of special interest in this critical discussion is *Three Guineas*, which has garnered a full spectrum of judgments, from being clumsily "un-political" to being one of the finest ever testaments against fascism to espousing views both "offensive" and "obscene."[5] While I register these controversies in this chapter, my central purpose is neither to excuse Woolf for the limitations in her political vision nor to make claims for some hitherto undetected "realism" in her *Three Guineas* proposals. Instead, by situating *The Years* and *Three Guineas* within the context of the British peace movement, I argue for an appreciation of Woolf's centrality to debates about peace activism and nonviolence.

After staking her position in the 1920s that art should not succumb to politics, as she claimed it had done in novels by Edwardian social realists, her own writings of the 1930s grew more explicitly politically engaged, despite a deepening sense that her vision of striving for peace and social justice was destined for failure.[6] We have seen versions of this failure in previous chapters—the inability of the peace movement and antiwar fellow travelers to prevent war, and the ineffectual efforts toward wide-scale nonviolent social changes and political schemes that could thwart oppression and rectify injustices. Within these broader failures, Woolf's work is one more casualty of the conflict between passionately held idealism and situational exigencies.

In November 1936, as the International Brigades were fighting in Madrid, Woolf sketched her thoughts in a brief but agonized essay for the *Daily Worker* called "Why Art To-day Follows Politics." Her portrait of the artist, though displaced onto sculptors, musicians, and poets rather than her own novelistic craft, is acutely conscious of her desire to separate creative work from political agendas, and the essay was accompanied by an editorial note distancing the paper from Woolf's views.[7] Separating art and politics, however, is impossible, she admits, because she is compelled by "voices" saying that society in crisis can no longer protect artists, might need them for more useful things such as "making airplanes" and "firing guns," and wants to press them into glorifying state-sponsored "gospels" such as Fascism and Communism (*E*, 6:77). The pages of the *Daily Worker* were filled with images and reports of the bombings in Spain, making all the more pointed the incongruity of her desire for art unbeholden to politics.[8] Undesired yet unavoidable, these political pressures could not be shirked simply by asserting artistic independence, and the works she published in the wake of this thinking exhibit her struggle to achieve a politically committed art that she could accept.

The Years, which she often called a failure—even a "deliberate" failure—seemed to Woolf to rest too precariously on the narrow ridge between authentically artful literature and the sermonizing she despised in writers such as D. H. Lawrence and Aldous Huxley (*D*, 5:65). As she noted while reading Huxley's edition of Lawrence's letters: "it's the preaching that rasps me . . . Art is being rid of all preaching" (*D*, 4:126). Sidestepping her self-deprecation, we might find in the idea of "deliberate failure" the crux of her dilemma: art in these years cannot avoid political commitment, but it always strains when placed under the weight of an explicit agenda.[9] Only a deliberate-yet-doomed effort to work within this troubling dissonance will do, even though it cannot hope to fully succeed, at least not to the artist's own satisfaction. The aesthetic quandary Woolf faced in struggling with an inevitable failure situates her in good company alongside other peace activists of the 1930s, similarly working with limited means to prevent a war most Europeans assumed was unavoidable.

Skepticism about Woolf as an activist, as well as an assumption that the "outsider" imagined in *Three Guineas* is a determinative label for her, has obscured her place within the broader peace movement. Looking first at the ways Woolf did in fact participate in peace activist networks adds richer context for her arguments in *Three Guineas*, a text I analyze alongside neglected contemporary works in its genre. Despite criticisms of its social analysis and dismissal of its political theory as idealistic utopianism, *Three Guineas* remains a substantial effort to advocate strategic nonviolence. Turning to *The Years* in light of this theory of nonviolence, I argue that Woolf enacted a literary peace witness through a novel covering fifty years of British history, a work whose elliptical and recursive formal features enable pacifist social critique. Anna Snaith calls *The Years* a "quietly revolutionary novel" that is concerned with "new ways of living, new forms of social organisation" (introduction to *The Years*, xliii). My argument investigates those "quiet" elements and their importance to Woolf's nonpropagandistic, radical pacifist literary activism.

Between "Weevil" and Activist

Borrowing a device familiar from "Mr. Bennett and Mrs. Brown," in which the novelist's skill with characterization melds with the essayist's development of a claim, Woolf describes the Cockney proprietor Mrs. Crowe, doyenne of a distinctly English residence that she eulogizes in "Portrait of a Londoner," published in December 1932: "Thus, to know London not merely as a gorgeous spectacle, a mart, a court, a hive of industry, but as a place where people meet and talk, laugh, marry, and die, paint, write and act, rule and legislate, it was essential to know Mrs Crowe" (*E*, 5:596–97). We see Woolf's lyricism in a sentence built out of mounting phrases, encapsulating that city feeling reminiscent of *Mrs. Dalloway* and arriving, as that novel so often does with Clarissa, at the figure of a woman past her youth and richly significant without becoming purely mythical. In this list of things comprising a life—the passage of seasons, mundane connections and conversations, the creation of art, and the workings of government—Woolf shows in brief the salient features of the London she apprehends. These mundane things are the basis for the "moments of being" she later described in "A Sketch of the Past," the small stuff of life that matters more than grandiose ideologies such as nationalism and religion (*MOB*, 70). This "portrait" is the last of six essays she published in *Good Housekeeping* to describe the "London scene," and her inspiration for this project was partly sparked by an interaction with Aldous Huxley, whose transformation from scourge of the masses to compassionate sage was underway.[10] Noting all the global sites of poverty and social change visited by Aldous and Maria Huxley, Woolf reveals in her diary feelings of inadequacy, that she was merely subsisting "like a weevil in a biscuit" (*D*, 4:11). "Lord, how little I've seen, done, lived, felt, thought" she writes, "compared with the Huxleys—compared with anyone" (*D*, 4:11). Thus, in February 1931, we find Woolf in a mood of political self-doubt, and as Alice Wood persuasively suggests, this moment can be considered a starting point for the new, explicitly political writing that would occupy the last phase of her career (*Late Cultural Criticism*, 33–36).

Though Woolf was never to be seen corralling citizens for antiwar activities in the style of Dick Sheppard or Vera Brittain, the repeated description of her role as something other than an activist neglects the ways she did give political lectures, write for politically committed journals, and lend her name and celebrity to antifascist organizations.[11] This is not to say that she found these opportunities always congenial; most often she eschewed formal ties with antifascist groups and rebuffed invitations for deeper commitment, such as Storm Jameson's requests for assistance with the International PEN. But despite her personal discomfort and fear of contaminating art with didacticism, she still used her fame toward peace advocacy alongside the other writers in this study.

It is no small irony to find Woolf envying Huxley's position at the beginning of 1931, given how frequently she disparaged his writing style and political activity. While tangling with revisions to *The Years* in 1935, she expressed in her diary disdain for his fictional mode: "A very difficult problem; this transition business. And the burden of something that I wont call propaganda. I have a horror of the Aldous novel: that must be avoided" (*D*, 4:81).[12] Selecting Huxley as her literary bête noire is especially intriguing given their friendship, shared commitment to pacifism, and Huxley's own struggles at the time to write his modernist, pacifist novel *Eyeless in Gaza*, with its complex experimental form and explicit political agenda. Huxley and Woolf would continue crossing paths through the early 1930s as they became more deeply involved in antifascist causes. David Bradshaw has shown that two groups were particularly important in this regard—the International Association of Writers for the Defense of Culture (IAWDC) and For Intellectual Liberty (FIL)—because these organizations held formal meetings at the Woolfs' home and brought together Huxley, Macaulay, and many other writers and intellectuals who circulated through the various antifascist and antiwar groups of the period. Particularly noteworthy was a meeting on November 5, 1935, to discuss the British FIL's involvement in a possible conference with the French antifascist group *Comité de Vigilance des Intellectuels Antifacistes*. The meeting was convened by Philip Noel-Baker, who had been responsible for encouraging Jameson's *Challenge to Death* anthology, and among those present at the FIL gathering were Huxley, Jameson, Macaulay, and the Woolfs (Bradshaw, "British Writers I," 21).

Woolf was typically ambivalent about these meetings, and her increasing dissatisfaction with this sort of political action may be seen most pointedly in *Three Guineas*, in which, as Bradshaw notes, the satirical repetition of an appeal to defend "culture and intellectual liberty" has a specific target in FIL ("British Writers II," 58). Woolf's detachment has sources that distinguish her from the other writer-activists who gathered for the meetings, but by late 1935, they were all changing allegiances toward the pacifist wing of the broader antifascist intelligentsia. This flurry of political energy, which invigorated so many activists against war and fascism, had also captivated Woolf. As she wrote to Julian Bell, her nephew who in less than a year would be killed at the Spanish front in the Battle of Brunete, "politics are raging faster and fiercer. I've even had to write an article for the Daily Worker on the Artist and politics. Aldous is on the rampage with his peace propaganda; and Leonard is trying to convince the labour party that the policy of isolation is now the only one. Berties book [Russell's *Which Way to Peace?*] convinced him" (*L*, 83). Though still betraying signs of resistance to this political activity—she "had to write" for the *Daily Worker*, steers clear of Huxley's "rampage" for peace, and seems less convinced than Leonard about "isolation"—her news for Julian foregrounds the peace activist discussions around her and her awareness of the positions advocated by Huxley and Russell.

In addition to the IAWDC and FIL, she had similarly marginal yet consequential affiliations with an array of internationalist, antifascist, and pacifist groups, including the Fabians, the Labour Party, the Union of Democratic Control, the No More War Movement, and the Friends Anti-War Group. Many of these connections were created through Leonard's deeper, more official involvement and through his direction of the Hogarth Press, but Virginia was closely connected with these enterprises even when she resisted Leonard's politicking and disagreed with his tack. The Hogarth Press in particular shows the Woolfs' importance for antiwar politics through the 1920s and 1930s, beginning with their publication of Philip Noel-Baker's *Disarmament* (1926), which had a shaping effect on the policy programs of many interwar pacifist groups.[13] The internationalist Robert Cecil and pacifist Arthur Ponsonby would continue Noel-Baker's discussion about disarmament in Hogarth publications; both were members of Parliament whose rising and falling fortunes would coincide with the gains and losses of power for antiwar voices within British government during the thirties. In October 1935, Woolf recorded in her diary that her attendance at the Labour Party meeting at Brighton had left her shaken, because the pacifist MP and party leader George Lansbury was effectively outargued in the party debates about how to respond to Italy's invasion of Abyssinia. Woolf found herself "out of my stride" and in the throes of writing her novel, unable to "hitch on to The Years again" (*D*, 4:345). Her reaction to Ernest Bevin's attack on Lansbury was deeply emotional, and she reported tears coming to her eyes as well as disappointment that "the women delegates were very thin voiced & insubstantial," even as they planned a "no wash" protest that she called "a little reed piping" with no "chance against this weight of roast beef & beer—which she must cook" (*D*, 4:345). Though she was not one of the "insubstantial" female delegates, her sympathies were clearly with them and with the male pacifists whose views were drowned out by brute masculine power. She finds herself agreeing with Alfred Salter "who preached non-resistance," but the tide was clearly against this position, leaving Woolf feeling inconsequential and inadequate within the established political Left (*D*, 4:345). Following this turning of the tide, the Hogarth Press would publish one more pacifist pamphlet in 1936, *The Roots of War*, edited by J. W. Strange and written by members of the No More War Movement and the Friends Anti-War Group, but Leonard's nonpacifist internationalism became the more prominent voice with the press through works such as *The League and Abyssinia* (1936). Woolf's experience of antifascist gatherings as full of drudgery and ineffectual debate, book and pamphlet printing that stirred conversation but not definitive antiwar results, and Labour meetings that confirmed no place for pacifist and feminist voices—all conspired to encourage her development of the "outsider" position she would theorize in *Three Guineas*.

Woolf's position as one "of but not in" several political organizations was also true with the Peace Pledge Union.[14] Stoking controversy within her Bloomsbury network, Clive Bell's infamous pamphlet *Warmongers* (1938) was published by the PPU Press, becoming what S. P. Rosenbaum has called a "sadder" addition to the collection of "Bloomsbury credos" of 1938, alongside Forster's "What I Believe," Keynes's "My Early Beliefs," and Woolf's *Three Guineas* (*Platform*, 18). Bell's essay, which he offered as a kind of sequel to his earlier antiwar treatise, "Peace at Once" (1914), was firmly on the side of appeasement. Bell declared himself an "out and out pacificist" who believed that "there would be plenty of happiness in a Nazi world" and that though he personally would not like to live under fascism, he suspected that most Britons would not know the difference (*Warmongers*, 3–4).[15] Bell was not a PPU member, and his pamphlet understandably remains something of an embarrassment for the organization, particularly when treated as an official declaration of PPU policy. But like many of the pamphlets produced by the PPU that took on topics potentially viewed as treasonous, *Warmongers* came with a disclaimer reading: "The Peace Pledge Union does not necessarily endorse all the views expressed in this pamphlet, which is published by it as a valuable contribution to current thought." Many other pamphlets carried this statement, or a version of it, but Bell's seems to be one of the first to receive this distancing measure from its publisher. In other pamphlets the message is usually printed on its title page, but *Warmongers* has a separate label affixed to its interior, suggesting some last minute rethinking. Woolf remarked in her diary that she knew Bell was writing the essay "secretly" (*D*, 5:159), and after reading it, she appeared hesitant about its isolationist stance, writing to Quentin Bell: "I've not seen Clive; but have read his pamphlet—Warmongers. I wont say what I think till you do. L[eonard] wont even read" (*L*, 293). At least with Quentin, Woolf betrays no clear conviction about Clive's thesis, showing enough sympathy to read the pamphlet, unlike Leonard, but not proffering affirmation or dissent, and thus maintaining contact with PPU debates though not directly engaging them.

In her own writing against war, Woolf did not explicitly address Bell, but she did incorporate an anecdote from a prominent PPU member into *Three Guineas* as an example of what she called the Society of Outsiders. Her last volume of reading notebooks, in which she gathered research material for *Three Guineas*, includes a cutting from the December 20, 1937, issue of the *Evening Standard* with the headline "Mayoress Would Not Darn Socks for War / SPEECH UPSETS ARSENAL EMPLOYEES" (Silver, *Virginia Woolf's Reading Notebooks*, 314). Woolf quotes from this article in the published version of *Three Guineas* as evidence that "the Society of Outsiders is in being," noting that the "tactlessness" of Mayor Kathleen Rance's statement "publicly, in such circumstances" is beside the point since she "has made a courageous and effective experiment in the prevention of war" (*TG*, 136–37). In Woolf's cutting of the article, which she used only partly in *Three Guineas*, Rance's full statement announces: "So far as my husband and I are concerned, we shall do all we can for peace during our year of office. We are both members of the Peace Pledge Union, and neither of us would take part in a war. I myself would not even do as much as darn a sock to help in a war" (qtd. in Pawlowski, "*Seule la culture*," 229). Rance's stand against military assistance, supported by her membership in the PPU, becomes a model for Woolf of female power in political office and also represents the unacknowledged but actively engaged Society of Outsiders. Her society, though certainly not synonymous with the PPU, thus shares some of its aims and objectives as well as its members.

Woolf also demonstrated sympathy for Dick Sheppard and his active leadership of the PPU, saving in her reading notebooks an article about the minister for war calling church leaders "to denounce the 'insidious doctrine of pacifism' as heresy"—a clear reference to Sheppard, Charles Raven, Donald Soper, and their ilk (Silver, *Reading Notebooks*, 283). And, like many British peace activists, Woolf saw the unexpected death of the PPU's founder symbolic of a larger loss to the war prevention movement. While "revising the 1st Guinea" and thus devoted to thoughts of peace activism, she recorded: "Dick Sheppard died at his desk yesterday; just elected Rector some where. A pity, I expect; if peace is a cause, he had some gift that way" (D, 5:118). Sheppard's "gift" and its promise for finally bringing all Europeans to renounce war, was now lost along with the hope for peace.

"We Were All C.O.'s"

Despite these connections to the PPU and other organizations, as well as the thoroughness of Woolf's observations in her diaries and letters about her writing, her political involvements (and withdrawals), and her network of friends and associates, there is little explicit awareness of how much she shared with the other writers in this study in terms of politically engaged literary efforts. Storm Jameson's vision in "Documents" of a collaborative community of socialist writers seems largely absent in Woolf's theories of political art, at least in late essays such as "Why Art To-Day Follows Politics" or "The Leaning Tower." The latter, originally read to a gathering of the Workers' Educational Association in Brighton, shows Woolf separating herself from the younger generation of writers within a framework that criticizes literary "theories" for committing "to the belief that there is some force, influence, outer pressure which is strong enough to stamp itself upon a whole group of different writers so that all their writing has a certain common likeness" (E, 6:260). She does not renounce this theorizing altogether—begrudgingly, she admits its usefulness—but she is mindful of the diversity within any group. Resistance to the affiliations of others seems to be at work in her quite limited recognition that while she was toiling away at the project that would develop into The Years and Three Guineas, writers of her direct acquaintance were working with antifascist and pacifist organizations, attempting peace witnessing through writing, and skirting the pitfalls of reductive propaganda.

Woolf's fierce independence has been regarded as one of her most attractive qualities by many readers—particularly feminist critics who laud her agency in a culture that militates against female autonomy and voice—but her individualism was accompanied by a feeling of isolation. This is not to say that she was without rich networks of politically and creatively interconnected people, as many scholars have shown. Her attentiveness to her reading public, at times over and against her writing peers, is perhaps her most substantial enactment of the writer's political role.[16] But there is no question that the forcefulness of her antiwar polemics in a period of rising antifascism left her particularly open to critique from both her reading public and her peers in the London intelligentsia. As Phyllis Lassner describes it, the reaction to *Three Guineas* was for Woolf "personally and politically painful," especially in "the portentous silences of her friend Maynard Keynes and of her husband"; these silences supported Woolf's argument that women's voices were not even in the debate; they were excluded from the male-constructed and male-dominated sphere of political discussion, as she had witnessed firsthand at the Labour meetings in Brighton (*British Women Writers*, 28). The hostile and dismissive reactions plus their even more insidious silent partners were counterbalanced by the host of feminist and pacifist correspondents whose letters Woolf kept as a record of her ability to hearten others who felt themselves similarly marginalized.[17] But her private and public writings of the late 1930s indicate her feeling out of step with the surrounding culture, which had grown more accepting of a war against Hitler. And, even more troubling for her was the widening separation from her Bloomsbury compatriots.

Nowhere is that feeling of incongruity more present than in her often quoted notes for a memoir of Julian Bell following his death in Spain. She writes of Bell: "What made him do it? I suppose it's a fever in the blood of the younger generation which we cant possibly understand. I have never known anyone of my generation have that feeling about a war. We were all C.O.'s in the Great War" (*Platform*, 28). This memoir struggles to comprehend how someone like Julian could go to war despite his being so gifted and cultured and peace-minded—the editor, in fact, of the pacifist anthology *We Did Not Fight*, featuring contributions from peace movement luminaries such as Russell and Sassoon.[18] Her notes are tentative in their response to this question, and her falling back on a generational difference with a pseudobiological (or pathological) source sounds less like certain diagnosis or cultural analysis and more like a yearning for a past moment when her "generation" was unified in its opposition to war. Not only was this opposition expressed with regard to a specific war but in Woolf's version of things, there was shared resistance at a deeply affective level to all wars—even those with purportedly good aims. She continues in her reminiscence: "And tho' I understand that this is a 'cause,' can be called the cause of liberty & so on, still my natural reaction is to fight intellectually" (ibid.). She does not dispute the righteousness of the end goal, but she is dissuaded by the violent means, and this investigation of the ends-means dichotomy puts her once again squarely in the intellectual orbit of Aldous Huxley, whom, as we have seen, made this argument the centerpiece of his philosophy of pacifism. Woolf's yearning for bygone days of shared war resistance betrays mournfulness not only for Julian but for herself and nostalgia for a past that she characterizes as congruous with her values in ways now forsaken by formerly likeminded activists.

The phrase "we were all C.O.s" has acquired legendary status in Woolf studies and is routinely mentioned as epitomizing her pacifism and the pacifism of her Bloomsbury circle. The factual inaccuracy of the phrase on several levels even adds to its importance as a polemical position statement, not just a historical data point. Woolf's claim of conscientious objector status for herself is loaded with feminist import, of course, because as a woman she had no need to resist being drafted. And, while official exemption for conscientious objection was awarded to several men of her circle, including Lytton Strachey, E. M. Forster, Duncan Grant, and David Garnett, many others were disqualified for other reasons, as was Leonard Woolf for a hand tremor that prevented active service (Atkin, *War of Individuals*, 34–40).[19] As Jonathan Atkin has shown, the pervasive antiwar sentiment in Bloomsbury and affiliated groups was not in all cases immediate or consistently principled—for instance, J. M. Keynes's views about the war grew increasingly critical through his work in the Treasury, and Clive Bell and Duncan Grant initially thought of enlisting and only later became outspoken opponents of the war (22–30). Woolf's comment is best viewed not for its insight into Bloomsbury during the Great War but into herself in the 1930s, when she was lonely while trying to "fight intellectually." Alex Zwerdling has memorably described Woolf's predicament: "The events in Europe in the four decades of her adult life would stretch this pacifist commitment to the limit and increasingly bring her into conflict with those on her own side. To her, nonviolence was an article of faith rather than a discretionary tactic—the closest thing to a religion her secular skepticism permitted" (*Real World*, 273–74). That "article of faith," though intensely felt at the personal level, was pointedly lacking in any unified "church," and the mournfulness of Woolf's late writings responds to this lack of community and attempts to imagine some replacement.

Outside, Indifferent, Nonviolent

The radicalism of Woolf's vision has been challenged in recent years, most notably by critics who have shown that her antisemitism hampers her antifascism and limits the inclusiveness of her concerns for justice.[20] Woolf's comments about Jews in her private writings as well as the troubling scene with Abrahamson in *The Years* and her notorious story "The Duchess and the Jeweller" (1938) indicate, at best, what Maren Tova Linnett contends is Woolf's "allosemitism"—the objectifying use of imaginary Jewishness as an intellectual and literary device.[21] Though scholars such as Herbert Marder have argued that Woolf's last decade shows her becoming less bound by her former prejudices and more attuned to the oppression of others, this view, even if it can be defended, only moderately adjusts the sense that her racist, classist, and antisemitic perspectives diminish the supposed universalism of her appeals for equality.[22] Even her sympathies for peace activism and anti-imperialism are marred by occasions in which bigotry interfered with her political support, as in her diary entry about attending the National Peace Council conference on peace and colonialism, which she endured "by way of a joke" and found full of "baboon faced intellectuals" (*D*, 4:349). Her aspersions in this entry are partly cast toward the "pale white platitudes" of British liberals, whose anticolonial peace activism seems anemic to her, but her description of African participants in the conference indulges in simian and primitivist stereotypes largely incompatible with a universal vision of the "outsider." For reasons such as these, and in particular Woolf's representation of Jews, disparagement of the activism of Storm Jameson and others, and faulty equation of British patriarchy with Nazism, Marina MacKay has insisted that "praise for the radicalism of *Three Guineas* should probably be tempered" (*Modernism and World War II*, 29).

Keeping this caution in mind, it remains important not to lose sight of the ways that *Three Guineas* is, indeed, radical in the sense that it calls for a deep restructuring of society, renewed from the roots up, and thus shares certain traits with the most revisionary utopian thinkers. It is nevertheless perfectly true that Woolf's projection of a Society of Outsiders had limits based in the author's own prejudices and foreshortened scale of vision. Utopia, that nowhere place, is still circumscribed by the boundaries of imagination. But her failures in imagining an unlimited utopia point to an imaginative limitation rather than a fundamentally conservative project of only slightly modifying the status quo. Contrasted with a deeply engaged political writer such as Storm Jameson, Woolf can appear irresponsible, her evasiveness in effect seeming to condone persecution and injustice that she does not explicitly condemn.[23] And yet, *Three Guineas* demonstrates her idiosyncratic participation in revolutionary pacifist debates of the period.

Her program for ending war through social reconstruction, even if somewhat sketchy and hypothetical, includes several directives: the redistribution of women's salaries to give "a living wage in all the professions," along with unpaid workers and mothers; equal distribution of workloads across genders; education for particular professional skills in ways that allow experiment and creativity to flourish; the renunciation of jobs such as munitions work that directly contribute to war; and the formation of a "new religion" based in a critical and creative unshackling of Christianity from its institutional prison (*TG*, 130–33). These directives are among Woolf's many suggestions, always in a spirit of possibility rather than prescription, no less radical than Huxley's international theories in *Ends and Means* but without his tone of exasperated conclusiveness. John Whittier-Ferguson has sympathetically described readings by Christine Froula and others that "discover a utopian element in the open-endedness of Woolf's late work," though he counters: "I have grown less sure that its heroic-utopian orientation effectively counterbalances the nightmares of history, and I am convinced that it only occasionally comforted Woolf" ("Repetition," 244–45). While not achieving the long-term goals she imagined, and even finding little solace in those imaginings, *Three Guineas* and *The Years* still enter contemporary debates about war prevention and the renewal of civilization. Woolf insists on a revitalization of British culture with renewed potential for women, whose increased social and economic capital could position them for more substantial and effective antiwar protests, but she criticizes the existing antiwar efforts for their essentially conservative desire to save (male-dominated) "disinterested culture" and civilization from militaristic nationalisms (*TG*, 110).[24] At its core, there is in Woolf's imagined society a quality shared by all the writers we have looked at in this study, a striving toward Jay Winter's notion of a "minor utopia" distinct from Fascist, Nazi, and Stalinist "major" utopias.[25] Though Woolf's contribution to this minor utopianism is open to criticism for its gender essentialism, its emergence from her own genteel liberalism, and its refusal to give "straightforward" answers to political realist critiques, it remains a landmark of pacifist theory from an unusual position neither inside nor fully outside the broader peace movement.

Debates about the utopianism of large-scale reforms with the aim of war prevention were prominent in Woolf's circle, perhaps most apparently in Leonard Woolf's sustained contribution to international theory. As author or editor, he produced a series of works proposing international coordination and supranational government as solutions to the problem of war. These books and pamphlets, including *The Intelligent Man's Way to Prevent War* (1933), *Quack, Quack!* (1935), *Barbarians at the Gate* (1939), and *The War for Peace* (1940), show a progression in Leonard's thinking about the crises in Europe, mostly based in grave concern about the threat of fascism and belief that the League of Nations (or something like it) stood the best chance for effectively ending war. As he wrote in his introduction to *The Intelligent Man's Way to Prevent War*, "a discussion of the League of Nations, disarmament, arbitration, international co-operation, and the prevention of war will seem to many people at the moment academically utopian," but despite this concern about utopianism amid the failure of the League, the rise of "Fascism and Hitlerism and the more violent forms of nationalism," the impossibility of disarmament, the Japanese conquest of China, and the all-around obstruction of "pacifism, liberty, democracy, [and] Socialism," he insists that "the majority of people are . . . opposed to war and anxious to prevent it" (*Intelligent Man's Way*, 17–18). This, he believes, may be accomplished if people "choose other aims and other policies" from those that make war inevitable, and he concludes that "there is nothing to be ashamed of in refusing to hurrah with the barbarians in those periods when the world turns back in full cry to barbarism" (ibid., 18). The remainder of this book, with essays by prominent antiwar, internationalist thinkers such as Norman Angell, Robert Cecil, and Harold Laski, offer theoretical and strategic policy proposals toward an alternative world system that even at this late date aimed to steer Europe away from the much-predicted war.[26]

Virginia Woolf's political writings are less schematic than Leonard's and seek a less direct engagement with academic theorists, though they are not less concerned with the task of reaching a common reader (or Leonard's "intelligent man") and advocating for radical social change as a deterrent to war. Her theories in *Three Guineas* have been criticized for their lack of political savvy, and when compared with Leonard's more strategic admonitions, it is understandable to regard her hopes for an alternative world as wanting in specific action plans. The stance that Virginia takes in her polemic, however, resonates strongly with Leonard's thoughts about "refusing to hurrah with the barbarians," which he later developed in *Quack, Quack!* For the vision she casts in *Three Guineas* to take root, some radical transformation of society's structures is needed. Differing from Huxley's emphasis on individual conversion or Jameson's appeal for a socialist economy and international reconfiguration, Woolf still demands large-scale change, from the economic base to the educational superstructure. Looking back at 1930s efforts to prevent war in a reprint of *The New Pacifism*, Sylvia Strauss writes of the essays by Heard, Huxley, Milne, Sheppard and company: "The one drawback with respect to all the proposals was that they required a long-range effort when time was of the essence."[27] Much the same might be said of Woolf's injunctions in *Three Guineas*.

While *Three Guineas* is her most well-developed pacifist treatise, Woolf's last years give other important signs of her public peace witness. Her talk on the Dreadnought Hoax at the Women's Institute in Rodmell in 1940, later reprised with the Memoir Club, appears in Forster's account for its humor, leaving the assembly "helpless with laughter" (*Woolf*, 6) and showing her ability to communicate despite her feeling that "she was living in a world with 'no audience. No echo'" (Lee, *Virginia Woolf*, 719). Regaling an audience in 1940 with the success of the hoax and its aftermath also has a clear political importance that Forster leaves unmentioned. In the surviving typescript for her talk, Woolf's narrative focuses not just on the hoax itself, when she and five friends in "exotic" costumes tricked their way into a guided tour of the British navy's *H.M.S. Dreadnought*, but on the immediate consequences of their stunt. A highlight of Woolf's story is a set piece involving her cousin Willy Fisher, a navy man and "Commander of the Dreadnought" (*E*, 6: 566), furiously upbraiding her brother Adrian about the admiral's loss of face; children were purportedly chasing him crying, "Bunga Bunga" (ibid., 574). "Did we realise" Fisher protested, "that we owed our lives to the British Navy?" (ibid.). Though humorous and farcical, this detail indicates that, at least in retrospect, the hoax was a significant affront to military power. Recalling this successful political theatre from 1910 for audiences in 1940 may have been amusing, but it also had serious stakes when many in Britain felt that their security rested on military preparedness. As Clara Jones observes, Woolf's talk involved a "conspiratorial dimension" that invited members of the conservative Women's Institute into a pacifist witness linked "theoretically and imaginatively to *Three Guineas*" (*Virginia Woolf: Ambivalent Activist*, 173). Fisher, in Woolf's narrative, coaxed names and addresses of the remaining conspirators from Adrian, whose confession led to a scene with Duncan Grant's being kidnapped for a naval ritual of corporal punishment. Woolf's narration at this point, though still drawing out the humor and absurdity of the scene, provides an account of effective nonviolence. As the navy men gather around him with their canes, Woolf reports that "Grant stood there like a lamb," confounding one of the officers, who says: "I can't make this chap out . . . He doesn't put up any fight. You can't cane a chap like that" (*E*, 6:574). Ultimately, Grant's nonresistance deescalates the violence, and the sailors can only bring themselves to administer "two ceremonial taps" (ibid., 575). The meek acceptance of violence in the face of an attacker thwarts the attacker's ambitions and defuses the hostile scenario.

Obviously, this story, surviving only as a fragment, is not a full-blown program of passive resistance. But Woolf's narrative of an unarmed group of artists who undermine self-serious military authority and escape drastic retribution through meekness echoes a common strategy among nonviolence advocates from Woolf's time to the present: the use of narrative and case studies as data for proving strategic effectiveness.[28] In *Which Way to Peace?* (1936), the book that Woolf noted had "convinced" Leonard, Bertrand Russell compares Nazis to "Mongols" in China and "Mohammedans" in the Eastern Empire, conquerors who were effectively civilized by those whom they conquered, causing their "militarist attitude" to be destroyed psychologically rather than militarily (*Which Way*, 142–43). Even more like recent works on nonviolence, Richard Gregg's *The Power of Non-Violence* (1934) begins with a chapter on "Modern Examples of Non-Violent Resistance" that includes reports of civil disobedience against Austrian imperialism in mid-nineteenth-century Hungary, a discussion of the 1926 General Strike in England, and, of course, descriptions of Gandhi's campaigns in South Africa and India.[29] Woolf's comic recounting of the Dreadnought Hoax and its successful nonvio-

lent protest resonates with the decades-long process of theorizing nonviolence, and its place in her thinking of 1940 indicates a nostalgia for the
prewar era, when peaceful, prankish demonstration had more manage-
able stakes.

As a method for convincing skeptics that nonviolence is the best tool
for social change and conflict resolution, the accumulation of examples
is undeniably limited. To any particular story about successful nonviolent
action, the unconvinced can always point to circumstances that enabled
this particular action to succeed and might not be so optimal when attempted again. Likewise, additional examples of the effectiveness and
necessity of violence or the inadequacy of nonviolence can be adduced.[30]
Even Gandhi criticized this rhetorical strategy when asked, "Is there any
historical evidence as to the success of what you have called soul-force or
truth-force [satyagraha]?" (*Hind Swaraj*, 50). Instead of citing examples,
he offered a wider-angle perspective, replying: "You cannot expect silver
ore in a tin mine. History, as we know it, is a record of the wars of the
world . . . The greatest and most unimpeachable evidence of the success of this force is to be found in the fact that, in spite of the wars of the
world, it still lives on . . . History, then, is a record of an interruption of the
course of nature. Soul-force, being natural, is not noted in history" (ibid.,
50–51). Demonstrating the utility of nonviolence within particular sce-
narios was less important for Gandhi than embracing satyagraha as a way
of being, practiced because it is righteous and harmonious with nature,
regardless of its historical successes or failures.

Gandhi's satyagraha and its related strategies of nonviolent direct action have a corollary in Woolf's thought with one of the most censured
elements of *Three Guineas*: her contention that "indifference" is the best
posture for women in a culture building toward war (*TG*, 129). Even her
earliest readers balked at this notion, as we see in Naomi Mitchison's
cautiously critical letter, which Woolf preserved among the dozens of
responses she received after publishing *Three Guineas*. Mitchison praises
Woolf's writings, especially *The Years*, but observes that within the real
world of ideological and economic entanglements, "I can't see anyone
but a saint getting rid of all motives, being as utterly disinterested as you
would have us be . . . Thus I am questioning the whole policy of 'indifference'" (qtd. in Snaith, "Wide Circles," 41). Mitchison takes Woolf to
mean "unfeeling," and unconcerned about whether children go to war or

whether revolutions fail to achieve their intended results. Unfortunately, Woolf's reply remains lost, but Mitchison's next letter thanks Woolf for clearing up their confusion, and adds that what had bothered her "was the 'indifference'; perhaps it is a word which has wrong connotations and should have something else substituted for it" (ibid., 48). What Mitchison seems to miss, whatever the infelicities of Woolf's word choice, is that Woolf does not treat indifference as an affective category or an untrained default position. Rather, she offers examples of the ways that women are drawn into public displays that act as support for, encouragement of, and submission to militaristic nationalism. To foil these displays, Woolf advocates the "use of indifference," a telling phrase that shows how indifference is a chosen, self-defining action rather than aloofness or dispassion (*TG*, 129). As Alice Wood intriguingly suggests, Woolf's "indifference" might be viewed as synonymous with nonviolent action, and that it, rather than being "a passive denial of, or refusal to engage with, the pressing political situation, in fact represents an active position of protest, if an idealistic one" (*Late Cultural Criticism*, 98).[31]

Woolf's "indifference" is embedded within her explanation of the "outsider," whose declaration "as a woman, I have no country. As a woman I want no country. As a woman my country is the whole world" is one of her most famous and frequently quoted passages (*TG*, 129). Often, however, this quotation is not explained within its context in the book, a context that makes it hypothetical and tentative rather than simply and directly Woolf's personal position statement. Thus, it is more imaginative than has sometimes been assumed. Woolf's turn to discussing "indifference" comes immediately after a passage that complicates the famous "no country" comment: "And if, when reason has said its say, still some obstinate emotion remains, some love of England dropped into a child's ears by the cawing of rooks in an elm tree, by the splash of waves on a beach, or by English voices murmuring nursery rhymes, this drop of pure, if irrational, emotion she will make serve her to give to England first what she desires of peace and freedom for the whole world" (ibid.). Woolf clearly admits that absolute nonattachment, as advocated by Gregg and Huxley, is not very likely possible; the best way to deal with lingering emotional attachments to land and to ideologies otherwise harmful to the female outsider is to channel these emotions toward making England more peaceful and free. It is in this context of unavoidable love for country, even patriotism, that Woolf describes the outsider: "Such then will be the nature of her 'indifference' and from this indifference certain acts must follow" (ibid.). Her setting "indifference" within quotation marks suggests the tentativeness of the term, a recognition in the text itself of her feeling that the word might not convey precisely what she wants it to, much in the way peace activist terminology such as "nonviolence," "non-resistance," and even "pacifism" often fail to capture the active, engaged, constructive meanings of the terms. She also gives several examples of ways that "certain acts must follow," clarifying her point that indifferent does not mean inactive.

Seen in this light, Woolf's indifference bears noticeable similarities to the passive resistance techniques famously advocated by Gandhi and popularized by Gregg. Among the several critics who have pointed out that Woolf's attraction to nonviolence was related to Gandhi's version, the common observation has been that Gandhi's antifeminist views, his arguing for the masculine integrity of nonviolence over its supposed feminine passivity, put him (and his translation through Gregg) at odds with Woolf's feminism.[32] That Woolf and Gandhi/Gregg espoused differing views about gender seems true. But stopping the comparison at this point precludes our understanding more of the character of Woolf's nonviolence as a part of the debates about pacifism and nonviolent strategies in the 1930s. Gregg's coinage "moral jiu-jitsu" is the main thrust of his nonviolence, a learned practice in which an attacker can be repelled not by fighting back—which Gregg argues only encourages the perpetrator—but by "accept[ing] the blows with good-tempered reasoning" and "offer[ing] resistance, but only in moral terms . . . Thus nonviolent resistance acts as a sort of moral jiu-jitsu. The non-violence and good will of the victim act like the lack of physical opposition by the user of physical jiu-jitsu, to cause the attacker to lose his moral balance" (*Power of Non-Violence*, 26). Gregg's theory offers an alternative way to resist assault by shifting the moral ground and reacting to the predator unpredictably.

Woolf similarly suggests the destabilizing power of nonviolent indifference. In the same paragraph in which she advocates "the use of indifference," she provides an example of its effect that she contends is analogous to militaristic patriotic displays: "For psychology would seem to show that it is far harder for human beings to take action when other people are indifferent and allow them complete freedom of action, than when their actions are made the centre of excited emotion. The small boy struts and trumpets outside the window: implore him to stop; he goes on; say nothing; he stops" (*TG*, 129). As with children, so with an inflamed patriotic society. Instead of jumping into the furor, Woolf recommends abstention as a way to clear the ground for better action: "they should shut the bright eyes that rain influence, or let those eyes look elsewhere when war is discussed—that is the duty to which outsiders will train themselves in peace before the threat of death inevitably makes reason powerless" (129–30). Refusing to engage on others' terms, even avoiding public antiwar displays, invokes a logic similar to Gregg's concern for the moral grounding of conflict. The Society of Outsiders that Woolf imagines functioning anonymously and diffusely, without the institutional mechanisms of pacifist groups such as the PPU, supplies a network of loose affiliation. This society imaginatively fills the gap Woolf potently expressed in her memoir of Julian Bell, the generational gap as well as the distance between herself and her peers who once seemed more uniformly opposed to war.

These related concepts of nonviolence, moral jiu-jitsu, and active indifference, as well as the support network of a Society of Outsiders, have been much disparaged for their lack of political realism. The weakest element of Gregg's argument for moral jiu-jitsu (and Woolf's story of the badly behaving boy) is the assumption that in practice, calmly accepting blows (or ignoring misbehavior) will have the salutary effect predicted. The skeptic might understandably counter: but what if it doesn't? Argumentation by example is designed to address this concern, and theorists such as Gene Sharp have built on Gregg's use of this strategy by employing examples not as logical proof but rather as case studies from which new techniques can be developed. But in Woolf's less technical approach to this sort of thinking, written well before conflict studies research had moved in its current direction, her injunctions remain open to charges of chilly disconnection from the suffering of others as well as irresponsible or merely wishful thinking. Furthermore, the links between deflecting personal violence and repelling state-sponsored military aggression are imperfectly explained in Gregg's theories. As a matter of policy or "civilian-based defense," *Three Guineas* is open to similar criticisms. More germane, however, than assessing how well Woolf's political theories and nonviolence strategies square with later developments in these fields or testing their living feasibility is to see how elements of her thought are enacted in her literary writing.

Cyclical, Elliptical, Repetitive: Pacifist Aesthetics in *The Years*

Turning to *The Years* offers a valuable resource for examining Woolf's literary peace witness, in part because of her own perception that *The Years* and *Three Guineas* once completed were "the end of six years floundering" and could be lumped "together as one book," and in part because readers have been slow to find in the earlier novel the pacifist advocacy of the later polemic (*D*, 5:148). This common oversight indicates one kind of success for the novel, at least according to Woolf's stated intentions that it would not become didactic, preachy, or Huxley-ish. It is with her exploration of fifty years in the lives of a British family and the revelation of forces that motivate them and push them toward war that we might see the kinship between *The Years* and *Three Guineas* as peace activist writing.

Though critics of *Three Guineas* commonly extract quotations from select locations in its circuitous arguments and use them for evidence of Woolf's precise claims about political matters, a sequential reading experience of the book contradicts this practice. Unlike many other antiwar polemics from the thirties, Woolf's style resists the logical structures familiar in propositional writing. For some readers, this has been a mark of weakness, as if Woolf's uncertainty and political naivety manifested in her compositional form. Valentine Cunningham, for instance, links her treatise with Huxley's "most strongly spiritual fictions of the period" (including *Eyeless in Gaza*), claiming that his books are "as skittishly wayward as Virginia Woolf's feminist-pacifist resistance to meeting the war issue head-on" and describing *Three Guineas* as "vexingly round about" (*British Writers of the Thirties*, 70). Cunningham's disparaging intent to one side, we can see the aptness of his connecting Woolf and Huxley, despite their own protestations, and his terms "skittish" and "round about" strike on an important aspect of Woolf's form. For Cunningham, her style obfuscates, rendering the politics useless. A more sympathetic approach to the same stylistic issue is Pamela L. Caughie's insight, declared for Woolf's entire oeuvre but particularly relevant with *Three Guineas*: "Equivocation . . . is for Woolf a stance against such certainty, a guard against the desire to prevail" (*Virginia Woolf*, 8). For Caughie, this rejection of mastery demonstrates a rejection of such male modernist enterprises as encyclopedic fiction, densely allusive long poems, or totalizing "mythic" methodologies. Though I am less concerned with how equivocation places Woolf in the modernist canon or in the history of feminist discourse, Caughie's comment assists with praising rather than condemning "equivocation," a device that gives *Three Guineas* its constantly shifting ground and to-and-fro argumentation. The conceit of a Society of Outsiders is often presented without its original context, and thus sounds more definitive, commanding, or "prevailing." The tentativeness and textual layering one finds in the full text suggests one way Woolf resists supplying a new hegemonic force to combat masculinist, militaristic patriotism. Rather, akin to the moral jiu-jitsu that Gregg recommends, she enacts at the formal level a response to force that destabilizes it by changing the terms of the conflict. Pursuing this idea further, we might consider Phyllis Lassner's attentive eye toward "Woolf's use of ellipses in *Three Guineas*," which, she argues, "suggests the two-way silences that prevent women from shaping, much less influencing, political culture" (*British Women Writers*, 28).[33]

I would add to this analysis the suggestion that the "dotted lines" in her argument also enable a form of nonviolent communication. Current theories of nonviolence contend that stylistic devices such as ellipses enable rhetoric that avoids unnecessary escalations of conflict and seeks instead the open spaces and common grounding necessary for collaborative conflict resolution.[34] Those elliptical moments, rather than being the "skittish" effects of indecision or denial of reality, speak through their silence by demonstrating exclusion from masculine political discourse. Ellipses, then, become a textual sign of "indifference," of the passive resistance to speech that is otherwise forged in molds unfavorable to women's voices. Along these lines, Sarah Cole argues that Woolf's cyclical and repetitive style in *Three Guineas* acts as a counter to violence. Besides the repeated phrases that become refrains in the book, the very possibility of defeating violence arises through absorption: "Antiviolence has to consume violence, to swallow it" (*Violet Hour*, 267). These prominent features of

Three Guineas—equivocal, elliptical, cyclical, and repetitive—are the text's way of representing, and even becoming, nonviolent discourse on Woolf's chosen terms: outside and "indifferent."

The formal "indifference" of *Three Guineas* is also readily apparent in the published version of *The Years*, a version that for many decades was overshadowed by the material Woolf cut from the book during her long period of revision.[35] Grace Radin, voicing a criticism often heard of the novel, claims that Woolf's revisions damaged its political meaning: "*Three Guineas* shows that the positions that Sara and Nicholas take bear a close resemblance to her own views. In *The Years* she seems to have been so concerned with avoiding a one-sided polemic that she ended by burying some of her ideas in obscurity and circumlocution" (*Virginia Woolf's* "The Years," 78).[36] Obscurity and circumlocution are in this reading seen as authorial failure, part of Woolf's inability to marshal her disparate ideas into a fictional form that could explore competing ideologies without compressing her characters into ideological mouthpieces. But another way to view these "circumlocutions" is in light of her elliptical *Three Guineas* structure, as a methodology for enacting textually the nonviolence that she advocates overtly in her polemical treatise. *The Years* is far removed from the style of other antiwar fictions, such as Helen Zenna Smith's *Not So Quiet . . . Stepdaughters of War* (1930), in which repulsive battlefield conditions serve as the primary device to shock readers into pacifism. Instead, Woolf's novel is "indifferent" in her *Three Guineas* sense, obviously rejecting jingoistic pomp but also refusing to sound a simplistic rallying cry for pacifism. Instead, as Gill Plain has argued, *The Years* becomes an "iconoclastic challenge to the dangerous inertia of the socio-cultural status quo" through its formal fragmentation and contradictoriness (*Women's Fiction*, 86).

With the exception of its allusions to British imperial and military history and its one true wartime chapter set during an air raid in 1917, *The Years* can appear uninterested in war. Among the first critics of the novel, few mention war as a central concern, and those who do largely refer to the obliqueness with which Woolf handles her depiction of World War I. In the *Evening Standard*, Howard Spring names the several important historical events left undepicted in the novel as examples of Woolf's off-center interests and observes: "During the Great War there are no telegrams from the front, no medals, no mentions in despatches" (qtd.

in Majumdar and McLaurin, *Critical Heritage*, 377). Spring's largely affirmative review still records the absence of material familiar from the previous decade's "war books" whose antiwar conventions we have considered with Siegfried Sassoon. Feminist scholarship on women and war writing has corrected the biased perception that the absence of (masculine) battlefield imagery disqualifies a work from being serious about war. Even so, many recent critics who have enriched our understanding of the historical and political contexts of *The Years* still describe the novel as though war were merely incidental to Woolf's larger concerns about patriarchy and the late Victorian influence on the long turn of the century.[37] Even critics who do find war to be a notable feature of the novel typically focus on the dread of aerial bombardment rather than on the ways her fiction enacts her pacifism.[38] As a source for understanding Woolf's efforts toward peace activist literature, then, *The Years* has scarcely registered.

Her 1920s novels are also oblique in their approaches to the Great War, but the death of significant characters in combat in *Jacob's Room* (1922) and *To the Lighthouse* (1927) and the devastating effects of war trauma on Septimus Warren Smith and his social network in *Mrs. Dalloway* (1925) put in relief Woolf's antiwar advocacy. With *The Years*, by contrast, shell shock and the deleterious effects of the Great War on a generation and a society are far less obvious. North Pargiter, the one main character who is also a combatant, survives the war apparently intact—a remarkable exception among Woolf's soldier characters. Through the novel's pervasively elliptical style, however, "wholeness" itself is questioned. At almost any key juncture—in the thick of conversation or as we approach a momentous time such as 1914—the narration omits crucial details and plot developments with seemingly willful disregard for our attention. If North has been damaged by the war, we never quite find out, apart from the detail that he has been many years abroad, seeking fortune in the imperial reaches and thus disconnected from the home he once knew. Elliptical and evasive, the narrative style obscures the sort of details we might find most useful in construing a pacifist agenda. It is a rich irony that in 1945 Harcourt Brace published a U.S. Armed Services Edition of *The Years*, describing its story as "the passing of the last fifty years, seen through the everyday life of separate individuals," affected by "all the forces that mould society, from fear and love to war and politics."

Unlike early reviews, war is named in this blurb, perhaps as an entice-
ment to servicemen, although those "forces" sound rather neutral and
amorphous. Presumably, no amount of clever ad copy could have made
an Armed Services Edition of *Three Guineas*. But *The Years*, in a kind of
vindication of its author's worries about politicized preachiness, passes
muster as "serious fiction" for bored soldiers.[39]

During her writing process, when the focus of the book changed from
its earliest inception as a sequel to *A Room of One's Own*, treating the
sexual lives of women, Woolf's thinking reveals the importance of militarism and antifascism to her novel in progress. On the same day that she
noted in the margins of her diary that the work would be called *The Years*,
she offers one of her most explicitly political entries from the first half of
the decade. The papers have declared September 4, 1935, "the most critical day since Aug 4th 1914" (*D*, 4:337). Before turning to the mundane,
with an anecdote about her new tasseled umbrella, and the professional,
with barbs at "Queenie Leavis['s] . . . priggish letter . . . in that prigs
manual, Scrutiny," she describes the growing Fascist threat while in London: "Writings chalked up all over the walls. 'Dont fight for foreigners.
Briton should mind her own business.' Then a circle with a symbol in it.
Fascist propaganda, L[eonard] said. Mosley again active" (ibid.). Though
it would be stretching the point to say that Woolf knowingly combined
these several thoughts into some cohesive statement, the unstated links
remain important. The title for *The Years* "dropped like a billiard ball
into a pocket" just as Woolf's concerns about Fascism and the coming
war intensify (4:342).

The "narrative pacifism" Nancy Knowles distills from *Three Guineas*
and applies to *Between the Acts* can also illuminate the subtle antiwar
agenda of *The Years*. Fragmentation emerges through its evasiveness and
the myriad concrete details left for the reader to meaningfully assemble.
Even in scenes in which war is not directly mentioned, its presence is
noticeable in anticipation. In addition, the saga of the Pargiters is rife
with inequality within their own family dynamics and particularly in their
treatment of others. The slim chapter set in 1913 demonstrates the workings of this pacifist aesthetics, subtly evoking the end of the prewar world.
In this chapter, the Pargiters' caretaker Crosby is moving to her own
small place after forty years of life and service in the recently sold Pargiter
home. The usually sympathetic Eleanor struggles to handle Crosby's

emotions, and their parting is tortured with internal conflict as Eleanor cannot fully reach across the gap of their experience and social class: "It was a dreadful moment; unhappy; muddled; altogether wrong. Crosby was so miserable; she was so glad" (TY, 206). In the muddle, Eleanor suggests that Crosby might be better off without the family's "smelly, wheezy and unattractive old dog" Rover, who much like Crosby herself no longer fits into the Pargiters' new life (ibid.). Crosby begs to keep the dog, one remaining vestige of her old life, but shortly, and with great pathos, the sick dog must be put down. The death of this dog clearly contrasts with Huxley's "dog episode" in *Eyeless in Gaza,* in which the animal's fall from an aeroplane splatters on lovers and evokes war from the air. Rover's death is quieter and becomes a key image in the depiction of Crosby's rough handling at the end of her career, produced by the Pargiters' blindness to the strains of class difference.

Almost in passing, slipped into the narrative texture woven from several strands of emotion surrounding Crosby, Martin Pargiter thinks about international trouble in Eastern Europe—a clear signal of the war to come. While sitting "in his room reading his newspaper," the narrative voice, in a free indirect fusion with Martin's thoughts, reports: "The war in the Balkans was over, but there was more trouble brewing—that he was now quite sure. He turned the page" (TY, 209). This description functions as a transition into Martin's mind, which predominates for the remainder of the chapter, as he finds himself irritated with Crosby, incapable of responding charitably to her personal turmoil, and chastising her for allowing the laundry woman to burn with the iron his "brand new pyjamas" that were "made of the finest silk, she could tell" (ibid.). Ever so briefly, Martin is aware through newspaper reportage that all is not well in Europe—trouble brews—but turning the page, he avoids further thought and, like many other Britons, supposes that he will be unaffected by the ongoing internecine violence in European hinterlands. Martin's obliviousness to the imminent war captures the tenor of 1914 among the sheltered elite, but it also reverberates with Woolf's growing anxiety through the 1930s about the next war.

Though her feelings about the coming war were less intense during the writing and revising of *The Years* than they were in, say, 1938, there is still a way in which writing about 1913 (and revising this section as late as 1936) corresponds to the mood of her time. Tamar Katz has described the novel as having a "future obsession," and while this might pertain most obviously to the final "Present Day" chapter, it can also be found in the cyclical sense of history in chapters such as "1913" ("Pausing," 3). This technique has an experimental quality, provoking readers in the 1930s to recall the last days before a violent outbreak in their own foreboding time. This provocation heightens what Paul K. Saint-Amour calls "a collective syndrome . . . instigated by expectation—that is, by the *eventuality* of a future-ordained war" (*Tense Future*, 7). Much as the Balkans War prefigured the First World War, the context for Woolf's work on *The Years* includes the Spanish Civil War's foreshadowing the larger scale conflict with Nazism. Woolf's use of all-encompassing snow at the chapter's end is explicitly political, covering palaces and monuments, and "1913" concludes by leaving anticipation of the war up to the reader, filling in ellipses in the story to awaken the dread of international violence.

Martin's newspaper, partly by informing the public about regional wars and partly by allowing readers to ignore real consequences of those wars, anticipates Judith Butler's analysis of the "frames of war." Butler explores the conditions under which societies agree that killing is acceptable when it is recognized as warfare rather than murder, and she observes that "the frame initiates (as part of weaponry) or finishes off (as part of reporting) a whole set of murderous deeds . . . its success depends upon a successful conscription of the public" (*Frames*, xiii–xiv). Playing with the term "conscription" by suggesting that noncombatants also participate in wars through their assent to military apparatuses, Butler follows a line of thinking we have seen in *Three Guineas* and the "Memoir of Julian Bell." In "The War from the Street," an earlier essay, in which Woolf reviewed D. Bridgman Metchim's *Our Own History of the War: From a South London View*, she criticized a phenomenon much like this noncombatant conscription, directing ire at the insularity of the "south London view," which seems little affected by the war, only glancing off of it through gossip and half-heard news stories. She writes: "Soon your mind, if one may distinguish one part of the jelly from another, has had certain inscriptions scored upon it so repeatedly that it believes that it has originated them; and you begin to have violent opinions of your own" (*E*, 3:4). In *The Years*, she would also attack that jelly-like lack of discrimination and immersion in the frame of war so deep that it cannot begin to be recognized.

Martin Pargiter, whose picture in uniform Crosby cherishes, has for the most part a genteel and casual association with military ancestry, most obviously through his father, the colonel, but his father was a more seasoned combatant, losing a finger in the 1857 Indian Mutiny. By 1913, Martin is a member of the middle-class reading public, conscious that the "end" of the Balkan Wars does not mean the end of all violence in the region, and his perusal of the newspaper suggests the casual acceptance of this violence as a natural order of things. Butler's call to action implores: "Our responsibility to resist war depends in part on how well we resist that daily effort at conscription" (*Frames*, xiv). Antiwar literature thus might be seen as an intercession into that frame, a way of interrupting the frame's persuasive hold on the public narrative of war and a means for recasting that narrative in terms less favorable to war's success. In *The Years*, Woolf—ever vigilant to resist propaganda—avoids any strong use of pathos, but the background of the Balkans conflict and a foreground of nonchalant class prejudice place within the reader's grasp the unease that attends our realization that war is coming. Giving readers the agency to compile disparate fragments and to realize the shaping influence of war even when characters themselves do not is a key strategy through which the novel enacts nonviolence.[40]

One of the most striking "evasions" in *The Years* is Woolf's choice to set the "1914" chapter in the "brilliant" springtime on a "radiant" day made singing and alive by air that "seemed to have a burr in it" (*TY*, 212). The beautiful country, with shimmering trees, red clover, and flying rooks mirrors the London cityscape with its spires, hooting horns, and flying flags. England's rural and urban beauty is troubled somewhat by the sound of church clocks that "were irregular, as if the saints themselves were divided," but this mild disturbance in an otherwise splendid spring is the only foreshadowing of much worse divisions to come (ibid.). Martin lunches with Sara and tells her of his connection to St. Paul's Cathedral, where he found himself "wishing I'd been an architect . . . But they sent me into the Army instead, which I loathed" (217). Like much of the novel, the restaurant scene is pointedly mundane, consumed with fragmentary talk of little real substance and providing instead succinct descriptions of food and wine. Peppering the mundanity are little moments in which the reader is allowed to glimpse rich characterization in the subtlest of forms—Martin denies Sara her fourth glass of wine, and Sara admits that she must see her militant suffragette sister Rose in prison, where she is being held for throwing a brick. Then, the waiter at their meal attempts a small scam when Martin pays the bill, hiding a coin he intends to pocket. Martin is understandably outraged, but there is a telling detail: "He felt exactly like his father in a rage; as if he had white spots above his temples" (220). This passing of masculine rage on through generations of patrilineal descent is crucial to Woolf's portrayal of structural violence. Martin is far from being an ardent militarist—he loathed the army, after all—but he still retains a corrupted version of his father's character, the rage at insubordination or incompetence from servants, and a need to control everything in his social space, from the conversation to Sara's alcohol intake. In a more jingoistic character than Martin, it would have been difficult for Woolf to avoid preachiness, but through her evasion of grand historical events or self-styled ideologues, she shows that in the spring of this fateful year, the last real months of peace are attended by petty and callous people who hardly seem to notice the violence all around them. By focusing in "1914" on these characters, Woolf offers no idealized portrait of people from her set displaying themselves "all" as COs and focuses neither on radicals nor policy makers. With this concentration on ordinariness and typicality, the pacifist agenda takes root at a deeper, structural level.

"Beauty, Simplicity and Peace"

For Siegfried Sassoon, as we have seen, the decades before the war were thick with nostalgia, an idyllic time shattered, though later understood as ripe with violent ideologies leading toward its own dissolution. Woolf offers an even less sanguine portrait of the "old century," and The Years suggests that progress is a matter of increasingly ossified militarism broken only by occasional shafts of peace. Beginning the novel in 1880, Woolf introduces her saga with an "uncertain spring" (TY, 3) that finds paterfamilias Colonel Abel Pargiter at his club—most likely the Naval and Military Club of Piccadilly—a setting that establishes the colonel's situation in the social fabric of the novel through his status as a military figure and patriarch.[41] From the very beginning, the descriptions of weather that Woolf added late in her drafting to introduce each chapter create an uncertain mood that pervades the narrative, an uncertainty with multiple causes, but most palpably, the anticipation of war. The civilization Woolf depicts, even in the relatively peaceful last two decades of Victoria's reign, is built around preparations for war, rewards for engaging in war, and an all-around tolerance of violence. With a point of view that tours several London landmarks, including Apsley House with its statue of Achilles and the Marble Arch with its Roman warriors in relief, the novel begins with immersion in unstated reminders that military history supplies much of what feels essential to Britain's capital.

Portraying masculinist-militarist ideologies as fundamental to British culture means that Woolf's criticism in *The Years* gestures toward the radical and utopian vision more fully articulated in *Three Guineas*. In her contribution to Mark Hussey's seminal collection, *Virginia Woolf and War*, Patricia Cramer interprets *The Years* as a "recording of unpleasant 'facts' of patriarchal life in the tradition of the realistic chronicle," in which "Woolf simultaneously weaves a matriarchal myth building a vision of 'another life,' another 'state of being'" ("Loving," 204). This idea of a "matriarchal myth" that builds a new sense of "life" and "being" shares with my argument a recognition of Woolf's utopian imagination. In one of her own descriptions of the published book, Woolf wrote to Stephen Spender in April 1937: "what I meant I think was to give a picture of society as a whole . . . turn them towards society, not private life; exhibit the effect of ceremonies; Keep one toe on the ground by means of dates, facts; . . . Compose into one vast many-sided group at the end; and then shift the stress from present to future; and show the old fabric insensibly changing without death or violence into the future" (*L*, 116). The forward progress of a "many-sided" constellation of people, shaped and molded by ceremony and ideology and narratively grounded by attention to concrete details such as "dates" and "facts," would, Woolf hoped, evoke a "future [that] was gradually to dawn" (ibid.). Her insistence that this movement might occur without violence signals her polemical refashioning of history.[42] Woolf notes that the form of her radical history will suggest "that there is no break, but a continuous development, possibly a recurrence of some pattern; of which of course we actors are ignorant" (ibid.) Those cyclical patterns, used for antiviolent effects in *Three Guineas*, are named as the basis for a restructured approach to progress, one with greater capaciousness and a nonviolent mode. In typical self-deprecating fashion, Woolf concludes: "Of course I failed completely" (ibid).

In the scene most closely connected to combat, the air raid in the "1917" chapter, the interactions of the characters swerve away from sharply defined position statements, and through this evasive point of view Woolf exposes the powerful way the frame of war conscripts these otherwise peace-minded noncombatants. The discussions among Sara, Maggie, Renny, and Eleanor, like much of the novel, attend to the mundane, as in their argument about the plates from Maggie and Eleanor's "drawing-room at home," which Renny snidely observes are broken at the rate of one a week (*TY*, 269). Maggie blankly responds: "They'll last the war" (ibid.). Renny's face changes, assuming a "curious mask-like expression," which Eleanor attributes to his underlying French patriotism (ibid.) Regarding herself, Eleanor feels "a little light-headed" and "blurred" from wine drinking, which seems to her like "light after the dark; talk after silence" (ibid.). The mixture of emotion and observation culminates in a free indirect moment with Eleanor supposing that it was "the war, perhaps, removing barriers" (ibid.). This removal of barriers, flush of wine and patriotism, and time's passing marked by broken dishware are all signals of the war's frame. Each moment in their lives, no matter how banal and supposedly distant from the centers of power and diplomatic hierarchies that generate war, each of these minute changes in affect and apparently trivial actions takes some of its shape from the context of war. Through Renny's gibe about the plates, his insinuation that women in the household cannot even be trusted to manage responsibly their trifling domestic duties, Woolf renders a scene with patriarchal inequality in the foreground that is heightened by the war in the background.

All of these characters are effectively conscripted by the war, even while opposing it. Sara is the most overtly pacifist character in the scene, ridiculing North's exuberant militarism by calling him a lieutenant in the "Royal Regiment of Rat-catchers or something" (270). Though Sara expresses views we might readily associate with Woolf's own—particularly her mockery of military pomp—Woolf resists propaganda by lacing Sara's character with bitterness and militancy that undermine the virtuousness of her position. Sara describes her last encounter with North, sitting in what she calls his "mud-coloured uniform, with his switch between his legs, and his ears sticking out on either side of his pink, foolish face"—a description that fails to contain her rage at his attitude and appearance (ibid.). Most infuriating is his impassiveness while repeating "Good, Good" and manipulating his switch, a lame yet irksome reminder of his phallic power sustained by militarism. But rather than finding a thoroughly nonviolent response to North, Sara indulges in militancy herself and grasps at phallic power, drowning out North's murmuring by taking up a "poker and tongs . . . and play[ing] 'God save the King'" (ibid.). While relating this anecdote to Eleanor and the others, she repeats her performance with silverware, holding "her knife and fork as if they were weapons" (ibid.). In Sara's militant pacifism, even her antiwar protests grow violent and link her with the militant suffragette Rose whom we later learn has patriotically joined the war effort.

In this scene, Sara is not merely hindered or oppressed by patriarchal social structures, she reproduces them, displaying an inability to imagine some moral alternative. The problem with Sara's behavior is not that her rhetoric is forceful or associated with violence. After all, Woolf was not averse to violent metaphors on behalf of peace, such as her often quoted diary entry about *Three Guineas* in which she notes that she has "collected enough powder to blow up St Pauls" (*D*, 4:77). Rather, the problem with Sara's position is its failure to be more than reactionary; hers is a politics based in response to the thing she despises, and she conducts her opposition by using the enemy's own terms. The "use of indifference" Woolf advocates in *Three Guineas* offers another kind of engagement from the one that Sara models. Though Sara could be seen as reclaiming the enemy's language and using his own tools against him, Woolf's broader agenda in *The Years* shows that violence cannot successfully bring an end to violence. To combat the inevitability of war, Woolf suggests, we need a revolutionary change in our social structures.

Woolf signals the failure of a "war for peace" by puncturing the emotional uplift that the characters experience once the raid ceases. When the raid is over, none of them can remember what they were talking about before it started, and its interruption—like the devastating interruption of the Great War itself—rigidly separates them from their earlier train of thought. The broken form of the scene enacts the content of Woolf's critique. Sara proposes a toast to the New World, and they all momentarily join in exhilarated optimism at the thought of the postwar world to come. But in the distance, they hear the guns still firing and "a sound like the breaking of waves on a shore far away" (*TY*, 277). Not only are they reminded that the end of war has not yet begun, a more sinister element resurfaces in Renny's angry effort at reassurance, when he kicks a wooden box and "savagely" says: "They're only killing other people" (ibid.). As with his previous eruption of patriotic sentiment, his appearance changes and "the mask had come down over his face" (ibid.). Not simply a shift in facial expression, the "mask" signifies hardened submission to violent impulses and self-preservation—precisely the attitudes that allow otherwise good people to affirm a war conducted for their benefit. The emotional uplift felt during the cessation of active violence is thus undercut by a reminder that peace is not the same thing as the absence of immediate warfare. As long as Renny and others like him perpetually sink into violence, and thoughtful yet ambivalent people like Eleanor are conscripted by the frame, and politically active people like Sara resort to militancy, then the socially structured preconditions of war will remain intact.

Those violent social structures are subtly yet powerfully attacked in the novel's elliptical, allusive form with its fragmentary assemblage of voices that require active reading. The final "Present Day" chapter set in the early 1930s exhibits most clearly Woolf's choral mode, bringing together many of the characters, voices, themes, and incidents into a collage that demands the reader's synthesis. Sara and North discuss their last meeting, years before in 1917, and engage in a process of reconciliation while eating a wretched meal whose centerpiece is a joint of mutton, a "rather stringy disagreeable object which was still bleeding into the well" on a "willow-pattern plate" now "daubed with gory streaks" (304). This evocative, sacrificial feast evokes Sara and North's earlier disagreement about military killing and the blood between them, yet it is through this meal that they come to terms with each other and restore something of their former friendship. Throughout the "Present Day" chapter, Woolf returns to sites of conflict, presents the ineffaceable stain of bloodshed, war, and violence, and still manages a glimmer of hope for a "another world, a new world"—the mantra of her characters during the lull in the air raid and in the aftermath of the novel's final party (401).

This last party does not eliminate conflict or neutralize the structural violence inherent in a society barreling toward another war, but Woolf infuses the final scene with some of her most romantic optimism. The revelers at Delia's party emerge into the strange light of dawn to realize that omnibuses and the underground have stopped running, and the usually belligerent Rose invites them to walk together home: "Walking won't do us any harm," she says (411). In the open air, the concluding single-sentence paragraph offers a last look at the seasonal weather that marks the passage of time throughout the novel: "The sun had risen, and the sky above the houses wore an air of extraordinary beauty, simplicity and peace" (412). This calm ending may seem insufficiently ironic and skeptical, a romantic excess in a work so thoroughly laced with cynicism about the progress of time and the violence of "civilization." Yet I would contend that this last paragraph is not a solution to the problems posed by the rest of the narrative but instead functions like the final voice in a choral work—meaningful as the concluding tone but not wholly dismissive of the range of voices preceding it. While writing this ending, Woolf noted: "I want a Chorus. a general statement. a song for 4 voices. how am I to get it? . . . And how to make the transition from the colloquial to the lyrical, from the particular to the general?" (D, 4:236). Instead of seeking tidy conclusiveness, the active reader must work to make connections, assemble fragments, and hold together disparate voices in opposition to the ideologies of patriarchy and militarism. Through cyclical, elliptical, and "indifferent" narration, The Years achieves a form of textual nonviolence that requires a reader to participate actively in the peace witness that Woolf creates. The novel thus becomes an artistic testament against bloodshed, challenging the frame of war through Woolf's narrative pacifism.

The Death of Pacifism?

Deviating from Woolf's misgivings about her conclusion to The Years, which she immediately felt was "Such feeble twaddle—such twilight gossip" (D, 5:8), critics have found in her final revised version a "rather blurred message of hope" (Levenback, Virginia Woolf and the Great War, 143) or "a tenuous peace" (Cole, Violet Hour, 260). If the last lines of The Years embrace a limited hopefulness and even romanticism, her subsequent writings can be read as a retreat from even that tentative optimism.

Critical biographers often portray these years as ones of tragic failure. Thus, Marder writes of Woolf's disposition in 1940: "if hearty patriotism was suspect, pacifism no longer served her either, and she had nothing to put in its place" (*Measure of Life*, 296). Even more pithily, Zwerdling's penultimate chapter of *Virginia Woolf and the Real World* is titled "Pacifism without Hope." Woolf's diary shows a torturous struggle to maintain her convictions and sense of self during the rising crises, recording in the middle of September 1940: "Could it be the end of resident servants for ever? This I pray this lovely fitful evening, as well as the usual Damn Hitler prayer" (*D*, 5:321). These comments contain a perfectly Woolfian sentiment: a bit of classism (worrying about the end of resident servants) combined with a succinct description of the evening mood and a reference to a religious practice made agnostic, political, and cheeky. The "prayer" to damn Hitler shows her still fighting with her mind, even though the London Blitz had been underway for several days, and, as we now know, would continue several weeks more. In the ongoing scholarly discussion of these last months in Woolf's life, there is general consensus that the changing crisis around her placed extraordinary pressures on her heretofore uncompromising political views, though whether her final writings constitute an abandonment of pacifism remains a subject of debate.[43]

Many controversies surround Woolf's posthumously published novel, *Between the Acts*, and its relation to her politics at the end of her life. Instead of directly responding to these critical disagreements, I wish to point out a problematic dimension of the debate about Woolf's late pacifism, which is that it often retains the polarized logic that my entire study has sought to trouble. As long as we remain fixated on whether Woolf *was* or *was not* a pacifist at the end of her life, we will reproduce the pacifism/antipacifism binary that plagues so many attempts to examine peace activism. As I have maintained throughout this study, there are many varieties of pacifism and possibly even more numerous expressions of pacifist conviction, not to mention the many ways nonviolence can be endorsed and enacted by people who do not claim any ideological pacifism. One reason that, with equal plausibility, some critics can claim that Woolf's pacifism never wavered and some that her last novel signals an endorsement of military force is that her aesthetic practices, with their refusal to supply single-minded visions, allow for a range of competing positions to be expressed. Sifting through her diaries and letters for evidence of a definitive change of heart can at times neglect the ephemeral and transitory ways these documents work, the diary especially being a place to preserve and record thoughts as they arose without belabored deliberation.

With these qualifications in mind, I turn briefly to "Thoughts on Peace in an Air Raid," Woolf's essay for an American audience, which she read in condensed form to a meeting of the Rodmell Local Labour Party. As an argument for Americans, a country not yet officially involved in the war, there is a strong activist edge to her writing and a seeming abandonment of her earlier writings that had urged artists to eschew politics. During the process of composition, the essay developed into an extension of her *Three Guineas* arguments, in which she would make Lady Astor's exhortation to defeat "subconscious Hitlerism," the militarist energies that propel men toward war, into a refrain.[44] She divides the fighting men of England and Germany from weaponless women, deprived of direct combat experience because of gender, but still suggests that making munitions, clothes, and food are just one way to fight. Of greater appeal to her is to "think peace into existence" (*E*, 6:242). Amid the material realities of bombs crashing around her and the "hornet" sounds of airplanes overhead, she says that women are uniquely suited for thought because men are occupied with fighting. Blake's notion of a "mental fight," which she cites approvingly, requires going past simplistic cries for disarmament; she knows how futile those same cries had been after 1918 and demands instead something more fundamental to eradicate the desire for war, which is deeply rooted at the emotional, ideological, and possibly even biological level.[45] Something must be done to "compensate the man for the loss of his gun" (6:244). To undo the conditions that have led to this renewal of violent conflict, drastic measures are needed that get to the heart of what Woolf diagnoses as a masculinist enterprise—the phallic appropriation of weaponry while "all the searchlights are erect" (ibid.).[46] "Access to creative feelings" is her prescription for freeing Englishmen from slavery to the war machine, and she admits that unless German and Italian men are similarly free, then war will not cease (6:245). In her list of beautiful, art-filled moments that she finds personally restorative— signs of the better life being swallowed up in war—she mentions "the memory of other Augusts—in Bayreuth, listening to Wagner; in Rome, walking over the Campagna" (ibid.). These are gestures toward Germany and Italy, places of beauty that could be crucial to restoring peace. But she ends the essay in a lull from explosions, with a wish for Americans to keep seeking peace while they still can. "Thoughts on Peace in an Air Raid" is far from a straightforward renunciation of pacifism, but it is also not a systematic program for waging nonviolent struggle or even a promotion of a specific pacifist agenda in wartime. It remains a version of "indifference," the effort to think against violent forces and outside established peace organizations.

After Woolf's death, Vera Brittain would make an early case for seeing her suicide as a form of antiwar activism, writing in the *Peace News-Letter* that "her end was perhaps a kind of protest, the most terrible and effective that she could make, against the real hell which international conflict creates for artists" (*Testament*, 69–70).[47] Brittain's take on Woolf's death has been disputed by later scholars, but what it does show, regardless of its biographical accuracy, is how important Woolf was as a figure among pacifists during World War II.[48] The *Peace News-Letter*, which had ties with the Peace Pledge Union and Anglican Pacifist Fellowship, was Brittain's way of staying connected to a large group of pacifist and peace-minded readers eager for community and for ideas about how to think about and engage with day-to-day operations of the war effort. That her death required commentary in this enterprise suggests Woolf's significant symbolic role as a high-profile, celebrity pacifist whose self-inflicted death might easily be taken as a broader failure for peace activism. Brittain's obituary gives a highly politicized account of Woolf's action, spinning it for a reading public desperate for a silver lining in the otherwise bleak forecast.

Another memorialization of Woolf's legacy stands today in Tavistock Square along with the bust erected in 2004 by the Virginia Woolf Society of Great Britain. On the plinth beneath the bust, a plaque informs us that Woolf lived on the south side of the square "from 1924 to 1939 where most of her greatest novels were written and published" and below this a quotation from "A Sketch of the Past," her recollection of walking in Tavistock Square and making up *To the Lighthouse* in "an involuntary rush." This monument highlights great literary production and Woolf's treasured particularity of place. Unmentioned directly, though hovering unspoken in the background, is that in 1939, the same year she was writing "A Sketch of the Past," she would move from that long tenure at 52

Tavistock Square to another Bloomsbury residence—the latter damaged and the former destroyed by German bombs. Near Woolf's monument, there are several other memorials of note for peace activists, including a statue of Gandhi, a cherry tree for the victims of Hiroshima, and an inscribed stone memorializing conscientious objectors.[49] This last artifact, commissioned and installed by the Peace Pledge Union, has an especially poignant quality, placing Woolf near other objectors to war. Quite fittingly, her own memorial says nothing about peace activism, but instead recognizes her literary art and places her as a pacifist outsider working alongside the British peace movement.

Perceiving the Peace Movement

Huxley went abroad, a prophet for the new world. Jameson embraced pragmatism, deciding that war was a lesser evil than Nazism. Sassoon, morbidly obsessed with what he had seen and done in combat, gave up antiwar crusading and offered qualified support to the Allied effort. Macaulay dwelt in despair over the ruins of civilization. Woolf remained the unaffiliated outsider whose death alleviated her need to find a third way between violence and submission. In each case, the failure to effectively stop war by stopping Nazism through peaceful means became an endpoint for absolute pacifism. All five writers demonstrated their advocacy for peace through fiction and political activity, but the unstoppable war made their efforts—at least when measured by short-term efficacy—a collective failure. The legacy of their writings, as well as the activities of the peace movement, however, carries on, providing resources for modern peace activists and for artists integrating creative complexity with political commitment. By way of a coda, I touch on two writers whose fiction continues to explore our perceptions of the British peace movement.

In 1948, still holding to her unwavering though subtly modified pacifism, Vera Brittain published her novel *Born 1925*, a piece of historical fiction that imagines a character modeled on Dick Sheppard living through the Second World War. Brittain's Robert Carbery is a decorated veteran of the Great War whose Victoria Cross gives greater weight to his later pacifism. A popular Anglican vicar appointed to St. Saviour's, Armada Square (stand-in for St. Martin's, Trafalgar), Carbery spends his celebrity capital forming a Christian peace organization called "Builders of Jerusalem." The BOJ takes its name from Blake's poem, wresting from conservative, imperialist nationalism the vision of England's "green and pleasant lands" and refashioning this utopia for radical, religious-pacifist ends. Brittain's novel never fully becomes a utopian fantasy or counter-factual history in which an Anglican leader prevents global war, but the BOJ develops her speculations about significant Christian peace witness during wartime.

As Brittain renders it, the essential role for the peace activist in an age of total war is that of the prophet. Throughout the war, Carbery is despised by most of his fellow citizens, who rally to the war effort, and he even for a time loses the allegiance of his son, Adrian—the titular youth whose midtwenties birthdate puts him squarely in the new war genera-tion. Adrian repudiates his father's pacifism and joins the army, though eventually he comes to admire Robert's independence and fortitude. Those traits forge Robert's prophetic stance, along with his perseverance on a righteous course despite an absence of visible, effective results. His prophecy is especially on display in his last major public appearance (he, like Sheppard, dies at his desk from exhaustion), a sermon at St. Saviour's delivered after V-E Day and broadcast throughout the country. Unlike the 1918 armistice, Brittain's narrator tells us, when crowds were uni-formly jubilant at the end of hostilities, the V-E Day gathering "did not appear triumphant and excited" because "too many of its members were still dazed by their years of anxiety and peril," and "they had all emerged too recently from the shadow of death" (*Born 1925*, 311). To a packed house and innumerable listeners over the airwaves, Robert proclaims their collective need for confession and forgiveness and leads a prayer for the end of conflict in Japan as well as a prayer for their German enemies. Enemy love, reconciliation, and a return to the "missed opportunity" for peace and national renewal are the core of his message (ibid., 317). He looks "ill and frail" but bears "a strange appearance of transfigura-tion," and he exhorts his hearers "to build Jerusalem—not only here, but throughout the world" (ibid., 312, 317). He does not live to see the fruits of his prophecy, and the novel leaves his son as the bearer of that vision alongside the implied reader.

Brittain's novel is not as rhetorically subtle or formally adventurous as the novels by Huxley, Jameson, Sassoon, Macaulay, and Woolf that I have discussed. It provides, however, an intriguing glimpse into cultural perceptions of the peace movement after the 1930s. She all but avoids thorny questions about nonviolent responses to Hitler, the pacifist's engagement with the Holocaust, or tactical objectives for postwar peace activism. Instead of a tract, she gives a narrative vision, urging readers to reach for those best traits of activists like Sheppard now that another chance has been granted to prevent future wars. Rather than detailed prescriptions for the future or historical revisionism, her attitude in *Born 1925* is one of cautious optimism for peacebuilding after V-E Day, when international relations might once more be forged against war.

Less sympathetic to the peace movement, but still clearly invested in a thoughtful representation of its quandaries and contradictions is Sophie Hardach's recent novel *Of Love and Other Wars* (2013). The relationships in Hardach's story are all based in conflicting positions about war and faith: a Quaker father versus his RAF son, a PPU signatory engaged to a Jewish munitions factory worker, a Friends ambulance driver separated from her Jewish German fiancée by his internment first in Britain and then by the Nazis. All of these relationships ask questions about the viability of absolutism in the face of the complexities of lived experience both in international conflicts and in romance. Late in the novel, siblings Charlie and Paul Lamb debate their respective positions about fighting. Paul is impulsive and contrarian, and had encouraged his brother to join the PPU in opposition to their family's Quaker expression of pacifist quietism. The New Pacifism of Gerald Heard, Aldous Huxley, and Dick Sheppard gives Charlie purpose, meaning, and a modern twist to inherited values of his youth, and he remains committed to the PPU despite his brother's defection and eventual military service. Charlie challenges Paul by showing his old pledge card, "dog-eared" and with "a jagged boyish ink scrawl across the bottom" (*Of Love*, 289). Paul accuses Charlie of naivety and childishness for clinging to this card when realities have changed, but the narration gives space to a lengthy speech from Paul, who aligns his current peace witness with their family history, in which "all the men in our family have honoured *their* pledge . . . and every single one of them must have had a niggling doubt as to whether their particular war was different" (291). The scene ends with a sense that Paul's absolutism is largely foolish, but Hardach strives to make it intelligible. Though somewhat mechanical in its representation of divisions among people arguing about war and pacifism, the novel does portray internal contradictions that show lived pacifism to be less simple and homogeneous than its stereotypical version. The peace movement provides a testing ground in this novel for considering essential values and the costs inherent in choices we make to stay fixed in beliefs or modify them according to circumstances.

Whereas Brittain's novel leans toward utopia through its glimpse of a world made better by Dick Sheppard's prolonged influence, Hardach's book takes conflict, division, and failure as its narrative catalysts. That looming sense of failure is perhaps more consistent with the 1930s writings by Huxley, Jameson, Sassoon, Macaulay, and Woolf. But as I have argued throughout this book, we need not take failure as an endpoint or as grounds for ignoring the efforts of peace activist writers. In their writings we see how idealistic revolutionary impulses coexist with skepticism and self-doubt, and how creative expression joins political passion within art that is both complex and exhortative. For we who live in this century of perpetual war that gives little sign of abating, the creative visions of pacifist revolutionaries who imagined nonviolent alternatives to war and—however briefly—believed in the realism of their cause may be worthy of inspiration. Out of their visions may arise resources for our own writing against war.

Introduction

1. See especially Lassner, *British Women Writers of World War II*; Brothers, "British Women Write the Story of the Nazis."

2. Storm Jameson to Vera Brittain, March 10, 1933, Vera Brittain Collection, McMaster University Library, Hamilton, Ontario.

3. Among the many histories of the British peace movement during the twentieth century and before, I am especially indebted to Brock, *Freedom from Violence and Freedom from War*; Brock and Young, *Pacifism in the Twentieth Century*; Carsten, *War against War*; Ceadel, *The Origins of War Prevention*, *Pacifism in Britain 1914–1945*, *Semi-Detached Idealists*, and *Thinking about Peace and War*; Cortright, *Peace*; Laity, *The British Peace Movement 1870–1914*; Robbins, *Abolition of War*.

4. An excellent resource on peace/war terminology is Ceadel, *Thinking about Peace and War*, which proposes a shared lexicon for these issues. Ceadel himself admits that "pacific-ism" is inelegant (*Thinking*, 102) and betrays its awkwardness through his changing usage from "pacificism" (1980) to "pacific-ism" (1989) to "pacificism" (2003).

5. "Just war" thinking has a long legacy, perhaps as far back as Aristotle but continued in Augustine and solidified by Aquinas. The successful integration of just war language into popular and political discourse does not come until the post-Vietnam era. See Walzer, *Arguing about War*, 3–22; Yoder, *Nonviolence*, 49–62.

6. The best resource for encountering the diversity within pacifism is Yoder, *Nevertheless*.

7. Kurlansky, *Nonviolence*, 5. See also Cortright, *Gandhi and Beyond*.

8. Howes, "The Failure of Pacifism," 430. Howes offers a further distinction pertinent to understanding Gandhi's promotion of satyagraha ("truth force" or "insistence upon truth"), noting that the concept "plac[es] special emphasis on methods that may put those taking action at physical risk" (430). For a provocative application of satyagraha to World War II, see Howes, *Toward a Credible Pacifism*, 121–48.

9. Sharp, *Waging Nonviolent Struggle*, 21, 3. The core of Sharp's work can be found in *Waging Nonviolent Struggle* and in his three-volume opus *The Politics of Nonviolent Action*.

10. See, for instance, Andrew Rigby's critique of the Peace Pledge Union in "The Response of British Pacifists to World War II."

11. Hershberger is an important exception, claiming a prophetic stance of total nonresistance and arguing against Gandhian nonviolence — a position he later modified during his support for the American civil rights struggles of the 1960s (*War, Peace and Nonresistance*, vii–viii, 190–97).

12. See the organization's website, http://www.ppu.org.uk.

13. See Wollaeger, *Modernism, Media, and Propaganda*.

14. See, for example, Beauman, *A Very Great Profession*; Humble, *The Feminine Middlebrow Novel 1920s to 1950s*; Joannou, *Women Writers of the 1930s*; Kershaw and Kimyongür, *Women in Europe between the Wars*; Kohlmann, *Committed Styles*; Montefiore, *Men and Women Writers of the 1930s*; Williams and Matthews, *Rewriting the Thirties*.

15. Valuable recent works include Ashe and Patterson, *War and Literature*; Favret, *War at a Distance*; McLoughlin, *Authoring War*; Margot Norris, *Writing War in the Twentieth Century*; Sheehan, *Modernism and the Aesthetics of Violence*.

16. See http://www.gf.org/fellows/all-fellows/sarah-cole/.

17. Jameson attributes this idea to John Aldridge (*The Antinomies of Realism*, 257).

18. Laurence Lerner's hope for "peace studies" to become a literary subfield like queer and feminist studies has not gained much traction ("Peace Studies: A Proposal"). White's *Pacifism and English Literature* expresses similar ambitions for a new mode of literary history that emphasizes peace (1–12). For a survey with a smaller scale, see Patterson, "Pacifists and Conscientious Objectors."

19. White's use of natural law cannot be adequately examined in these pages, but I will note that I find it unfortunate that he takes the natural basis for pacifism as self-evident rather than developing an argument about this point. Within a natural law paradigm, one might still support the need to protect weaker victims of injustice with violent force. White's assumptions about the naturalness of a life drive make too many literary works available to the pacifist lens, because so much creative work affirms life in one way or another.

20. Lewis's essay was first given as a talk to a pacifist organization in 1940 (*The Weight of Glory*, 80).

21. White's study is not especially contentious in his presentation of these pacifist moments throughout English literature, and nowhere does he explicitly reference C. S. Lewis. It would be interesting to apply White's theory of reading through a "pacifist lens" to Lewis's fiction. Stanley Hauerwas offers a thorough critique of Lewis's essay from a Christian pacifist perspective, affirming Lewis's criticism of what Hauerwas calls "liberal pacifism"—a belief in pacifism as a strategy for eliminating war and based in values such as civilization and reason—but noting that Lewis fails to address the strongest arguments for religious pacifism and betrays an unfortunately limited imagination regarding conflict ("C. S. Lewis and Violence").

22. Though many peace studies programs include coursework in theology, history, philosophy, and some even in literary studies, the dominant models still emphasize fields such as political science, global affairs, anthropology, and sociology. See, for example, the Kroc Institute for International Peace Studies at Notre Dame, http://kroc.nd.edu; Wallensteen, *Peace Research*.

23. Among literary studies that draw on Lederach, see Russell, *Poetry and Peace*.

24. Knowles, "Active Pacifism in a World at War."

25. See, for instance, Lassner, *British Women Writers*. The philosopher most indebted to Woolf's version of feminist thinking about war is Sara Ruddick in *Maternal Thinking* and "Notes Toward a Feminist Peace Politics."

26. Ceadel reproduces the survey and adds "that half a million volunteers helped distribute and collect the forms was more impressive than the fact that 11,640,066

people, an estimated 38.2 per cent of the UK population aged over 18, were persuaded to fill them in" (*Semi-Detached*, 318).

27. See Lynch, *Beyond Appeasement*; Cortright, *Peace: A History*, 79–81; Neville, *Hitler and Appeasement*; Ascher, *Was Hitler a Riddle?*

28. See the epigraph for this chapter, from Brittain and Holtby, *Testament of a Generation*, 210.

29. Morrison notes that this comment in West's 1949 version of the book was removed from the later edition which was called *The New Meaning of Treason*. Silent emendation of the offensive passage appeared "after a lengthy correspondence between the General Secretary [of the PPU] and the publishers," but Morrison tartly adds: "Rebecca West herself consistently refused to see the General Secretary or to make any apology" (*I Renounce*, 51).

30. On Orwell's changing views about war, see William T. Ross, "Words, War, and Peace," 187–96. Among historians following Orwell's line, see Gilbert, "Pacifist Attitudes to Nazi Germany."

31. See Ackerman and Kruegler, *Strategic Nonviolent Conflict*, 213–50; Sharp, *Waging Nonviolent Struggle*, 135–42.

32. See Fixdal, *Just Peace*.

33. *The Pledge of Peace* compiles Murry's essays for the PPU's *Peace News* and his own *Adelphi* from May 1937 to February 1938.

Chapter 1

1. See Hynes, *A War Imagined*, 423–63.

2. Bradshaw argues that "much of what Huxley is presumed to have feared—such as the state use of eugenics, planning and propaganda—he actually embraced as desirable at the time he wrote the novel. In fact, Huxley was a vehement anti-democrat until the mid-1930s, when he committed himself to absolute pacifism" ("Modern Life," 226).

3. *The Hidden Huxley* was published in the United States as *Between the Wars: Essays and Letters* (Chicago: Ivan Dee, 1994).

4. See Murray, *Aldous Huxley*, chap. 5, including a list of guests that included Bertrand Russell, Virginia Woolf, and Clive Bell.

5. See Dunaway, *Huxley in Hollywood*, 14–17.

6. S. Krishnamoorthy Aithal conducts an elaborate reordering of the chapters as evidence for a claim that Huxley composed the novel chronologically and then shuffled the chapters. Aithal idiosyncratically suggests that the order of the chapters lends itself to six groups that correspond to the letters in "HUXLEY" or "BEAVIS." Aithal, "Huxley's *Eyeless in Gaza*." For examples of less far-reaching analyses that connect formalist readings to Huxley's philosophical influences, see Keith M. May, *Aldous Huxley*; Wasserman, "Huxley's Either/Or." Dunaway also tentatively repeats the apocryphal story that Huxley drafted the novel chronologically and cut his typescript with scissors ("Introduction," ix). Bradshaw dismisses this speculation by quoting Huxley's letter to Richard Mealand, which reveals that Huxley added the 1934 and 1935 sections at the end of his writing process ("Flight from Gaza," 16).

7. Bradshaw writes: "it is essential to appreciate how let down the PPU felt when Huxley left for the United States in April. Although he fully intended to return to Britain, Huxley's decision to lecture abroad when he was at the height of his popularity and influence at home baffled his admirers and detractors alike" ("Flight from

Gaza," 24). Huxley's departure to North America during the war puts him in the company of other figures, such Benjamin Britten, Peter Pears, W. H. Auden, and Christopher Isherwood—friends and acquaintances whose flight from Europe also sparked controversy.

8. A lengthy letter of July 30, 1939, to his brother Julian describes this commitment to the "Bates Method" (*LAH*, 441–43). Huxley's experience with blindness and eye exercises is most fully examined in *The Art of Seeing*.

9. Sarah Cole claims that Sheppard's initial appeal "called explicitly for the votes of men, the reasoning being that a peace movement made up primarily of women would have little political force" (*Violet Hour*, 228). She likens Sheppard to C. E. M. Joad whose misogyny Woolf attacked in *Three Guineas*. Cole's miscasting of Sheppard as a Joad-like misogynist is belied by the history of the PPU's formation. Sheppard's appeal to men had more to do with the gendering of combatants than fearfulness about a women's peace movement, and even the Royal Albert Hall rally, which primarily comprised men who had signed the peace pledge, featured Maude Royden as a keynote speaker. Once it officially began in 1936, the PPU had women such as Vera Brittain in leadership positions, which quickly led to full acceptance of female membership (Hetherington, *Swimming*, 9).

10. Personal interview with Bill Hetherington, January 23, 2014. As a testament to the enduring value of Huxley's thought, today's PPU still offers a collection of his writings, *Pacifism and Philosophy*.

11. Nugel argues that Heard's *The Third Morality*, published in January 1937, predates Huxley's *Ends and Means* and signifies a difference in their thinking that undermines the critical assumption that *Ends and Means* is simply a "result of their collaboration" ("Aldous Huxley as Moral Philosopher," 47). Notwithstanding this nuanced interpretation, the sense of the two men's sharing a productive working relationship during these years is unavoidable, amounting to what Richard Overy describes as a noticeable effect on the PPU: "The Heard-Huxley axis distorted the aims of the Union and exposed it to the accusation that it was run by cranks" (*Morbid Age*, 253).

12. See Schneiderman's introduction, which repeatedly contrasts "Huxley's utopian mentality" and "Weber's realist sociology" (xix).

13. This longstanding treatment of Huxley's thought contradicts Hermione Lee's assertion that, by contrast with Virginia Woolf, "Bertrand Russell and Aldous Huxley did not get derided for mental instability or ludicrous Utopianism" (*Virginia Woolf*, 680).

14. See Peter van den Dungen, "Bart de Ligt, Aldous Huxley and 'The Conquest of Violence'"; de Ligt, *The Conquest of Violence*; Garland's 1972 edition of de Ligt's book is a reprint of the English translation (1937), revised and expanded from the French translation (1935), which itself was revised from the original Dutch version *De overwinning van het geweld* (1934). For publication history and biography, see Peter van den Dungen's introduction to *The Conquest of Violence*, available at http://www .satyagrahafoundation.org/bart-de-ligt-1883-1938-non-violent-anarcho-pacifist/.

15. Gregg's book went through multiple editions, with updates and revisions beginning in 1934. The first draft of the book was *The Psychology and Strategy of Gandhi's Nonviolent Resistance* (1929). After the first edition from 1934, Gregg published a revised and expanded edition in 1935. The most recent version, published by Greenleaf Books and featuring a foreword by Martin Luther King Jr., removes the hyphen from "non-violence" and includes examples of nonviolent resistance to the Nazis during

World War II. For an extended discussion of King's Greggist and Gandhian influences, see Kosek, *Acts of Conscience*. In another instance of Gregg's legacy, Gene Sharp used this martial arts metaphor in the 1970s, calling nonviolent warfare a matter of "political jujitsu" (*Politics of Nonviolent Action*, 2), though Sharp's more recent works have adopted the confrontational language of "political defiance" (*From Dictatorship to Democracy*, 25).

16. Bradshaw quotes from Huxley's *Vanity Fair* article of July 1930, "What Gandhi Fails to See" ("Flight from Gaza," 11–12).

17. On charismatic magnetism, see the first biography of Sheppard by his friend R. Ellis Roberts, *H. R. L. Sheppard: Life and Letters* (London: John Murray, 1942), vii.

18. Huxley's use of the word *agape* is idiosyncratic. He may be thinking of an *agape* feast, which would have been a gathering of early Christians around a meal distinct from the Eucharist. The more common term for an early Christian commune is *koinonia*.

19. McGann, "The Grand Heretics of Modern Fiction," 316.

20. Bradshaw has argued for these "three broad periods" of Huxley's intellectual and political development, admitting that "this parabola is crude and almost certainly contentious" ("Flight from Gaza," 9).

21. Huxley's November 27, 1941, letter to his brother Julian comments on speculation about the difference between "managerial wars" and "capitalist wars" and reiterates his insistence on social and economic revolution (*LAH*, 471–72).

Chapter 2

1. Milne, *Peace with Honour*, 18. Giving Zwerdling's implied disparagement of children's literature more than its fair consideration, I might point out that Huxley's *The Crows of Pear Blossom*—which was written in 1944 for his young niece and which tells of birds tricking a killer snake into swallowing clay eggs and then hanging him for a clothesline—may be one of its author's strongest endorsements of realpolitik.

2. See Lassner, "On the Point of a Journey."

3. For Jameson's productivity, see Maslen's bibliography (the most detailed to date), which runs to fifteen closely printed pages listing novels, stories, plays, adaptations, poems, nonfiction, and much more (*Life*, 514–29).

4. See Briganti, "Stern Cassandra"; Maslen, "A Cassandra with Clout."

5. Jameson to Brittain, September 6, 1941, Vera Brittain Collection, McMaster University Library.

6. See also Jameson, "Socialists Born and Made."

7. Jennifer Birkett's biography, *Margaret Storm Jameson: A Life*, situates Jameson within a broad French literary tradition from Balzac to Beckett. See also Birkett, "Re-Imagining Nations, Rewriting Lives."

8. Lukács identified Scott as the greatest progenitor of typicality through realism, a writer whose "greatness lies in his capacity to give living human embodiment to historical-social types" (*Historical Novel*, 35). For an extended discussion of the importance of Lukács to British literature of the 1930s, see Montefiore, *Men and Women Writers of the 1930s*, chapter 5.

9. Jameson discontinued the *Mirror in Darkness* series in 1936, but its characters recur in several other novels throughout her career, demonstrating their usefulness for helping frame her thoughts about England and its place in the world. Hervey returns

in Jameson's experimental autobiography, *The Journal of Mary Hervey Russell* (1945). David Renn becomes a witness to postwar devastations of Europe in the connected novels *Before the Crossing* (1947) and *The Black Laurel* (1947). Minor characters such as Marcel Cohen and Sally Rigden reappear in *The Green Man* (1952) and *A Cup of Tea for Mr. Thorgill* (1957).

10. Maslen points out the connection to Dos Passos's style and that even the name William Gary is a direct reference to *U.S.A.* (*Life*, 130).

11. A PPU pamphlet, *The Futility of Air Raid Precautions*, for instance, reprints a "Speech delivered in the House of Lords by Lord Arnold," making the case that ARP prepares Britons not for safety but for acceptance of war as a political solution. Peace Pledge Union file, Swarthmore College Peace Collection.

12. For discussion of Jameson's pre-1930s antiwar writing, including her novel *The Happy Highways* (1920), see Vance, "Lorca's Mantle."

13. On Chapman's complicated relationship with his military service in World War I as well as his return to the army in 1940 at age fifty, see Bond, *Survivors of a Kind*, 27–35.

14. Jameson to Brittain, March 10, 1933, Vera Brittain Collection. McMaster University Library.

15. Jameson to Brittain, Oct. 28, 1933, Vera Brittain Collection, McMaster University Library.

16. Sources are inconsistent regarding whether Noel-Baker or Jameson initiated this idea. Maslen notes the ambiguity as well as the problem of deciphering Jameson's "facts" about such meetings, which shifted depending on her audience (*Life*, 129).

17. Cecil's views about pacifism were complicated. After winning his Nobel Prize, he told students at Columbia University that if they had signed peace pledges, they should "give that up and join the League of Nations Societies instead." "Nobel Prize Awarded to Cecil," *New York Times*, November 19, 1937.

18. Birkett says that the opening essay is "something of a rant" that "piled up clichés" and parrots Viscount Cecil's views (*Margaret Storm Jameson*, 124). Mary Anne Schofield disagrees, arguing that "The Twilight of Reason" appeals to sanity and reason through a (feminine) counterbalance to Churchill's (masculinist) "finest hour" rhetoric, which ignores the realities of human suffering in wartime ("'Less Than a Whisper'").

19. See Addams, "Patriotism and Pacifists in Wartime"; Bertrand Russell, *Which Way to Peace?*

20. "Rooted cosmopolitanism" comes from Appiah, "Cosmopolitan Patriots." Rod Mengham describes Jameson as "an idiosyncratic, uncompromising, uncomfortable, elegiac, and prophetic writer, who for more than fifty years would not let go of the idea that English culture seen outside of its European context is incomprehensible and even invalid" ("Come Back," 192–93).

21. Lassner also discusses Jameson's use of panoramic form in "On a Point," 120–21.

22. Graham Greene, review of *Company Parade*.

23. In 1936, the year Jameson published her final *Mirror in Darkness* novel, Greene would supply his own "entertainment" on the theme of impending war with *A Gun for Sale*, his thriller about a hare-lipped hit man provoking World War II through an assassination. With its cast of corrupt politicians and quasi-fascist capitalists, Greene appears to have learned something from Jameson's calling "Bogy."

24. Birkett goes as far as to say that "the story of Margaret and Guy is at the centre of *Love in Winter*," and while this might be the overdetermined view of a biographer, the ways that Jameson mined her own life for material are inescapable (foreword, 9). Maslen notes the autobiographical elements but sees them as part of a "collage effect" that dwells equally in literary criticism and political prognostication and finds moments of "sheer sensual delight in the world" that match Woolfian high modernist aesthetics (*Life*, 142–43).

25. For more on the displayed items at this exhibition, see Richard Overy, *The Morbid Age*, 277; Walkowitz, *Night Out*, 126–132.

26. See Willis, *Leonard and Virginia Woolf as Publishers*, 237.

27. Woolf's depiction of Mosley concurs with P. G. Wodehouse's lampooning of the BUF in *The Code of the Woosters* (1938), which introduced Sir Roderick Spode and the Saviours of Britain, clad in "black shorts."

28. Lewis's *The Apes of God* (1930) concludes with a tour de force satire on the strike and the reactions of privileged bohemians. For a recent discussion of the General Strike as it pertains to Ford's works, see O'Malley, "Listening for Class."

29. Jameson to Brittain, August 8, 1940, Vera Brittain Collection, McMaster University Library.

30. Jennifer Birkett examines the relationship between Jameson's writing and her PEN work in "Margaret Storm Jameson and the London PEN Centre," and "'The Spectacle of Europe.'"

31. See Berry and Bostridge, *Vera Brittain*, 413–18.

32. Schofield notes that "after war was declared, [Jameson] was equally active, in 1941, defining her pacifist position in *The End of This War*" ("Whisper," 43).

Chapter 3

1. Jean Moorcroft Wilson reports the Sassoon family's King David myth but notes that "it is not until the birth of Sason ben Saleh in 1750 that any reliable documentary evidence exists" (*Siegfried Sassoon: Soldier, Poet*, 6). Sassoon's comment about women sounds less aggressive in context. He was writing to Edward Carpenter in praise of Carpenter's pioneering book *The Intermediate Sex: A Study of Some Transitional Types of Men and Women* (1912), and he explains how he came to understand himself more deeply because of this work: "What ideas I had about homosexuality were absolutely prejudicial, and I was in such a groove that I couldn't allow myself to be what I wished to be, and the intense attraction I felt for my own sex was almost a subconscious thing, and my antipathy for women a mystery to me" (qtd. in Caesar, *Taking It*, 66).

2. Wilson's recent *Siegfried Sassoon: Soldier, Poet, Lover, Friend—A Life in One Volume* updates and condenses her two-volume *Siegfried Sassoon: The Making of a War Poet, 1886–1918* and *Siegfried Sassoon: Journey from the Trenches, 1918–1967*. See also Egremont, *Siegfried Sassoon*; Roberts, *Siegfried Sassoon*. Hibberd's comment comes from "To Endure Their Ache," his review of Egremont's biography.

3. For instance, Parker, *The Old Lie*; Cole, *Modernism, Male Friendship, and the First World War*.

4. Half a century ago, in the first comprehensive monograph on Sassoon, *Siegfried Sassoon: A Critical Study*, Michael Thorpe similarly commented on the relative neglect of his prose.

5. Chatfield, "Thinking about Peace in History," 37.

6. Paul Moeyes disagrees with Fussell's assessment of Sherston's cavalry life but affirms his use of juxtaposed binaries: "as in his war poetry, juxtaposition is one of the key devices of his prose writings" (*Siegfried Sassoon*, 148). T. G. Ashplant accepts the binary logic while focusing on "four apparently contradictory elements" among which Sassoon oscillated (*Fractured Loyalties*, 79).

7. Williams's main argument, which is not directly relevant to my discussion, explores a fascinating link between Sassoon's writings and film theory, suggesting that ontological doubling is adapted from early concepts of film spectatorship.

8. For this image, see http://siegfried-sassoon.firstworldwarrelics.co.uk/html/his_library.html.

9. Sassoon made numerous appearances for the PPU to read antiwar poetry. Wilson writes that "SS read his poems at a PPU rally at the Albert Hall on 27 November 1936, at Bristol on 13 January 1937, Salisbury on 31 January 1937 and Southend-on-Sea on 6 February 1937. (He refers to having given at least five readings in 1936)" (*Siegfried Sassoon: The Journey*, 471n40).

10. Brittain to Storm Jameson, January 17, 1937, Vera Brittain Collection, McMaster University Library.

11. See Eastman, "The *Clarté* Movement"; Racine, "The *Clarté* Movement in France, 1919–1921."

12. Moeyes discusses this episode but makes no reference to Sassoon's work for the PPU (*Siegfried Sassoon*, 105)

13. Russell's handwritten additions to Sassoon's letter can be found in the Russell papers at McMaster University. The most substantive change is that Sassoon's "the war would now be at an end" is crossed out and replaced with "would now be attainable by negotiation," which appears in the final published versions. Brian Bond's essay contrasting Sassoon's self-serving, deeply conflicted protest with Max Plowman's more ideologically consistent objection appears in *Survivors of a Kind*, 93–112. Bond is especially critical of Morrell and Russell, whom he regards as pacifists who secretly detested anyone in uniform and used Sassoon for their own ends. Bond's source on this matter is primarily Egremont, and he does not cite any primary or secondary works on Morrell or Russell to support his claims.

14. For additional discussion of the role of the *Cambridge Magazine* in the peace movement, see Atkin, *A War of Individuals*, 53–56.

15. Another work that thoroughly rejects the "antiwar" assumptions of World War I criticism is Frantzen, *Bloody Good*. A noteworthy difference between Frantzen and Caesar, however, is that Caesar's criticism attempts to show how Sassoon and others effectively endorse the war that they superficially despise—a stance Caesar finds reprehensible. Frantzen, by contrast, argues in favor of medieval values of chivalry and sacrifice that give meaning, wholeness, and communal bonding in wartime.

16. Bond follows Caesar closely, claiming that "Fight to a Finish" is "anti-war poetry" with "a very nasty political tone" (*Survivors of a Kind*, 97).

17. For a persuasive rejoinder to Bond's argument that World War I was necessary for Britain and an explanation of Sassoon as a critic of the war's "human price," see Ashplant, *Fractured Loyalties*, 192.

18. For these readings, see, respectively, Fleishman, *Figures of Autobiography*; Kunka, "The Evolution of Mourning"; Hemmings, *Modern Nostalgia*; Berberich, *The Image of the English Gentleman*.

19. Many critics read these works against their reception as antiwar; see, for example, Eide, "Witnessing and Trophy Hunting."

20. For elaboration of this phenomenon, see Adams, *The Great Adventure*.

21. Thorpe noted in his second edition of *Siegfried Sassoon: A Critical Study* that the one point Sassoon objected to in the first edition was Thorpe's claim that "The Kiss" was initially written in praise of bayonet training (xi). Robert Graves suggested the same in *Good-Bye to All That* (237). Caesar takes as a matter of fact that Sassoon covered up his early bloodthirstiness by claiming intentional satire (*Taking It*, 78).

22. Michael Walzer has strongly criticized "just war absolutism," noting that it amounts to a covert return of pacifism into the tradition meant to replace it (*Arguing about War* 13–14).

23. Caesar's claims pertain to the *Memoirs* rather than Sassoon's own actions, though he implies that Sassoon also espouses the futility of individual protest. Bond and Egremont criticize Sassoon for political naivety in thinking that his protest could be effective, while Caesar criticizes Sassoon's fiction for pointing out that his protest could have no effect. Both sides neglect the propaganda dimension of Sassoon's protest and how it positioned him within the broader antiwar discourse.

24. Elaine Showalter suggests that Maccamble is a doppelgänger for Rivers (*The Female Malady*, 185–86). Ashplant notes that no real life analogue for Maccamble appears in Sassoon's diaries or letters (*Fractured*, 173), despite Sassoon's device in the *Memoirs*, in which he claims not to know whether Maccamble is still alive (*CMGS*, 528).

25. Moeyes observes that Rivers, presumably unbeknownst to Sassoon, was finally convinced by his patient that unconditional surrender was not better than a negotiated peace (*Siegfried Sassoon*, 188). In an even more critical take on Rivers, Ashplant argues that his treatment of Sassoon amounts to emotional manipulation verging on a breach of medical ethics (*Fractured*, 168–69). See also Showalter, "Rivers and Sassoon," 61–69.

26. Bernard Bergonzi sounds a typical complaint when he writes that *Sherston's Progress* "is the least satisfactory of the three; it attempts to compress too large and varied a range of experiences in a small compass, and lacks unity of feeling, having neither the poignancy of the remembered rural pleasures of the *Fox-Hunting Man* or the concentration of the battle scenes in the *Infantry Officer*" (*Heroes' Twilight*, 154). For additional formalist objections, see Thorpe, *Sassoon: Critical Study*, 97; Sternlicht, *Siegfried Sassoon*, 90; Moeyes, *Siegfried Sassoon*, 185.

27. Williams provocatively argues that Sassoon cinematically adapted his dreams while revising the diaries into fiction (*Media, Memory*, 144–47).

28. Perhaps the clearest moment in which the *Memoirs* alludes to the coming European crisis is in this third volume where Sherston writes: "In these days of incalculable dictators, (and in my humble opinion the proper place for a dictator is a parenthesis) one cannot help wondering whether an acute Continental crisis could not quite conceivably be caused by an oncoming chill" (*CMGS*, 551). In his letters to Blunden in 1935, Sassoon would show his own vacillations, writing on April 13: "Do not be alarmed by Hitler! I feel sure he is a good hand once you get at him, and will be at the old X-roads at the exact time with the rations, as he undertook. I refuse to believe in Wars" (*SLSB*, 113). Then, on Easter Monday: "Personally I am so prejudiced against Hitlerism and all its works that I can believe nothing good of it and am unable to trust it an inch. In fact I think it almost worth fighting against!" (*SLSB*, 115).

29. Anne Olivier Bell notes that Woolf was reading *The Old Century* (Woolf, *D*, 5:173n16); Meg Albrinck, however, says Woolf's "diaries indicate that she was reading Sassoon's final installment of the Sherston series" ("Silent Citations," 3).

30. In a typical judgment, Moeyes interprets *The Road to Ruin* as Sassoon in "prophet-role" and finds that "the poems themselves have little merit" (*Siegfried Sassoon*, 125).

Chapter 4

1. Jane Emery writes that *Going Abroad* was a formulaic, lightweight bestseller that "produces easy laughs" and that *I Would Be Private* is "much weaker" (*Rose Macaulay*, 236–37).

2. Two unpublished theses are the major exceptions to this neglect of Macaulay's peace activist writing: Ha-Birdsong, "To Seize Fragments of Truth," and Vance, "The Art of Peace: Pacifism and Women Writers of the 1930s." For Macaulay as a middlebrow, see Humble, *The Feminine Middlebrow*; Hinds, "Domestic Disappointments"; Sullivan, "The Middlebrows of Hogarth Press."

3. Macaulay's poignant reflections on this period can be found in "Losing One's Books." Included in the destruction were books once belonging to her famous relative, Thomas Babington Macaulay.

4. Woolf's June 22, 1940, diary entry reports on the fighting in France, her irritation over losing at bowls, and her recourse to pleasure reading: "My book is Coleridge; Rose Macaulay" (*D*, 5:298). Anne Olivier Bell speculates that the novel is the newly published *And No Man's Wit* (*D*, 5:298n18).

5. LeFanu corrects Emery, showing that Macaulay had a customary six-month contract that officially began in May 1915, with a formal discharge in November (*Rose Macaulay*, 326).

6. See Fromm, "Re-inscribing *The Years*."

7. See Emery, *Rose Macaulay*, 250; Scott, *Sheppard*, 238.

8. Smith's comment is from the published version of her Marie Stopes Memorial Lecture given on March 1, 1973 (qtd. in Passty, *Eros and Androgyny*, 167n8). See also John Guest, ed., *Essays by Divers Hands: Being the Transactions of the Royal Society of Literature* (London: Oxford University Press, 1973). On Macaulay's journalism, see Collier, *Fleet Street*, 137–68.

9. Smith glosses Macaulay's term "the Brotherhood" as "the Brotherhood Movement," an ecumenical organization to which Sheppard had been elected president (*LTS*, 76n1). See also Scott, *Sheppard*, 212.

10. John Howard Yoder's slim book *What Would You Do?* offers a convincing rebuttal to the question of what a pacifist would do if someone tried to hurt a loved one, arguing that it presupposes too many conditions to be truly persuasive as a counterargument.

11. Rory Miller has written extensively on the scale of force, training law enforcement and civilians to have a range of options in hopes of reducing lethal outcomes. See, for instance, Miller and Kane, *Scaling Force*. Among Gene Sharp's many publications, *Making Europe Unconquerable* and *Civilian-Based Defense* in particular investigate nonmilitary forms of defense to advocate strategies that evaluate the use of force in anticipation of Miller's more individualized theories of scaling.

12. Rose Macaulay file, PPU Archives, London.

13. See Gottlieb, *Feminine Fascism*, 267–68.

14. That Macaulay refers to the letters section of *Peace News* rather than to official articles or leading members is often elided. Gottlieb makes this omission and also cites the PPU's advocating members to visit Germany and befriend German people as evidence of their collaborationist tendencies toward fascism (*Feminine Fascism*, 257n39). The intention of the PPU's *Peace Service Handbook* (May 1939) was a response to the British Government's *National Service Handbook* (January 1939), which had outlined a process for all households to prepare for war. Rather than demonizing the enemy, the PPU encouraged relationships with citizens of opposing nations. The *Peace Service Handbook* inadvertently named two pro-Nazi groups (including the Link and its publication, the *Anglo-German Review*) as possible allies in building nonviolent international cooperation. As Hetherington notes, "this now obvious lack of judgement was naïve, but any notion that it demonstrated a pro-Nazi strain within the PPU was disproved by lengthy disclaimers in *Peace News* and withdrawal of the pamphlet" (*Swimming*, 14).

15. Qtd. in Preston, *The Spanish Civil War*, 7.

16. See Overy, "Saving Civilization," 188.

17. On Spain's inaugurating total war, see Patterson, *Guernica and Total War*, 4–5.

18. The most substantial discussion of Brown and the WRI is Devi Prasad's *War Is a Crime against Humanity*.

19. See Cunningham, "Neutral?"

20. See, for instance, Berman, *Modernist Commitments*, 184–236.

21. See Boxwell, "Macaulay's *And No Man's Wit* and Hemingway's *For Whom the Bell Tolls*"; Mazlin, "Rose Macaulay's *And No Man's Wit*." Jameson's 1937 Spanish Civil War novel, *No Victory for the Soldier*, which she published under the name "James Hill," is even more neglected than Macaulay's novel. Regrettably, Gayle Rogers's *Modernism and the New Spain*, which pays considerable attention to English writers' use of the Spanish war, mentions neither Macaulay nor Jameson.

22. Likewise, for LeFanu, the "trudge" is "redeemed by a fantastical strand of the story" (*Macaulay*, 224).

Chapter 5

1. See Quentin Bell, *Virginia Woolf* and *Bloomsbury Recalled*. In context, Leonard's description of Virginia as "the least political animal that has lived since Aristotle invented the term," suggests that by "politics" he meant organized political parties—a thought muddled by his witticism about Aristotle. He then praises her acute sense of observation and deep interest in all people and things around her, claiming that she "was the last person who could ignore the political menaces under which we all lived" and noting that she was greatly involved in "pedestrian operations" of groups like the Rodmell Labour Party and the Women's Co-operative Guild (*Downhill All the Way*, 27).

2. Marcus, introduction to *Three Guineas*. For another denier of Woolf's activism, see Zwerdling, *Woolf and the Real World*, 274. Clara Jones provides the fullest response to claims that Woolf was not an activist and argues that Marcus's debates with Quentin Bell lacked specific references to Woolf's political activity. For a rich history of Woolf's involvement with political groups such as the People's Suffrage Federation and the Women's Co-operative Guild, see Jones, *Virginia Woolf: Ambivalent Activist*.

3. For discussion of Woolf's work with the women's movement, see Black, *Virginia Woolf as Feminist*, 23–50; and Jones, *Virginia Woolf: Ambivalent Activist*, 65–107.

4. See Ellis, *British Writers*, 7. Ellis anchors his discussion of 1939 on Forster's essay "The 1939 State," published in *New Statesman and Nation* (10 June 1939), 888–89.

5. For these three coordinates in the debate, representative texts include Quentin Bell, *Bloomsbury Recalled*, 212–20; Pawlowski, *Virginia Woolf and Fascism*; Spiro, *Anti-Nazi Modernism*, 174–86.

6. See Woolf, "Character in Fiction," *E*, 3:420–37.

7. Woolf claims that true artists, such as Keats, Titian, and Mozart, give us art that does not tell us anything about the context in which it was produced. The editorial note demurs: "We doubt whether artists in the past have been so peacefully immune from the conditions and issues of the society in which they live as she suggests" (*E*, 6:78).

8. Elizabeth F. Evans suggests that the *Daily Worker*'s coverage of the violence in Madrid may be an overlooked source of the photographs Woolf references throughout *Three Guineas* ("Air War," 64–65). For additional discussion of the *Daily Worker* photographs, see Berman, *Modernist Commitments*, 62–76.

9. Woolf's assertion of a "deliberate" failure remains puzzling. For an early explication, see Middleton, "The Years: 'A Deliberate Failure.'" More recently, Judy Suh has argued that Woolf's admission of failure comes from her inability to successfully oppose "bourgeois liberal representation with fascism" and claims that *The Years* records Woolf's "fall from idealist pacifism" (*Fascism and Anti-Fascism*, 100). My argument offers another perspective on the novel, suggesting that a radical pacifist critique remains crucial to its political agenda.

10. See Wood, *Virginia Woolf's Late Cultural Criticism*, 33–36, which draws heavily on David Bradshaw's commentary on Huxley's essays in *Hidden Huxley*.

11. On June 24, 1937, Woolf was onstage at the Royal Albert Hall behind the speakers at "Spain and Culture," a rally to aid refugees in Spain (Lee, *Virginia Woolf*, 674–77; Rogers, *New Spain*, 147).

12. On Woolf's complex relationship with "propaganda," see Wollaeger, *Modernism, Media, and Propaganda*, 71–127.

13. See Willis, *Leonard and Virginia Woolf as Publishers*; Southworth, *Leonard and Virginia Woolf, Hogarth Press*.

14. Gillian Beer claims that "as the 1930s go on [Woolf] clings to the frail hope of the Peace Pledge movement, and grits her teeth in the knowledge of the coming war" (*Virginia Woolf*, 122). Beer's comment is more suggestive than precise; though Woolf discusses women's efforts to "pledge themselves" to protect culture, she appears to be without formal ties to the PPU (*TG*, 110).

15. Grace Brockington notes that "Peace at Once," which argues for similarly passive responses to Germany, was not taken well either: "Bell's contention that the average working man would be no worse off under German rule provoked an editorial rebuke" (*Above the Battlefield*, 237n98).

16. See especially Chapman and Manson, *Women in the Milieu*. Recently, Jean Mills argues for Woolf's "transpersonal" connection with the classicist and pacifist Jane Ellen Harrison against previous assumptions that Woolf's pacifism was mostly indebted to G. E. Moore and the Cambridge Apostles (*Modernist Classicism*, 6). See also Froula, "War, Peace, and Internationalism." Studies of Woolf's relationship with her reading public include Snaith, *Virginia Woolf*; Cuddy-Keane, *Virginia Woolf*; Ellis, *British Writers*, 188–233.

17. An early analysis of these letters is in Silver, *"Three Guineas* Before and After." See also Snaith, "Wide Circles."

18. Victoria Stewart notes that Bell was ambivalent about this project from the start and had to be convinced by David Garnett (*Women's Autobiography*, 67–68). See also Laurence, *Julian Bell*.

19. Levenback even argues that "Leonard would not have claimed conscientious objector status if he had not received medical exemptions" (*Virginia Woolf and the Great War*, 22).

20. Numerous studies have addressed Woolf's relationships with and writing about Jews. Of particular note is *Woolf Studies Annual* 19 (2013) on the special topic "Virginia Woolf and Jews" including a forum with several major scholars on this topic as well as feature essays including Schröder, "'A Question Is Asked Which Is Never Answered': Virginia Woolf, Englishness and Antisemitism," 27–57; and, Phyllis Lassner and Mia Spiro, "A Tale of Two Cities: Virginia Woolf's Imagined Jewish Spaces and London's East End Jewish Culture," 58–82. See also MacKay, *Modernism and World War II*, 27–32; Linett, *Modernism, Feminism, and Jewishness*, 1–110; Suh, *Fascism and Anti-Fascism*, 99–128; Spiro, *Anti-Nazi Modernism*, 139–98; Phyllis Lassner, "'The Milk of Our Mother's Kindness Has Ceased to Flow': Virginia Woolf, Stevie Smith, and the Representation of the Jew," in *Between "Race" and Culture: Representations of "the Jew" in English and American Literature*, ed. Bryan Cheyette (Stanford, Calif.: Stanford University Press, 1996), 129–44. A few studies have attempted to dispute charges of antisemitism in Woolf's writings, such as Hargreaves, "I should explain," and, most frequently cited, Bradshaw, "Hyams Place." The first half of Bradshaw's essay offers a rich history of the BUF and its relation to Woolf's writings, but less convincing is the second half which attempts to prove Woolf's affirmation of Jews through her repeated use of the colors white and blue in *The Years*.

21. Linnett draws the term "allosemitism" from Artur Sandauer and Zygmunt Bauman (*Modernism, Feminism, and Jewishness*, 3).

22. Marder argues that "later in the 1930s," we find "no more racial slurs or disparaging remarks about the poor"; instead, when "the dictators consolidated their hold on the Continent," Woolf "increasingly identified with the rebels and victims of oppression, declaring herself an 'outsider,' a pacifist, and (by virtue of her marriage) a Jew" (*Measure of Life*, 8–9).

23. On Woolf's evasiveness, see Walkowitz, "Virginia Woolf's Evasion," 119–44.

24. On Woolf's "disinterested culture" versus Eliot's *Notes towards the Definition of Culture* (1948), see Pawlowski, "*Seule la Culture*," 216–17.

25. On minor utopias, see Jay Winter, *Dreams of Peace and Freedom*; Gregory and Kohlmann, eds., *Utopian Spaces of Modernism*.

26. On Leonard Woolf's political thought and realism/idealism debates, see Wilson, *The International Theory of Leonard Woolf*.

27. Sylvia Strauss, introduction to *The New Pacifism*, ed. Gerald K. Hibbert (1936; New York: Garland, 1972), 10.

28. Current models of argumentation by example include Ackerman and Jack Duvall, *A Force More Powerful*; Gene Sharp, *Waging Nonviolent Struggle*, 69–358.

29. See also de Ligt, *The Conquest of Violence*, chapters 6 and 7, for examples of successful nonviolent campaigns and violent failures.

30. See Biggar, *In Defence of War*, 5–8.

31. Wood's comment is highly suggestive; however, she overstates the importance of a lone mention of Gandhi in Woolf's diary when there is no evidence of any further engagement with Gandhian thought (*D*, 4:8). Also, Wood's notion of nonviolence derives from Mark Kurlansky's problematic *Nonviolence*, which unhelpfully claims: "Pacifism is passive, but nonviolence is active" (6). See Howes, Sharp, and Ceadel for superior theorization of these terms.

32. See Stec, "Gandhian Non-Violence"; Zwerdling, *Real World*, 298–301; Cole, *Violet Hour*, 228–32. Gandhi's relationship with feminism may be more complex than is usually admitted by critics who focus on his insistence on traditional, patriarchal family structures. As he wrote in "To the Women of India" (1930), "if non-violence is the law of our being, the future is with woman" (*Non-Violent Resistance*, 325).

33. In "The Dotted Line," Rachel Bowlby similarly argues that ellipses disrupt conventional, masculine discursive practices to produce a more distinctly feminist style.

34. See Gorsevski, *Peaceful Persuasion*.

35. In "Re-inscribing *The Years*," Gloria Fromm astutely critiques scholarship that she claims "redeemed" *The Years* only by restoring material Woolf herself cut.

36. See also McNees, "The 1914 'Expurgated Chunk,'" 55–62.

37. The introductions to three critical editions of the novel describe it mostly in terms of its feminist response to patriarchy: McNees (Harcourt, 2008), Bradshaw and Blythe (Wiley-Blackwell, 2012), Snaith (Cambridge University Press, 2012). According to Bradshaw and Blythe, "the unspeakable and the unspoken; the marginalized, the concealed and the excluded; the malignant, obligatory reticence of the patriarchal system, would become the driving concerns of her ninth novel" (xiii). Christine Froula's engaging study, despite her subtitle, emphasizes gender politics in the novel rather than war (*Virginia Woolf and the Bloomsbury Avant-Garde: War, Civilization, Modernity*, 213–56). See also Davis, "The Historical Novel at History's End"; Bradshaw, "History in the Raw."

38. See Saint-Amour, *Tense Future*, 90–132; Stonebridge, *The Writing of Anxiety*. Air war scholarship includes Evans, "Air War"; Cole, *Violet Hour*, 252; Clarke, "Virginia Woolf in the Age of Aerial Bombardment"; Saint-Amour, "Air War Prophecy"; Ellmann, "Death in the Air."

39. Reception history of *The Years* among soldiers is uncertain; however, Mary Chinery has noted that misperceptions about novels from the Armed Service Editions program were common, partly because of the democratization of the series, which placed trashy pulp alongside works such as Willa Cather's *Death Comes for the Archbishop*. One soldier purportedly "grabbed [Cather's novel] under the delusion that it was a murder mystery, but he discovered, to his amazement, that he liked it anyway" ("Wartime Fictions," n.p.).

40. In "Where Am I?" Merry Pawlowski claims that the structure of *The Years* comes from Woolf's feminist approach to history, an argument that dovetails with mine.

41. The suggestion that Colonel Pargiter's club is the Naval and Military Club of Piccadilly comes from Bradshaw and Blythe's edition of *The Years*, 307.

42. Erica Gene Delsandro, for instance, claims that the novel critiques "the detrimental consequences of nationalistic historiography-cum-mythology dominated by imperial progress, war, and patriotic heroics" ("To 'make that country,'" 121).

43. A core sample in this debate includes MacKay, *Modernism and World War II*, 30;

Suh, *Fascism and Anti-Fascism*, 99–128. Suh cites Zwerdling's claim that Woolf was dissuaded from pacifism by reading Freud (Zwerdling, *Virginia Woolf and the Real World*, 296). Many critics insist on the continuity of Woolf's views, including Gillian Beer (*Virginia Woolf: Common Ground*, 125–48) and Anna Snaith, who writes: "Woolf's commitment to pacifism, however, allowed no oscillation. This is the one issue on which Woolf did not waver; here, her reaction was not contingent, but constant" (*Public and Private*, 145).

44. On "Thoughts on Peace in an Air Raid" as an extension of *Three Guineas*, see Deer, *Culture in Camouflage*, 91–96.

45. On Woolf's use of Blake, see Mackay, *Modernism and World War II*, 24–27.

46. For further discussion of the gender politics of Woolf's "Thoughts on Peace in an Air Raid," see Cooper, Munich, and Squier, "Arms and the Woman."

47. This particular "letter" by Brittain also contrasts Woolf with Huxley, whom she criticizes for attempting to "escape from totalitarian warfare . . . by retiring to California"; she suggests that Woolf wrote politically in the way Storm Jameson advocated in *Civil Journey* (1939) (*Testament*, 70). Woolf's epitaph, Brittain says, should be her words from *The Waves*: "Against you I will fling myself, unvanquished and unyielding, O Death!" (ibid., 71).

48. For a critique of Brittain's reading of Woolf, see Victoria Stewart, *Women's Autobiography*, 83.

49. Christine Froula also notes the association of Bloomsbury with conscientious objection, including photographs from Tavistock Square of the Conscientious Objector Memorial and the bust of Woolf, though not linking these images with Gandhi or the PPU ("War, Peace, and Internationalism," 95–96).

BIBLIOGRAPHY

Adams, Michael C. C. *The Great Adventure: Male Desire and the Coming of World War I*. Bloomington: Indiana University Press, 1990.

Addams, Jane. "Patriotism and Pacifists in Wartime." In *The Jane Addams Reader*, edited by Jean Bethke Elshtain, 352–64. New York: Basic, 2001.

Adolf, Antony. "What Does Peace Literature Do? An Introduction to the Genre and Its Criticism." *Peace Research: The Canadian Journal of Peace and Conflict Studies* 42, nos. 1–2 (2010): 9–21.

Ackerman, Peter, and Jack DuVall. *A Force More Powerful: A Century of Nonviolent Conflict*. New York: St. Martin's, 2000.

Ackerman, Peter, and Christopher Kruegler. *Strategic Nonviolent Conflict: The Dynamics of People Power in the Twentieth Century*. Westport, Conn.: Praeger, 1994.

Aithal, S. Krishnamoorthy. "Huxley's *Eyeless in Gaza*." *Explicator* 42, no. 3 (1984): 46–49.

Albrinck, Meg. "Silent Citations in *Three Guineas*." *Virginia Woolf Miscellany* 60 (2002): 3.

Appiah, Kwame Anthony. "Cosmopolitan Patriots," *Critical Inquiry* 23, no. 3 (1997): 617–39.

Ascher, Abraham. *Was Hitler a Riddle?: Western Democracies and National Socialism*. Stanford, Calif.: Stanford University Press, 2012.

Ashe, Laura, and Ian Patterson, eds. *War and Literature*. Cambridge: Boydell and Brewer, 2014.

Ashplant, T. G. *Fractured Loyalties: Masculinity, Class and Politics in Britain, 1900–30*. London: Rivers Oram, 2007.

Atkin, Jonathan. *A War of Individuals: Bloomsbury Attitudes to the Great War*. Manchester: Manchester University Press, 2002.

Beauman, Nicola. *A Very Great Profession: The Woman's Novel 1914–1939*. London: Persephone, 1983.

Beer, Gillian. *Virginia Woolf: The Common Ground*. Ann Arbor: University of Michigan Press, 1996.

Bell, Clive. *Warmongers*. London: Peace Pledge Union, 1938.

Bell, Julian, ed. *We Did Not Fight: 1914–1918 Experiences of War Resisters*. London: Cobden-Sanderson, 1935.

Bell, Quentin. *Bloomsbury Recalled*. New York: Columbia University Press, 1995.

———. *Virginia Woolf: A Biography*. New York: Harcourt Brace Jovanovich, 1972.

Berberich, Christine. *The Image of the English Gentleman in Twentieth-Century Literature: Englishness and Nostalgia*. Aldershot, UK: Ashgate, 2007.

Bergonzi, Bernard. *Heroes' Twilight: A Study of the Literature of the Great War*, 3rd ed. Manchester, UK: Carcanet, 1996.

Berman, Jessica. *Modernist Commitments: Ethics, Politics, and Transnational Modernism*. New York: Columbia University Press, 2012.

Berry, Paul, and Mark Bostridge. *Vera Brittain: A Life*. London: Chatto and Windus, 1995.

Biggar, Nigel. *In Defence of War*. Oxford: Oxford University Press, 2013.

Birkett, Jennifer. Foreword to *Love in Winter*, by Storm Jameson, 9–15. London: Capuchin, 2009.

———. *Margaret Storm Jameson: A Life*. Oxford: Oxford University Press, 2009.

———. "Margaret Storm Jameson and the London PEN Centre: Mobilising Commitment." *E-rea: Revue électronique d'études sur le monde anglophone* 4, no. 2 (2006): 81–89.

———. "Re-Imagining Nations, Rewriting Lives: The Image of France in the Autofictions of Storm Jameson and Assia Djeb." *Romance Studies* 23, no. 1 (2005): 15–28.

———. "'The Spectacle of Europe': Politics, PEN and Prose Fiction—The Work of Storm Jameson in the Inter-War Years." In *Women in Europe between the Wars*, edited by Angela Kershaw and Angela Kimyongür, 25–38. Burlington, Vt.: Ashgate, 2007.

Birkett, Jennifer, and Chiara Briganti, eds. *Margaret Storm Jameson: Writing in Dialogue*. Newcastle: Cambridge Scholars, 2007.

Black, Naomi. *Virginia Woolf as Feminist*. Ithaca, N.Y.: Cornell University Press, 2003.

Bluemel, Kristin, ed. *Intermodernism: Literary Culture in Mid-Twentieth-Century Britain*. Edinburgh: Edinburgh University Press, 2011.

Bond, Brian. "British 'Anti-War' Writers and Their Critics." In *Facing Armageddon: The First World War Experienced*, edited by Hugh Cecil and Peter Liddle, 817–830. London: Leo Cooper, 1996.

———. *Survivors of a Kind: Memoirs of the Western Front*. New York: Continuum, 2008.

Bowlby, Rachel. "The Dotted Line." In *Feminist Destinations and Further Essays on Virginia Woolf*, 137–45. Edinburgh: Edinburgh University Press, 1997.

Boxwell, D. A. "The (M)Other Battle of World War One: The Maternal Politics of Pacifism in Rose Macaulay's *Non-Combatants and Others*." *Tulsa Studies in Women's Literature* 12, no. 1 (1993): 85–101.

———. "Rose Macaulay's *And No Man's Wit* and Ernest Hemingway's *For Whom the Bell Tolls*: Two Spanish Civil War Novels and Questions of Canonicity." *WILLA* 1 (1992): 17–19.

Bradshaw, David. "British Writers and Anti-Fascism in the 1930s, Part I: The Bray and Drone of Tortured Voices." *Woolf Studies Annual* 3 (1997): 3–27.

———. "British Writers and Anti-Fascism in the 1930s, Part II: Under the Hawk's Wings." *Woolf Studies Annual* 4 (1998): 41–66.

———. "The Flight from Gaza: Aldous Huxley's Involvement in the Peace Pledge Union in the Context of his Overall Intellectual Development." In *Now More than Ever: Proceedings of the Aldous Huxley Centenary Symposium Münster 1994*, edited by Bernfried Nugel, 9–27. Bern, Switzerland: Peter Lang, 1994.

———. "History in the Raw: Searchlights and Anglo-German Rivalry in *The Years*." *Critical Survey* 10, no. 3 (1998): 13–21.

———. "Hyams Place: *The Years*, the Jews and the British Union of Fascists." In *Women Writers of the 1930s: Gender, Politics and History*, edited by Maroula Joannu, 179–91. Edinburgh: Edinburgh University Press, 1999.

———. "Modern Life: Fiction and Satire." In *The Cambridge History of Twentieth-Century English Literature*, edited by Laura Marcus and Peter Nicholls, 218–31. Cambridge: Cambridge University Press, 2004.

Bradshaw, David, and Ian Blyth. Introduction to *The Years: The Shakespeare Head Press Edition*, by Virginia Woolf, xii–xxxii. London: Wiley-Blackwell, 2012.

Briganti, Chiara. "Mirroring the Darkness: Storm Jameson and the Collective Novel." In *Margaret Storm Jameson: Writing in Dialogue*, edited by Jennifer Birkett and Chiara Briganti, 71–91.

———. "Stern Cassandra: Storm Jameson, War, and Modernity." *HJEAS: Hungarian Journal of English and American Studies* 5, no. 2 (1999): 63–80.

Brittain, Vera. *Born 1925: A Novel of Youth*. 1948. London: Virago, 1982.

———. "Letter." *Peace News*, June 2, 1939: 1.

———. *Testament of a Peace Lover: Letters from Vera Brittain*, edited by Winifred Eden-Green and Alan Eden-Green. London: Virago, 1988.

Brittain, Vera, and Winifred Holtby. *Testament of a Generation: The Journalism of Vera Brittain and Winifred Holtby*, edited by Paul Berry and Alan Bishop. London: Virago, 1985.

Brock, Peter. *Freedom from Violence: Sectarian Nonresistance from the Middle Ages to the Great War*. Toronto: University of Toronto Press, 1992.

———. *Freedom from War: Nonsectarian Pacifism, 1814–1914*. Toronto: University of Toronto Press, 1991.

Brock, Peter, and Nigel Young. *Pacifism in the Twentieth Century*. Syracuse, N.Y.: Syracuse University Press, 1999.

Brockington, Grace. *Above the Battlefield: Modernism and the Peace Movement in Britain, 1900–1918*. New Haven, Conn.: Yale University Press, 2011.

Brothers, Barbara. "British Women Write the Story of the Nazis: A Conspiracy of Silence." In *Rediscovering Forgotten Radicals*, edited by Angela Ingram and Daphne Patai, 244–64. Chapel Hill: University of North Carolina Press, 1993.

Brown, H. Runham. *Spain: A Challenge to Pacifism*. London: Finsbury/Detloff, 1936.

Butler, Judith. *Frames of War: When Is Life Grievable?* London: Verso, 2009.

Caesar, Adrian. *Taking It Like a Man: Suffering, Sexuality and the War Poets: Brooke, Sassoon, Owen, Graves*. Manchester: Manchester University Press, 1993.

Cambridge Exhibition: Fascism and War. Cambridge: British Women's World Committee against War and Fascism, 1935.

Carsten, F. L. *War against War: British and German Radical Movements in the First World War*. Berkeley: University of California Press, 1982.

Case, Clarence Marsh. *Non-Violent Coercion: A Study in Methods of Social Pressure*. 1923. New York: Garland, 1972.

Caughie, Pamela L. *Virginia Woolf and Postmodernism: Literature in Quest and Question of Itself*. Champaign: University of Illinois Press, 1991.

Ceadel, Martin. *The Origins of War Prevention: The British Peace Movement and International Relations, 1730–1854*. Oxford: Oxford University Press, 1996.

———. *Pacifism in Britain 1914–1945: The Defining of a Faith*. Oxford: Clarendon, 1980.

———. *Semi-Detached Idealists: The British Peace Movement and International Relations, 1854–1945*. Oxford: Oxford University Press, 2000.

———. *Thinking about Peace and War*. Oxford: Oxford University Press, 1989.

Chapman, Wayne K., and Janet M. Manson, eds. *Women in the Milieu of Leonard and Virginia Woolf: Peace, Politics, and Education*. New York: Pace University Press, 1998.

Chatfield, Charles. "Thinking about Peace in History." In *The Pacifist Impulse in Historical Perspective*, edited by Harvey L. Dyck, 36–51. Toronto: University of Toronto Press, 1996.

Chinery, Mary. "Wartime Fictions: Willa Cather, the Armed Services Editions, and the Unspeakable Second World War." *Cather Studies* 6 (2006). http://cather.unl.edu/cs006_chinery.html.

Clarke, Stuart N. "Virginia Woolf in the Age of Aerial Bombardment." In *The Theme of Peace and War in Virginia Woolf's Writing*, edited by Jane M. Wood, 101–18. Lewiston, N.Y.: Edwin Mellen, 2010.

Cohen, Debra Rae. *Remapping the Homefront: Locating Citizenship in British Women's Great War Fiction*. Boston, Mass: Northeastern University Press, 2002.

Cobley, Evelyn. *Representing War: Form and Ideology in First World War Narratives*. Toronto: University of Toronto Press, 1993.

Cohrs, Patrick O. *The Unfinished Peace after World War I: America, Britain and the Stabilisation of Europe 1919–1932*. Cambridge: Cambridge University Press, 2006.

Cole, Sarah. *At the Violet Hour: Modernism and Violence in England and Ireland*. Oxford: Oxford University Press, 2012.

———. *Modernism, Male Friendship, and the First World War*. Cambridge: Cambridge University Press, 2007.

Collier, Patrick. *Modernism on Fleet Street*. Burlington, Vt.: Ashgate, 2006.

Connon, Bryan. *Beverly Nichols: A Life*. Portland, Ore.: Timber, 2000.

Cooper, Helen, Adrienne Munich, and Susan Squier, "Arms and the Woman: The Con[tra]ception of the War Text." In *Arms and the Woman: War, Gender, and Literary Representation*, edited by Helen Cooper, Adrienne Munich, and Susan Squier, 19–24. Chapel Hill: University of North Carolina Press, 1989.

Cortright, David. *Gandhi and Beyond: Nonviolence for a New Political Age*. Boulder, Colo.: Paradigm, 2009.

———. *Peace: A History of Movements and Ideas*. New York: Cambridge University Press, 2008.

Cramer, Patricia. "'Loving in the War Years': The War of Images in *The Years*." In *Virginia Woolf and War: Fiction, Reality, and Myth*, edited by Mark Hussey, 180–202. Syracuse: Syracuse University Press, 1991.

Crawford, Alice. *Paradise Pursued: The Novels of Rose Macaulay*. Cranbury, N.J.: Associated University Presses, 1995.

Cuddy-Keane, Melba. *Virginia Woolf, the Intellectual, and the Public Sphere*. Cambridge: Cambridge University Press, 2003.

Cunningham, Valentine. *British Writers of the Thirties*. Oxford: Oxford University Press, 1988.

———, ed. *Spanish Front: Writers on the Civil War*. Oxford: Oxford University Press, 1986.

Davies, Norman. *Europe at War, 1939–1945: No Simple Victory.* London: Macmillan, 2006.

Davis, Thomas. "The Historical Novel at History's End: Virginia Woolf's *The Years.*" *Twentieth-Century Literature* 60, no. 1 (2014): 1–26.

Day Lewis, Cecil. *We're Not Going to Do Nothing!: A Reply to Mr. Aldous Huxley's Pamphlet, "What Are You Going to Do About It."* 1936. London: Folcroft, 1970.

Deer, Patrick. *Culture in Camouflage: War, Empire, and Modern British Literature.* Oxford: Oxford University Press, 2009.

Delafield, E. M. "The Past or the Present? An Autobiography from Miss Storm Jameson." *Morning Post*, April 25, 1933.

de Ligt, Bartélemy. *The Conquest of Violence: An Essay on War and Revolution*, translated by Honor Tracy. 1937. New York: Garland, 1972.

Delsandro, Erica Gene. "To 'Make That Country Our Own Country': *The Years*, Novelistic Historiography, and the 1930s." In *Woolf and the City: Selected Papers of the 19th Annual Conference on Virginia Woolf*, edited by Elizabeth F. Evans and Sarah E. Cornish, 120–29. Clemson, S.C.: Clemson University Digital Press, 2009.

Dunaway, David King. *Huxley in Hollywood.* New York: Harper and Row, 1989.

———. Introduction to *Eyeless in Gaza*, by Aldous Huxley, vii–xiii. New York: Harper-Perennial, 2009.

Dungen, Peter van den. "Bart de Ligt, Aldous Huxley and 'The Conquest of Violence': Notes on the Publication of a Peace Classic." In *Bart de Ligt: Peace Activist and Peace Researcher*, edited by Herman Noordegraaf, Peter van den Dungen, and Wim Robben. Boxtel, Netherlands: Bart de Ligt Fund, 1988.

Eastman, Max. "The *Clarté* Movement." *Liberator* 3, no. 4 (April 1920): 40–42. https://www.marxists.org/archive/eastman/1920/clarte.htm.

Egremont, Max. *Siegfried Sassoon: A Life.* New York: Farrar, Straus and Giroux, 2005.

———. *Some Desperate Glory: The First World War the Poets Knew.* New York: Farrar, Straus and Giroux, 2014.

Eide, Marian. "Witnessing and Trophy Hunting: Writing Violence from the Great War Trenches." *Criticism: A Quarterly for Literature and the Art* 49, no. 1 (2007): 85–104.

Ellis, Steve. *British Writers and the Approach of World War II.* Cambridge: Cambridge University Press, 2015.

Ellmann, Maud. "Death in the Air: Virginia Woolf and Sylvia Townsend Warner in World War II." In *Virginia Woolf: Writing the World*, edited by Pamela L. Caughie and Diana L. Swanson, 77–90. Clemson, S.C.: Clemson University Press, 2015.

Emerson, Caryl. "Leo Tolstoy on Peace and War." *PMLA* 124, no. 5 (2009): 1855–58.

Emery, Jane. *Rose Macaulay: A Writer's Life.* London: John Murray, 1991.

Eros, Paul. "'A Sort of Mutt and Jeff': Gerald Heard, Aldous Huxley, and the New Pacifism." *Aldous Huxley Annual* 1 (2001): 85–115.

Evans, Elizabeth F. "Air War, Propaganda, and Woolf's Anti-Tyranny Aesthetic." *Modern Fiction Studies* 59, no. 1 (2013): 53–82.

Ewins, Kristin. "'Revolutionizing a Mode of Life': Leftist Middlebrow Fiction by Women in the 1930s. *ELH* 82 (2015): 251–79.

Favret, Mary A. *War at a Distance: Romanticism and the Making of Modern Wartime.* Princeton, N.J.: Princeton University Press, 2010.

Feinstein, Elaine. Introduction to *None Turn Back,* by Storm Jameson, v–vii. London: Virago, 1982.

Fixdal, Mona. *Just Peace: How Wars Should End.* New York: Palgrave Macmillan, 2012.

Fleishman, Avrom. *Figures of Autobiography: The Language of Self-Writing in Victorian and Modern England.* Berkeley: University of California Press, 1983.

Ford, Ford Madox. *No More Parades.* 1925. Edited by Joseph Wiesenfarth. Manchester: Carcanet, 2011.

Forster, E. M. "The 1939 State." *New Statesman and Nation,* June 10, 1939, 888–89.

———. *Virginia Woolf.* New York: Harcourt, Brace and Company, 1942.

Frantzen, Allen J. *Bloody Good: Chivalry, Sacrifice, and the Great War.* Chicago: University of Chicago Press, 2003.

Fromm, Gloria G. "Re-inscribing *The Years*: Virginia Woolf, Rose Macaulay, and the Critics." *Journal of Modern Literature* 13, no. 2 (1986): 289–307.

Froula, Christine. *Virginia Woolf and the Bloomsbury Avant-Garde: War, Civilization, Modernity.* New York: Columbia University Press, 2005.

———. "War, Peace, and Internationalism." In *The Cambridge Companion to the Bloomsbury Group,* edited by Victoria Rosner, 93–111. Cambridge: Cambridge University Press, 2014.

Fussell, Paul. *The Great War and Modern Memory.* 1975. New York: Oxford University Press, 2000.

———. Introduction to *Siegfried Sassoon's Long Journey: Selections from the Sherston Memoirs.* Edited by Paul Fussell, ix–xx. New York: Oxford University Press, 1983.

Galtung, Johan. "Violence, Peace, and Peace Research." *Journal of Peace Research* 6, no. 3 (1969): 167–91.

Gandhi, Mahatma. *Hind Swaraj; or, Indian Home Rule.* 1908. Gloucester, UK: Dodo, 2008.

———. *Non-Violent Resistance (Satyagraha).* 1961. Mineola, N.Y.: Dover, 2001.

George, Daniel, and Rose Macaulay, eds. *All in a Maze.* London: Collins, 1938.

Gilbert, Mark. "Pacifist Attitudes to Nazi Germany, 1936–1945." *Journal of Contemporary History* 27, no. 3 (1992): 493–511.

Gorsevski, Ellen W. *Peaceful Persuasion: The Geopolitics of Nonviolent Rhetoric.* Albany, N.Y.: State University of New York Press, 2004.

Gottlieb, Julie V. *Feminine Fascism: Women in Britain's Fascist Movement, 1923–1945.* London: I. B. Tauris, 2003.

Graves, Robert. *Good-bye to All That.* 1929. New York: Anchor, 1998.

Greene, Graham. *Articles of Faith: The Collected "Tablet" Journalism of Graham Greene.* Edited and introduced by Ian Thomson. Oxford: Oxford University Press, 2006.

———. Review of *Company Parade,* by Storm Jameson. *Spectator,* April 20, 1934, 634.

Gregg, Richard B. *The Power of Non-Violence.* Philadelphia, Penn.: Lippincott, 1934.

Gregory, Rosalyn, and Benjamin Kohlmann, eds. *Utopian Spaces of Modernism: British Literature and Culture, 1885–1945.* New York: Palgrave Macmillan, 2012.

Guest, John, ed. *Essays by Divers Hands: Being the Transactions of the Royal Society of Literature.* London: Oxford University Press, 1973.

Ha-Birdsong, Seonae. "'To Seize Fragments of Truth': A Study of Rose Macaulay's Pacifist Novels." PhD diss., Oklahoma State University, 1996.

Hardach, Sophie. *Of Love and Other Wars*. London: Simon and Schuster, 2013.

Hargreaves, Tracy. "I Should Explain He Shares My Bath: Art and Politics in *The Years*." *English* 50 (2001): 183–98.

Hauerwas, Stanley. "C. S. Lewis and Violence." In *War and the American Difference: Theological Reflections on Violence and National Identity*, 71–82. Grand Rapids, Mich.: Baker Academic, 2011.

Hemmings, Robert. *Modern Nostalgia: Siegfried Sassoon, Trauma and the Second World War*. Edinburgh: Edinburgh University Press, 2008.

Hershberger, Guy Franklin. *War, Peace, and Nonresistance*. 1944. Harrisonburg, Vir.: Herald, 2009.

Hetherington, William. *Swimming against the Tide: The Peace Pledge Union Story, 1934–2009*. London: Peace Pledge Union, 2009.

Hibberd, Dominic. "To Endure Their Ache." Review of *Siegfried Sassoon: A Life*, by Max Egremont. *TLS*, November 20, 2005.

Hibbert, Gerald, ed. *The New Pacifism*. London: Allenson, 1936.

Hinds, Hilary. "Domestic Disappointments: Feminine Middlebrow Fiction of the Interwar Years." *Home Cultures* 6, no. 2 (2009): 199–212.

Hirsch, Marianne. "'What We Need Right Now Is to Imagine the Real': Grace Paley Writing against War." *PMLA* 124, no. 5 (2009): 1768–77.

Hitchens, Christopher. Foreword to *Brave New World and Brave New World Revisited*, by Aldous Huxley, vii–xxi. New York: HarperPerennial, 2005.

Howes, Dustin Ells. "The Failure of Pacifism and the Success of Nonviolence." *Perspectives on Politics* 11, no. 2 (2013): 427–446.

——. *Toward a Credible Pacifism: Violence and the Possibilities of Politics*. Albany, N.Y.: State University of New York, 2009.

Hulme, T. E. *The Collected Writings of T. E. Hulme*. Edited by Karen Csengeri. Oxford: Clarendon, 1994.

Humble, Nicola. *The Feminine Middlebrow Novel 1920s to 1950s: Class, Domesticity and Bohemianism*. Oxford: Oxford University Press, 2001.

Huxley, Aldous. *The Art of Seeing*. New York: Harper, 1942.

——. *Encyclopaedia of Pacifism*. 1937. New York: Garland, 1972.

——. *Ends and Means: An Inquiry into the Nature of Ideals*. 1937. New Brunswick, N.J.: Transaction, 2012.

——. *Eyeless in Gaza*. 1936. New York: HarperPerennial, 2009.

——. *The Hidden Huxley*. Edited by David Bradshaw. London: Faber, 1994.

——. *Letters*. Edited by Grover Smith. New York: Harper and Row, 1969.

——. *Pacifism and Philosophy: An Aldous Huxley Reader*. Edited and introduced by William Hetherington. London: Peace Pledge Union, 1994.

——. *Selected Letters*. Edited by James Sexton. Chicago: Ivan Dee, 2007.

——. *What Are You Going to Do About It? The Case for Constructive Peace*. London: Chatto and Windus, 1936.

Hynes, Samuel. *The Auden Generation: Literature and Politics in England in the 1930s*. Princeton, N.J.: Princeton University Press, 1972.

——. *A War Imagined: The First World War and English Culture*. New York: Atheneum, 1991.

Jameson, Fredric. *The Antinomies of Realism*. London: Verso, 2013.

Jameson, Storm. "About the Next War: What Are You Going to Do?" *New Clarion* 2, no. 34 (January 28, 1933): 144.

——. *Before the Crossing*. New York: Macmillan, 1947.

——. *The Black Laurel*. London: Macmillan, 1947.

——. *Challenge to Death*. New York: Dutton, 1935.

——. *Civil Journey*. London: Cassell, 1939.

——. *Company Parade*. 1934. London: Virago, 1982.

——. "Crisis" (review). *Left Review* (January 4, 1936): 156–59.

——. *A Cup of Tea for Mr. Thorgill*. London: Macmillan, 1957.

——. "Documents." *Fact*, no. 4 (July 15, 1937): 9–18.

——. *The End of This War*. London: Allen and Unwin, 1941.

——. *Europe to Let: The Memoirs of an Obscure Man*. New York: Macmillan, 1940.

——. "Fifteen Years Ago—We Said 'NEVER AGAIN!,'" *New Clarion* 3, no. 71 (October 21, 1933): 325, 327.

——. *The Green Man*. London: Macmillan, 1952.

——. *The Happy Highways*. London: Heinemann, 1920.

——. *In the Second Year*. 1936. Nottingham: Trent Editions, 2004.

——. *The Journal of Mary Hervey Russell*. London: Macmillan, 1945.

——. *Journey from the North: The Autobiography of Storm Jameson*. New York: Harper and Row, 1970.

——. *Love in Winter*. 1935. London: Capuchin Classics, 2009.

——. *None Turn Back*. 1936. London: Virago, 1984.

——. *No Time like the Present*. New York: Knopf, 1933.

—— [as James Hill]. *No Victory for the Soldier*. New York: Doubleday Doran, 1937.

——. "Socialists Born and Made." *Fact* 2 (May 15, 1937): 87–90.

——. "Storm Jameson on the P.E.N." *P.E.N. News* (October 1938): 3.

——. *That Was Yesterday*. 1932. New York: Berkley Medallion, 1976.

——. *The Writer's Situation and Other Essays*. London: Macmillan, 1950.

Joannou, Maroula, ed. *Women Writers of the 1930s: Gender, Politics, History*. Edinburgh: Edinburgh University Press, 1999.

Jones, Clara. *Virginia Woolf: Ambivalent Activist*. Edinburgh: Edinburgh University Press, 2016.

Katz, Tamar. "Pausing, Waiting, Repeating: Urban Temporality in *Mrs. Dalloway* and *The Years*." In *Woolf and the City: Selected Papers from the Nineteenth Annual Conference on Virginia Woolf*, edited by Elizabeth F. Evans and Sarah E. Cornish, 2–16. Clemson, S.C.: Clemson University Digital Press, 2010.

Kershaw, Angela, and Angela Kimyongür, eds. *Women in Europe between the Wars: Politics, Culture and Society*. Burlington, Vt.: Ashgate, 2007.

Knowles, Nancy. "Active Pacifism in a World at War: The Legacy of Virginia Woolf's Pacifist Theory on Narrative Structure." In *The Theme of Peace and War in Virginia Woolf's Writings: Essays in Her Political Philosophy*, edited by Jane M. Wood, 237–60. Lewiston, N.Y.: Edwin Mellen, 2010.

Kohlmann, Benjamin. *Committed Styles: Modernism, Politics, and Left-Wing Literature in the 1930s*. Oxford: Oxford University Press, 2014.

Kosek, Joseph Kip. *Acts of Conscience: Christian Nonviolence and Modern American Democracy*. New York: Columbia University Press, 2009.

Kunka, Andrew J. "The Evolution of Mourning in Siegfried Sassoon's War Writing." In *Modernism and Mourning*, edited by Patricia Rae, 69–84. Cranbury, N.J.: Associated University Presses, 2007.

Kurlansky, Mark. *Nonviolence: The History of a Dangerous Idea*. New York: Modern Library, 2006.

Kushner, Tony. *The Holocaust and the Liberal Imagination: A Social and Cultural History*. Oxford: Blackwell, 1994.

Laity, Paul. *The British Peace Movement 1870–1914*. Oxford: Oxford University Press, 2002.

Lassner, Phyllis. *British Women Writers of World War II: Battlegrounds of Their Own*. New York: St. Martin's, 1998.

——. "'The Milk of Our Mother's Kindness Has Ceased to Flow': Virginia Woolf, Stevie Smith, and the Representation of the Jew." In *Between "Race" and Culture: Representations of "the Jew" in English and American Literature*, edited by Bryan Cheyette, 129–44. Stanford, Calif.: Stanford University Press, 1996.

——. "'On the Point of a Journey': Storm Jameson, Phyllis Bottome, and the Novel of Women's Political Psychology." In *And in Our Time: Vision, Revision, and British Writing of the 1930s*, edited by Antony Shuttleworth, 115–32. Lewisburg, Penn.: Bucknell University Press, 2003.

Lassner, Phyllis, Ann Rea, and Geneviève Brassard. "Reading Sideways: Middlebrow into Modernism." *Space Between Journal* 9, no. 1 (2013): 7–10.

Laurence, Patricia. *Julian Bell: The Violent Pacifist*. London: Cecil Woolf, 2006.

Lederach, John Paul. *The Moral Imagination: The Art and Soul of Building Peace*. New York: Oxford University Press, 2005.

Lee, Hermione. *Virginia Woolf*. New York: Vintage, 1996.

LeFanu, Sarah. *Dreaming of Rose: A Biographer's Journal*. Bristol: Silverwood, 2013.

——. Foreword to *Non-Combatants and Others*, by Rose Macaulay, 7–11. London: Capuchin Classics, 2010.

——. *Rose Macaulay*. London: Virago, 2003.

Lerner, Laurence. "Peace Studies: A Proposal." *New Literary History* 26, no. 3 (1995): 641–65.

Levenback, Karen. *Virginia Woolf and the Great War*. Syracuse, N.Y.: Syracuse University Press, 1999.

Lewis, C. S. "Why I Am Not a Pacifist." In *The Weight of Glory and Other Addresses*, 64–90. New York: HarperOne, 2009.

Lewis, Wyndham. *The Apes of God*. 1930. Santa Rosa, Calif.: Black Sparrow, 1997.

Linnett, Maren Tova. *Modernism, Feminism, and Jewishness*. Cambridge: Cambridge University Press, 2007.

Lukács, Georg. *The Historical Novel*. 1937. Translated by Hannah and Stanley Mitchell. Lincoln: University of Nebraska Press, 1983.

Lynch, Cecelia. *Beyond Appeasement: Interpreting Interwar Peace Movements in World Politics*. Ithaca, N.Y.: Cornell University Press, 1999.

Macaulay, Rose. *And No Man's Wit*. Boston: Little, Brown, 1940.

——. "Aping the Barbarians." In *Let Us Honour Peace*. Introduced by H. R. L. Sheppard, 9–17. London: Cobden-Sanderson, 1937.

——. "Catchwords and Claptrap." In *The Hogarth Essays*, compiled by Leonard S.

Woolf and Virginia S. Woolf, 111–34. Freeport, N. Y.: Books for Libraries Press, 1970.

——. "Consolations of the War." In *Hearts Undefeated: Women's Writing of the Second World War*, edited by Jenny Hartley. London: Virago, 1994. Rpt. in *Wave Me Goodbye and Hearts Undefeated Omnibus*, edited by Anne Boston and Jenny Hartley, 549–553. London: Virago, 2003.

——. *Dearest Jean: Rose Macaulay's Letters to a Cousin*. Edited by Martin Ferguson Smith. Manchester: Manchester University Press, 2011.

——. Introduction to *All in a Maze*, edited by Daniel George and Rose Macaulay. 7–16.

——. "Letter." *Peace News* (June 9, 1939): 9.

——. *Letters to a Friend, 1950–1952*. Edited by Constance Babington-Smith. New York: Atheneum, 1962.

——. *Letters to a Sister*. Edited by Constance Babington-Smith. New York: Atheneum, 1964.

——. *Life among the English*. London: Collins, 1942.

——. "Losing One's Books." In *Articles of War: The Spectator Book of World War II*, edited by Fiona Glass and Philip Marsden-Smedley, 184–87. London: Grafton, 1989.

——. *Non-Combatants and Others*. 1916. London: Capuchin Classics, 2010.

——. *An Open Letter to a Non-Pacifist*. London: Collins and PPU, 1937.

——. *Pleasure of Ruins*. 1953. New York: Barnes and Noble, 1996.

MacKay, Marina. *Modernism and World War II*. Cambridge: Cambridge University Press, 2007.

Majumdar, Robin, and Allen McLaurin, eds. *Virginia Woolf: The Critical Heritage*. London: Routledge and Kegan Paul, 1975.

Marcus, Jane. Introduction to *Three Guineas*, by Virginia Woolf, xxxv–lxxii. Orlando, Fla.: Harvest/Harcourt, 2006.

Marder, Herbert. *The Measure of Life: Virginia Woolf's Last Years*. Ithaca, N.Y.: Cornell University Press, 2000.

Maslen, Elizabeth. "A Cassandra with Clout: Storm Jameson, Little Englander and Good European." In *Intermodernism: Literary Culture in Mid-Twentieth-Century Britain*, edited by Kristin Bluemel, 21–37. Edinburgh: Edinburgh University Press, 2009.

——. *Life in the Writings of Storm Jameson: A Biography*. Evanston, Ill.: Northwestern University Press, 2014.

McGann, Jerome. "'The Grand Heretics of Modern Fiction': Laura Riding, John Cowper Powys, and the Subjective Correlative." *Modernism/modernity* 13, no. 2 (2006): 309–23.

McLoughlin, Kate. *Authoring War: The Literary Representation of War from the "Iliad" to Iraq*. Cambridge: Cambridge University Press, 2011.

McNees, Eleanor. "The 1914 'Expurgated Chunk': The Great War in and out of *The Years*." In *Virginia Woolf: Writing the World*, edited by Pamela L. Caughie and Diana L. Swanson, 55–62. Clemson, S.C.: Clemson University Press, 2015.

Mengham, Rod. "Come Back: The Work and Life of Storm Jameson." *Kenyon Review* 32, no. 4 (2010): 191–98.

Middleton, Victoria. *"The Years: 'A Deliberate Failure.'" Bulletin of the New York Public Library* 80 (1977): 163–64.

Milne, A. A. *Peace with Honour*. New York: Dutton, 1934.

———. *War Aims Unlimited*. London: Methuen, 1941.

———. *War with Honour*. London: Macmillan, 1940.

Miller, Rory, and Lawrence A. Kane. *Scaling Force: Dynamic Decision Making under Threat of Violence*. Wolfeboro, N.H.: YMAA, 2012.

Mills, Jean. *Virginia Woolf, Jane Ellen Harrison, and the Spirit of Modernist Classicism*. Columbus: Ohio State University Press, 2014.

Milton, John. *The Complete Poems*. Edited by Gordon Campbell. London: Everyman, 1980.

Moeyes, Paul. *Siegfried Sassoon, Scorched Glory: A Critical Study*. New York: St. Martin's, 1997.

Montefiore, Janet. *Men and Women Writers of the 1930s: The Dangerous Flood of History*. London: Routledge, 1996.

Morrison, Sybil. *I Renounce War: The Story of the Peace Pledge Union*. London: Sheppard, 1962.

Mosley, Oswald. "From *The Greater Britain* (1932)." In *History in Our Hands: A Critical Anthology of Writings on Literature, Culture and Politics from the 1930s*, edited by Patrick Deane, 26–36. London: Leicester University Press, 1998.

Murray, Nicholas. *Aldous Huxley: An English Intellectual*. London: Abacus, 2002.

Murry, John Middleton. *The Pledge of Peace*. London: Herbert Joseph, 1938.

Mussolini, Benito. "The Political and Social Doctrine of Fascism," translated by Jane Soames, *Living Age* (November 1933): 235–44.

Nichols, Beverley. *Cry Havoc!* Toronto: Doubleday, 1933.

———. *Men Do Not Weep*. London: Jonathan Cape, 1941.

Neville, Peter. *Hitler and Appeasement: The British Attempt to Prevent the Second World War*. London: Hambledon Continuum, 2006.

Norris, Margot. *Writing War in the Twentieth Century*. Charlottesville: University of Virginia Press, 2000.

Nugel, Bernfried. "Aldous Huxley as Moral Philosopher: *Ends and Means* vis-à-vis Gerald Heard's *The Third Morality*." In *Aldous Huxley, Man of Letters: Thinker, Critic and Artist: Proceedings of the Third International Aldous Huxley Symposium*, edited by Bernfried Nugel, Uwe Rasch, and Gerhard Wagner, 47–63. New Brunswick, N.J.: Transaction, 2007.

O'Malley, Seamus. "Listening for Class in Ford Madox Ford's *Parade's End*." *Modernism/modernity* 21, no.3 (2014): 689–714.

Orwell, George. *My Country Right or Left, 1940–1943*. Volume 2 of *The Collected Essays Journalism and Letters of George Orwell*. Edited by Sonia Orwell and Ian Angus. Boston: Godine, 2000.

Overy, Richard. *The Morbid Age: Britain and the Crisis of Civilization, 1919–1939*. London: Penguin, 2010.

———. "Saving Civilization: British Public Opinion and the Coming of War in 1939." In *Justifying War: Propaganda, Politics and the Modern Age*, edited by Jo Fox and David Welch, 179–99. New York: Palgrave Macmillan, 2012.

Parker, Peter. *The Old Lie: The Great War and the Public-School Ethos*. London: Constable, 1987; rpt. London: Hambledon Continuum, 2007.

Passty, Jeanette N. *Eros and Androgyny: The Legacy of Rose Macaulay*. Rutherford, N.J.: Associated University Presses, 1988.

Patterson, Ian. *Guernica and Total War*. Cambridge, Mass.: Harvard University Press, 2007.

——. "Pacifists and Conscientious Objectors." In *The Edinburgh Companion to Twentieth-Century British and American War Literature*, edited by Adam Piette and Mark Rawlinson, 304–16.

Pawlowski, Merry M. "'*Seule la Culture Désintéressée*': Virginia Woolf, Gender, and Culture in Time of War." In *War and Words: Horror and Heroism in the Literature of Warfare*, edited by Sara Munson Deats, Lagretta Tallent Lenker, and Merry G. Perry, 215–34. Lanham, Md.: Lexington, 2004.

——. "'Where Am I?': Feminine Space and Time in Virginia Woolf's *The Years*." In *Literary Landscapes: From Modernism to Postcolonialism*, edited by Attie de Lange, Gail Fincham, Jeremy Hawthorn, and Jakob Lothe, 75–91. New York: Palgrave Macmillan, 2008.

——, ed. *Virginia Woolf and Fascism: Resisting the Dictators' Seduction*. New York: Palgrave Macmillan, 2001.

Pittock, Malcolm. "Max Plowman and the Literature of the First World War." *Cambridge Quarterly* 33, no. 3 (2004): 217–43.

Plain, Gill. *Women's Fiction of the Second World War: Gender, Power and Resistance*. New York: St. Martin's, 1996.

Plowman, Max. *The Faith Called Pacifism*. London: J. M. Dent, 1936.

——. *Bridge into the Future: Letters of Max Plowman*. Edited by Dorothy L. Plowman. London: Andrew Dakers, 1944.

Prasad, Devi. *War Is a Crime against Humanity: The Story of the War Resisters' International*. London: WRI, 2005.

Preston, Paul. *The Spanish Civil War: Reaction, Revolution, and Revenge*. Rev. ed. New York: Norton, 2006.

Query, Patrick R. *Ritual and the Idea of Europe in Interwar Writing*. Burlington, Ver.: Ashgate, 2012.

Racine, Nicole. "The *Clarté* Movement in France, 1919–1921." *Journal of Contemporary History* 2, no. 2 (1967): 195–208.

Radin, Grace. *Virginia Woolf's "The Years": The Evolution of a Novel*. Knoxville: University of Tennessee Press, 1982.

Raven, C. E. *War and the Christian*. London: SCM, 1938.

Rigby, Andrew. "The Response of British Pacifists to World War II." In *Twentieth-Century Peace Movements: Successes and Failures*, edited by Guido Grünewald and Peter van den Dungen, 145–59. Lewiston, N.Y.: Edwin Mellen, 1995.

Robbins, Keith. *The Abolition of War: The Peace Movement in Britain, 1914–1919*. Cardiff: University of Wales Press, 1976.

Roberts, John Stuart. *Siegfried Sassoon*. London: John Blake, 2000.

Roberts, R. Ellis. *H. R. L. Sheppard: Life and Letters*. London: John Murray, 1942.

Rogers, Gayle. *Modernism and the New Spain: Britain, Cosmopolitan Europe, and Literary History*. Oxford: Oxford University Press, 2012.

Ross, William T. "Words, War, and Peace: The Nature of Orwell's Pacifism." In *War and Words: Horror and Heroism in the Literature of Warfare*, edited by Sara Munson Deats, Lagretta Tallent Lenker, and Merry G. Perry, 187–96. Lanham, Md.: Lexington, 2004.

Ruddick, Sara. *Maternal Thinking: Toward a Politics of Peace*. Boston, Mass.: Beacon, 1989.

———. "Notes Toward a Feminist Peace Politics," in *Gendering War Talk*, edited by Miriam G. Cooke and Angela Woollacott, 109–27. Princeton, N.J.: Princeton University Press, 1993.

Russell, Bertrand. *Which Way to Peace?* London: Michael Joseph, 1936.

Russell, Richard Rankin. *Poetry and Peace: Michael Longley, Seamus Heaney, and Northern Ireland*. Notre Dame, Ind.: University of Notre Dame Press, 2010.

Saint-Amour, Paul K. "Air War Prophecy and Interwar Modernism." *Comparative Literature Studies* 42, no. 2 (2005): 130–61.

———. *Tense Future: Modernism, Total War, Encyclopedic Form*. New York: Oxford University Press, 2015.

Sassoon, Siegfried. *Letters to a Critic*. Edited and introduced by Michael Thorpe. London: John Roberts, 1976.

———. *Letters to Max Beerbohm with a Few Answers*. Edited by Rupert Hart-Davis. London: Faber, 1986.

———. *Collected Poems: 1908–1956*. London: Faber, 1961.

———. *The Complete Memoirs of George Sherston*. 1937. London: Faber, 1972.

———. *Siegfried Sassoon Diaries, 1915–1918*. Edited and introduced by Rupert Hart-Davis. London: Faber, 1983.

———. *Siegfried Sassoon Diaries, 1920–1922*. Edited and introduced by Rupert Hart-Davis. London: Faber, 1981.

———. *Siegfried Sassoon Diaries, 1923–1925*. Edited and introduced by Rupert Hart-Davis. London: Faber, 1985.

———. *Siegfried's Journey, 1916–1920*. New York: Viking, 1946.

Sassoon, Siegfried, and Edmund Blunden. *Selected Letters of Siegfried Sassoon and Edmund Blunden*. Volume 2: *Letters 1932–1947*. Edited by Carol Z. Rothkopf. London: Pickering and Chatto, 2012.

Saunders, Max. *Self Impression: Life-Writing, Autobiografiction, and the Forms of Modern Literature*. Oxford: Oxford University Press, 2010.

Scarry, Elaine. *The Body in Pain: The Making and Unmaking of the World*. New York: Oxford University Press, 1985.

Schneiderman, Howard. Introduction to *Ends and Means: An Inquiry into the Nature of Ideals*, by Aldous Huxley, vii–xxvi. New Brunswick, N.J.: Transaction, 2012.

Schofield, Mary Anne. "'Less Than a Whisper Raised against the Massed Music': British Women Writers Address 1930s Fascism." In *Women in Europe between the Wars*, edited by Angela Kershaw and Angela Kimyongür, 39–54.

Schröder, Leena Kore. "'A Question Is Asked Which Is Never Answered': Virginia Woolf, Englishness and Antisemitism." *Woolf Studies Annual* 19 (2013): 27–57.

Scott, Carolyn. *Dick Sheppard: A Biography*. London: Hodder and Stoughton, 1977.

Sharp, Gene. *Civilian-Based Defense: A Post-Military Weapons System*. Princeton, N.J.: Princeton University Press, 1990.

———. *From Dictatorship to Democracy: A Conceptual Framework for Liberation*. London: Serpent's Tail, 2012.

———. *Making Europe Unconquerable: The Potential of Civilian-based Deterrence and Defense*. Cambridge, Mass.: Ballinger, 1985.

———. *The Politics of Nonviolent Action*. 3 vols. Boston, Mass.: Porter Sargent, 1973.

———. *Waging Nonviolent Struggle: 20th Century Practice and 21st Century Potential*. Boston: Porter Sargent, 2005.

Sheehan, Paul. *Modernism and the Aesthetics of Violence*. Cambridge: Cambridge University Press, 2013.

Sheppard, H. R. L. *We Say NO! The Plain Man's Guide to Pacifism*. 1935. Critical Edition. Edited by Kerry Walters. Eugene, Ore.: Cascade, 2013.

Sheppard, Dick, and Aldous Huxley. *100,000 Say No! Aldous Huxley and "Dick" Sheppard Talk about Pacifism*. London: Athenaeum, 1936.

Showalter, Elaine. "Rivers and Sassoon: The Inscription of Male Gender Anxieties." In *Behind the Lines: Gender and the Two World Wars*, edited by Margaret Randolph Higonnet, Jane Jenson, Sonya Michel, and Margaret Collins Weitz, 61–69. New Haven, Conn.: Yale University Press, 1987.

Silver, Brenda. "*Three Guineas* Before and After: Further Answers to Correspondents." In *Virginia Woolf: A Feminist Slant*, edited by Jane Marcus, 254–76. Lincoln: University of Nebraska Press, 1983.

———. *Virginia Woolf's Reading Notebooks*. Princeton, N.J.: Princeton University Press, 1983.

Smith, Constance Babington. *Rose Macaulay*. London: Collins, 1972.

Smith, Stan. "'The Answer Would Appear to Be a Lemon': Rose Macaulay's Civil War." *English* 54, no. 208 (2005): 15–34.

Snaith, Anna. Introduction to *The Years: The Cambridge Edition of the Works of Virginia Woolf*, by Virginia Woolf, xxxix–xcix. Cambridge: Cambridge University Press, 2012.

———. *Virginia Woolf: Public and Private Negotiations*. New York: Palgrave Macmillan, 2000.

———. "Wide Circles: The *Three Guineas* Letters." *Woolf Studies Annual* 6 (2000): 1–168.

Southworth, Helen, ed. *Leonard and Virginia Woolf, the Hogarth Press and the Networks of Modernism*. Edinburgh: Edinburgh University Press, 2010.

Spiro, Mia. *Anti-Nazi Modernism: The Challenges of Resistance in 1930s Fiction*. Evanston, Ill.: Northwestern University Press, 2012.

Stec, Loretta. "Gandhian Non-Violence in Works of Ethel Mannin and Virginia Woolf." In *Literature of Region and Nation: Proceedings of the 6th International Literature of Region and Nation Conference*, edited by Winnifred M. Bogaards, 163–80. Saint John, N.B.: University of New Brunswick in Saint John Press, 1996.

Sternlicht, Sanford. *Siegfried Sassoon*. New York: Twayne, 1993.

Stewart, Victoria. *Women's Autobiography: War and Trauma*. New York: Palgrave Macmillan, 2003.

Stonebridge, Lyndsey. *The Writing of Anxiety: Imagining Wartime in Mid-Century British Culture*. New York: Palgrave Macmillan, 2007.

Strauss, Sylvia. Introduction to *The New Pacifism: Essays by Gerald Heard [and others]*. Edited by Gerald T. Hibbert, 5–10. 1936. New York: Garland, 1972.

Suh, Judy. *Fascism and Anti-Fascism in Twentieth-Century British Fiction.* New York: Palgrave Macmillan, 2009.

Sullivan, Melissa. "A Middlebrow Dame Commander: Rose Macaulay, the 'Intellectual Aristocracy,' and *The Towers of Trebizond.*" *Yearbook of English Studies* 42 (2012): 168–85.

——. "The Middlebrows of Hogarth Press: Rose Macaulay, E. M. Delafield, and Cultural Hierarchies in Interwar Britain." In *Leonard and Virginia Woolf, the Hogarth Press, and the Networks of Modernism,* edited by Helen Southworth, 52–73. Edinburgh: Edinburgh University Press, 2010.

Thorpe, Michael. *Siegfried Sassoon: A Critical Study.* London: Oxford University Press, 1967.

Tylee, Claire M. *The Great War and Women's Consciousness: Images of Militarism and Womanhood in Women's Writings, 1914–64.* Iowa City: University of Iowa Press, 1990.

Vance, Sylvia. "The Art of Peace: Pacifism and Women Writers of the 1930s," DPhil thesis, University of Oxford, 1997. D196285/98.

——. "Lorca's Mantle: The Rise of Fascism and the Work of Storm Jameson." In *Women Writers of the 1930s: Gender, Politics and History,* edited by Maroula Joannou, 123–37. Edinburgh: Edinburgh University Press, 1999.

Venter, Susan. "The 'Dog Episode' in Aldous Huxley's *Eyeless in Gaza.*" *Standpunte* 96 (1971): 16–19.

Walkowitz, Judith. *Night Out: Life in Cosmopolitan London.* New Haven, Conn.: Yale University Press, 2012.

Walkowitz, Rebecca L. "Virginia Woolf's Evasion: Critical Cosmopolitanism and British Modernism." In *Bad Modernisms,* edited by Douglas Mao and Rebecca L. Walkowitz, 119–44. Durham, N.C.: Duke University Press, 2006.

Wallensteen, Peter. *Peace Research: Theory and Practice.* New York: Routledge, 2011.

Walzer, Michael. *Arguing about War.* New Haven: Yale University Press, 2004.

Wasserman, Jerry. "Huxley's Either/Or: The Case for *Eyeless in Gaza.*" *Novel: A Forum on Fiction* 13, no. 2 (1980): 188–203.

Weinberg, Gerhard L. *A World at Arms: A Global History of World War II.* Cambridge: Cambridge University Press, 1994.

Weintraub, Stanley. *The Last Great Cause: The Intellectuals and the Spanish Civil War.* New York: Weybright and Talley, 1968.

West, Rebecca. *The New Meaning of Treason.* 1964. New York: Penguin, 1985.

White, R. S. *Pacifism and English Literature: Minstrels of Peace.* New York: Palgrave Macmillan, 2008.

Whittier-Ferguson, John. "Repetition, Remembering, Repetition: Virginia Woolf's Late Fiction and the Return of War." *Modern Fiction Studies* 57, no. 2 (2011): 230–53.

Williams, David. *Media, Memory, and the First World War.* Montreal: McGill-Queen's University Press, 2009.

Williams, Keith, and Steven Matthews, eds. *Rewriting the Thirties: Modernism and After.* New York: Longman, 1997.

Willis, J. H. *Leonard and Virginia Woolf as Publishers: The Hogarth Press, 1917–41.* Charlottesville: University Press of Virginia, 1992.

Wilson, Jean Moorcroft. *Siegfried Sassoon: The Journey from the Trenches, A Biography (1918–1967).* New York: Routledge, 2003.

———. *Siegfried Sassoon: Soldier, Poet, Lover, Friend: A Life in One Volume.* London: Duckworth Overlook, 2013.

Wilson, Peter. *The International Theory of Leonard Woolf: A Study in Twentieth Century Idealism.* New York: Palgrave Macmillan, 2003.

Winter, Jay. *Dreams of Peace and Freedom: Utopian Moments in the 20th Century.* New Haven, Conn.: Yale University Press, 2006.

Wodehouse, P. G. *The Code of the Woosters.* New York: Doubleday, 1938.

Wollaeger, Mark. *Modernism, Media, and Propaganda: British Narrative from 1900 to 1945.* Princeton, N.J.: Princeton University Press, 2006.

Wood, Alice. *Virginia Woolf's Late Cultural Criticism: The Genesis of "The Years," "Three Guineas" and "Between the Acts."* London: Bloomsbury, 2013.

Woodcock, George. *Dawn and the Darkest Hour: A Study of Aldous Huxley.* Montreal: Black Rose, 2007.

Woolf, Leonard. *Downhill All the Way: An Autobiography of the Years 1919 to 1939.* New York: Harcourt Brace Jovanovich, 1967.

———. *Quack, Quack!* New York: Harcourt, Brace, 1935.

Woolf, Leonard, ed. *The Intelligent Man's Way to Prevent War.* London: Gollancz, 1933.

Woolf, Virginia. *The Diary of Virginia Woolf.* Edited by Anne Olivier Bell with Andrew McNeillie. 5 vols. San Diego: Harvest/Harcourt, 1977–1984.

———. *The Essays of Virginia Woolf.* Edited by Andrew McNeillie and Stuart N. Clarke. Orlando: Harcourt Brace Jovanovich, 1987–2011.

———. *The Letters of Virginia Woolf.* Edited by Nigel Nicolson and Joanne Trautmann. 6 vols. New York: Harcourt Brace Jovanovich, 1975–80.

———. *Moments of Being: Unpublished Autobiographical Writings.* Edited and introduced by Jeanne Schulkind. New York: Harcourt Brace Jovanovich, 1976.

———. *Mrs. Dalloway.* 1925. Edited by Bonnie Kime Scott. Orlando: Harvest/Harcourt, 2005.

———. *The Platform of Time: Memoirs of Family and Friends.* Edited by S. P. Rosenbaum. London: Hesperus, 2007.

———. *Three Guineas.* 1938. Edited and introduced by Jane Marcus. Orlando: Harvest/Harcourt, 2006.

———. *The Years.* 1937. Edited and introduced by Eleanor McNees. Orlando: Harvest/Harcourt, 2008.

———. *The Years: The Shakespeare Head Press Edition.* 1937. Edited and introduced by David Bradshaw and Ian Blyth. London: Wiley-Blackwell, 2012.

Yoder, John Howard. *Nevertheless: The Varieties and Shortcomings of Religious Pacifism.* Scottsdale, Penn.: Herald, 1992.

———. *Nonviolence—A Brief History: The Warsaw Lectures.* Waco, Tex.: Baylor University Press, 2010.

———. *What Would You Do?* Scottsdale, Penn.: Herald, 1992.

Zwerdling, Alex. *Virginia Woolf and the Real World.* Berkeley: University of California Press, 1986.

World War II, 2, 4–5, 7, 14–16, 24–25, 49–50, 52–55, 86–87, 90, 92, 121, 129–30, 139–40, 156, 165, 191–92; fear of, 46–47, 78, 127; in literature, 3, 67, 150–53, 195–98; origins of, 32–33, 37, 84, 138, 141, 144, 150, 157, 161–62, 169

Wragg, Arthur, 96

Yeats, William Butler, 22, 38, 124

Yoder, John Howard, 133, 199n6, 208n10

Zwerdling, Alex, 51, 116, 166, 190, 203n1, 209n2, 212n43